TEXAS SPORTS
HEROES

SERIES EDITED BY
JORGE IBER

SEÑOR SACK

SACK

THE LIFE OF GABE RIVERA

JORGE IBER

TEXAS TECH UNIVERSITY PRESS

This book is typeset in Athleas. The paper used in this book meets the minimum requirements of ANSI/NISO Z39.48-1992 (R1997). ∞

Designed by Hannah Gaskamp
Cover design by Hannah Gaskamp
Cover photograph courtesy of TTU Athletics

Library of Congress Cataloging-in-Publication Data
Names: Iber, Jorge, 1961– author.
Title: Señor Sack: The life of Gabe Rivera / by Jorge Iber.
Description: Lubbock, Texas: Texas Tech University Press, 2021. | Series: Texas sports biographies | Includes bibliographical references and index. | Summary: "Biography of Mexican American football player for Texas Tech University Gabriel Rivera, voted all-American and into the College Hall of Fame"— Provided by publisher.
Identifiers: LCCN 2021005746 (print) | LCCN 2021005747 (ebook)
ISBN 978-1-68283-099-4 (cloth) | ISBN 978-1-68283-120-5 (ebook)
Subjects: LCSH: Rivera, Gabriel, 1961–2018. | Football players—Texas— Biography. | Texas Tech University—Football—History. | Texas—Biography.
Classification: LCC GV939.R558 I34 2021 (print) | LCC GV939.R558 (ebook)
DDC 796.33092 [B]—dc23
LC record available at https://lccn.loc.gov/2021005746
LC ebook record available at https://lccn.loc.gov/2021005747

Printed in the United States of America
21 22 23 24 25 26 27 28 29 / 9 8 7 6 5 4 3 2 1

Texas Tech University Press
Box 41037
Lubbock, Texas 79409-1037 USA
800.832.4042
ttup@ttu.edu
www.ttupress.org

For Raquel and Matthew. Thank you for your love and support and for willingly listening to so many stories about Gabe Rivera's life and Texas Tech and Pittsburgh Steelers football.

Contents

ILLUSTRATIONS

ACKNOWLEDGMENTS

I WOULD LIKE TO THANK the following persons for their help in fleshing out important parts of this manuscript: the Rivera family, and in particular Norbert Rivera; Ray Galindo; Jose Angel Gutierrez; Kim Pappas; Nancy Rivera; Derek Michael Zike; and Patti and Rob Randle.

SEÑOR SACK

INTRODUCTION

SEÑOR SACK—A TRAGIC AND TRIUMPHANT LIFE

OVER THEIR HISTORY, LIKE MOST large football programs, the Texas Tech University Red Raiders have had many great players, with a total of eleven individuals garnering selection as consensus first-team All-Americans.[1] An even more select few have merited both All-American status as well as induction into the College Football Hall of Fame. Among these legends of the Lubbock gridiron are the great E. J. Holub (inducted in 1986), Donny Anderson (1989), Dave Parks (2008), and Zach Thomas (2015).[2] The subject of this work, Gabriel Rivera, is another member of this august grouping. His legend, which would grow exponentially during his time in Lubbock, started to blossom in San Antonio and eventually generated national attention on and off the football field, for both positive and negative reasons, in the early 1980s. There were four key moments in Gabe's athletic and personal life that helped shape his story.

First, Rivera, who was born in Crystal City, Texas, began to gain notoriety as a two-way player (tight end and linebacker) for the Jefferson High School Mustangs in San Antonio. He made All-City as a junior after the 1977 season and followed that honor with selection to the nationally prestigious *Parade* All-American team and the Thom McAn Award (given to the best player in the San Antonio area) after the 1978 campaign. Needless to say, this recognition made Gabriel a highly

3

sought-after commodity among a plethora of collegiate recruiters. One local paper estimated the number of potential suitors at as many as fifteen, including the fabled Notre Dame Fighting Irish.[3] Among the institutions that he planned to visit were Arizona, Baylor, Texas Tech, and up to three more schools. By early February 1979, Gabe had made his (surprising) choice: he would become a Red Raider. Upon his arrival on campus in the late summer of that year, he began a meteoric rise that would bring him to the pinnacle of the football world: selection as a first-round choice in the NFL draft.

Second, while Rivera starred in many games, one in the 1982 season stood out clearly from the rest. Over the decades, the eyes of all of collegiate football have not often focused intently upon the Red Raiders, but the team certainly was in the national spotlight on October 23, 1982. On that day, Tech played in Seattle against the then-number-one-ranked University of Washington, a team that would finish ranked seventh that year.

Any aficionado of collegiate football can almost instinctively rattle off the names of the sport's most historically elite and celebrated programs. When discussing any chronicle of the game, teams such as the Alabama Crimson Tide, Notre Dame Fighting Irish, Ohio State Buckeyes, Texas Longhorns (painful for Texas Tech diehards to admit), Oklahoma Sooners, and the Michigan Wolverines stand out from the vast majority of institutions that field programs in the highest echelons of gridiron competition.[4] The Red Raiders have had memorable years, claiming a total of a dozen conference titles or cochampionships as of the end of the 2018 season. Nine of these came while in the Border Conference (which Texas Tech was a part of between 1932 and 1956), two during their time in the Southwest Conference (between 1957 and 1996), and one South Division co-title in the Big 12 (which Tech has been a member of since 1996).[5] The school's squads have played in a total of 38 bowl games, including the Cotton Bowl on four occasions (all defeats), with an overall mark of 13–24–1 in postseason competition.[6]

Going into this October 1982 contest against Washington, the Raiders sported a mediocre 3–3 record, with victories over Air Force, Texas A&M, and Rice, to go along with defeats suffered at the hands of New Mexico, Baylor, and Arkansas.[7] The Washington Huskies, conversely, came in undefeated at 6–0, with impressive triumphs over Pac 10 foes such as Arizona, Oregon, California, and Oregon State.[8] Not surprisingly, pigskin prognosticators forecasted that the home team would steamroll the visitors from Lubbock. This contest was supposed to be but a midseason tune-up with an also-ran before the mighty purple and gold moved on to play highly ranked sides from UCLA and Arizona State later in their conference schedule. The Huskies came into the contest averaging more than 40 points per game—a freakishly high total in the pre-"air-raid" offensive era of current college football. Texas Tech, it was understood, had little chance against Washington.[9] On that autumn afternoon, however, something totally unforeseen occurred as the team at the top of the polls barely survived an unexpectedly stern challenge by the upstarts from western Texas. The final score of 10–3 in favor of Washington was so surprising that the Huskies afterward actually dropped out of the top spot in the national polls.

After the final whistle, all that the national, Washington State, and Lubbock media could talk about was not the Huskies' nail-biting triumph, but rather how one Tech player on the defensive side of the ball—a six-feet-three, 285-pound behemoth—had totally dominated the action on the field. Texas Tech football beat writer for the *Lubbock Avalanche-Journal*, Norval Pollard, summarized the stupendous play of number 69 that day in the following manner:

> Gabe was like a mad hornet trapped in a fast-moving car with all the windows up. The Huskies didn't know whether to pull over, open all the doors, and wait until he escaped or keep traveling and hope he stayed at the rear window.

> [Washington coach Don] James and his players lauded Rivera following the contest, and rightfully so. James, who rushed out to midfield after the game to congratulate Gabe, called him everything from "Superman" to the "best defensive player I've seen."
>
> The fuss was something to see and hear, but the greatest tribute to Gabe's play came Sunday morning in the two Seattle newspapers, the *Times* and the *Post-Intelligencer*. Seldom, if ever, will you see a victory by the top team in the country—in its own stadium no less—upstaged by the play of one individual, especially a defensive player for the opposition, especially when the opposition happens to be non-conference from 1500 miles away. But Gabe couldn't be ignored.[10]

Such performances brought Gabe to the attention of several NFL teams and a profusion of agents who sought to make him their client. Additionally, with the advent of the USFL in the early 1980s, athletes such as Rivera were even more sought-after and were in an even stronger bargaining position. The sky, it appeared, was the limit.[11]

A third key moment in Gabe's life came as the various NFL franchises called out the names of their first-round selections in April 1983. Soon, attention focused on the Pittsburgh Steelers as they moved up to call out the 21st choice. At this time, the most dominant team of the 1970s was approaching a transitional phase. Among their needs were concerns such as, Who would (eventually) replace Terry Bradshaw under center? Who would be the next outside threat to supplant the legendary Lynn Swann? Should they look to shore up the other side of the ball and begin refortifying the fabled "Steel Curtain"? Did this draft class possibly contain someone who could be slotted to succeed another Texas legend, "Mean" Joe Greene? Pittsburgh's brain trust, the Rooney family and Coach Chuck Noll, decided to go with Rivera as their choice in the first round of the 1983 draft, eschewing another possibility: the selection of native son Dan Marino (who would, instead, go on to have a Hall of Fame career with the Miami Dolphins). Gabe signed a multiyear contract with the Steelers in May: he was now on his way to becoming a star and a millionaire.[12] The future seemed very bright indeed.

The fourth key moment took place when all these hopes, dreams, and aspirations came crashing down in late October of that same year. After finishing practice, Gabe went to a restaurant for dinner and had a few beers with his meal. Later that evening, as he was driving his newly purchased Datsun 280ZX, Rivera had a violent collision with another vehicle and was ejected through the rear window of his sports car. For several days he hovered close to death. He survived, but his spine was broken at vertebrae T5–6, paralyzing him from the chest down. He would remain a paraplegic for the rest of his life. The fans in western Pennsylvania, though greatly supportive, eventually came to refer to this former Red Raider great as "The Steeler Who Never Was."[13]

Beyond tragedy, several factors make Rivera's story distinctive. Not many Latinos (Mexican American in Gabe's case) were playing at the highest levels of collegiate football in the late 1970s and early 1980s; in fact, they still are not represented in substantial numbers, even in the early 2020s. Yet Gabe came from a family that had seized upon both education and football as mechanisms to carve out a middle-class life in segregated 1950s Texas. Indeed, Juan Rivera, Gabe's father, who also played football and who graduated from Crystal City High School (in 1948), went on to play collegiately at Howard Payne College (now Howard Payne University) in Brownwood; earned two degrees in education; and finally coached football and track in various communities in southern parts of the Lone Star State. Gabe would be among the select few Mexican American athletes to move on from playing Division I football to the NFL. Though the devastating accident would render his career among the shortest in NFL history, a mere six games, he would fight to overcome the physical and emotional trauma of this catastrophic event no less valiantly than he'd fought on the football field. While there were many difficult years, Gabe eventually summoned the diligence and wherewithal to give back to his adopted homes of Lubbock and San Antonio and became a highly respected and beloved community figure.

On July 17, 2018, aficionados of Texas Tech's football program awoke to learn of the passing of Gabriel Rivera. To those who followed the fortunes of the Red Raiders over the years, this giant of a man was more widely and affectionately referred to as Señor Sack. He was a shining star over the years 1979–1982 for a series of teams that finished with a combined mark of 13–28–3, with their best season being a mediocre 5–6 in 1980. The 1982 game versus the Washington Huskies was just one of Señor Sack's many memorable performances. According to his webpage on the College Football Hall of Fame website (he was inducted in 2012), Rivera was a consensus All-American after the 1982 season. Further, he was honorable-mention All-American in 1980 and 1981 and earned first-team All–Southwest Conference honors his senior year.[14]

Another legendary figure of Texas Tech football, Rodney Allison—who is now the director of the lettermen's association (the Double T Varsity Club) and who interacted with Gabe and his family constantly in recent years—recalled one particular play that showcased and exemplified Rivera's truly unique skill set. In a contest against Arkansas, the Razorback quarterback, running an option play, broke through the Red Raiders' line into the open field. He continued to run toward Tech's goal line only to be caught from behind, almost 60 yards beyond the line of scrimmage, by a lineman. Plays like these are what attracted and held the attention of the NFL.

This work includes eight chapters, plus a conclusion. Chapter 1 provides a brief history of the participation and significance of the Latino presence on the gridiron. I argue that the role of Spanish-surnamed athletes is of long duration in the sport and focus on some of the most important players from this background, Gabe Rivera certainly being one of the most significant at the collegiate level.

Chapter 2 sets the scene of Mexican American life in the place of Gabe's birth—Crystal City, Texas—from 1900 to 1948, one of the most researched and discussed locales of this group's twentieth-century history. Not only was this Zavala County municipality one of the epicenters of the Chicano-era civil rights struggle, the town also witnessed the manifestation of resistance in unexpected places, such as the football field and sidelines. The sport's significance in Texan life made the gridiron a place where Chicanos/as were able to stake a claim to broader civic life.

Athletics also played a role in the life and career of Gabe's father, Juan Rivera, as well as Gabe's three brothers. Chapter 3 covers the years between 1948 and 1972 and examines how Juan's abilities on the football field helped make it possible for him to gain access to a very rare commodity among Mexican Americans in the late 1940s: an opening to earn a collegiate education, as well as to play football beyond the high school level. This opportunity, in part facilitated by a powerful member of the local school administration, helped set the family onto the path of a middle-class, professional life and standing. Juan's status as a teacher and coach called for him to move the family often—with stops in Benavides (Duval County), Edinburg (Hidalgo County), back to his hometown of Crystal City (during the most tumultuous times of the Chicano era), and finally, to San Antonio, where the family would live for the final two decades of Juan's life, and where the athletic legend of Gabe Rivera began to gain nationwide attention.

Chapter 4 focuses on Gabe's time at Jefferson High School, his gridiron achievements for the Mustangs, the accolades earned, his selection of Texas Tech for his collegiate career, and his arrival on the Lubbock campus. This chapter covers the years 1972–1979. Chapter 5 discusses some of the highlights (including a particularly memorable tackle of Eric Dickerson) and lowlights (for example, a suspension for breaking team rules prior to his senior season) in his first seasons as a Red Raider, 1979–1981. This chapter also reviews the national press's perception of a "rare" Mexican American athlete who was making a name for himself in one of the most competitive and important conferences in the nation. Lastly, the chapter covers Gabe's 1982 campaign, particularly the contest against the Washington Huskies: the game that finally made him a household name. Now, he was not only recognized as a superb player in the Southwest Conference but also worthy of All-American status.

Chapter 6 reviews the end of Gabe's time at Texas Tech, his first marriage, and the process by which he moved on to the NFL in 1983. All seemed to be in place for a bright future, though there were some moments of consternation during negotiations with the Steelers, as well as concerns expressed by local media during training camp. Expectations were high, as the team's hope was that Rivera would anchor the Pittsburgh line for years to come. Many of the team's faithful reached out to Gabe in touching ways and welcomed him warmly to the environs of western Pennsylvania. Indeed, there was a sense among some in the area that this giant man from Texas would eventually be seen as a quintessential Steeler: an athlete who could identify with the working-man fan base of the black and gold. Unfortunately, it was not to be.

Chapter 7 covers Gabe's accident, the aftermath, the impact on his marriage, and his coming to grips with being paralyzed—roughly the years from 1983 to 1998. The story of this period includes a discussion of the unique relationship that developed between the Steelers' legendary owner, Art Rooney, and the Rivera family. The connection was, in part, due to their common Catholic faith, as well as Gabe being a part (albeit only briefly) of the Pittsburgh Steelers' family. The chapter also discusses some of the psychological difficulties that are common to individuals confronted with such a radical life change. I connect Gabe's circumstances with some of the psychological and sociological literature on this topic, as well as to the experiences of another NFL player similarly injured: Darryl Stingley of the New England Patriots. In hope of walking again, Gabe even made a trip to China to seek alternative medicinal cures and procedures (acupuncture), to no avail. The separation from his wife and son for nine months helped contribute to the end of his first marriage.

Chapter 8 examines the years 1999–2018, and the coverage pivots to Gabe's return to San Antonio. During these years, Gabe went through a second divorce, the deaths of his parents, and the passing of one of his brothers. By the late 1990s, however, Gabe also found a new purpose in life: volunteering with a community-based organization named Inner City Development. Interviews with the administrators of this entity, as well as an extensive collection of heartfelt drawings and letters from many of the children at the facility, show how Gabe helped to improve the lives of youths in an impoverished section of the city. This endeavor, as well as meeting his third wife, Nancy, and helping her with her children, shaped and gave purpose to Gabe's life. Additionally, he often returned to Texas Tech to be remembered and praised for his time as a Red Raider.

Several major honors came his way in his final years. Not only was he inducted into the College Football Hall of Fame, he was also awarded a spot in Texas Tech's Hall of Honor in 2014. The book's conclusion summarizes Gabe's life and career, and their significance. Though his time in the NFL spotlight was all too brief, his impact on his alma mater and San Antonio continued well past his playing days. He is an athlete worthy of recognition among the greats who have played collegiate football.[15]

Chapter 1

Latinos and Football in Texas

Pioneers Who Helped Open the Doors of Opportunity, 1920s–1975

THE GAME THAT WOULD BECOME American football first took root at the elite institutions that now make up the Ivy League; the rugged nature of the sport eventually attracted the attention and participation of athletes of varied racial, ethnic, and religious backgrounds. Many scholars have documented the participation of Native Americans, African Americans, Jews, Italian Americans, Asian Americans / Pacific Islanders, and other groups and their connections to the game.[1] By the early 1900s, the sport had spread to the entire nation, and for many of the young men who attended high school (granted, for the Spanish-surnamed, this was certainly a minority of the group) and college (even fewer), playing on the gridiron came to be seen as a rite of passage into a vigorous, masculine adulthood.

One population of football players that has not, until very recently, attracted much attention is now the largest minority group in the United States: Latinos/Hispanics.[2] A recent publication, *Bibliography of Books about American Football, 1891–2015*, compiled by Ralph Hickok, can serve as a handy reference of mostly popular literature concerning the few works extant on the topic.[3] The number of publications on the lives of Latinos involved with football is short indeed. A perusal of the section titled "Coaches" lists one item: a biography of the University of Wisconsin's legendary head coach Barry Alvarez (of Spanish descent). In the section on players, readers find mentions of popular biographies on Victor Cruz, Tony Romo, and Tom Flores.

While Hickok's work is a valuable resource, a recent book by Mario Longoria and myself, however, has thoroughly dispelled the notion that Spanish-surnamed athletes were and are extreme rarities on the gridirons of the United States (and, at the professional level, in Canada). Certainly, not all Latinos who played or coached football at the high school level, collegiately, or in the NFL and CFL or other pro leagues are worthy of biographical monographs, but more merit such treatment than just the aforementioned Alvarez, Cruz, Romo, and Flores.[4]

Latinos in American Football covers the Latino presence in football in various states. Since the story of Gabe Rivera and his family takes place in Texas, the following discussion primarily focuses on the Lone Star State through the time when Gabe began his career at Jefferson High School in the mid-1970s. The reasons for ending the discussion at this point are twofold. First, it is necessary to provide context concerning some of the issues Mexican American athletes faced when trying to take the field in Texas during the early decades of the twentieth century. Second, it is proper to take note of some of the pioneers who blazed the trail to make it possible for Gabe to have the opportunities he enjoyed in his home state, pioneers who included his father, Juan.

Beginning in 1927, with the signing of Ignacio Molinet (he was Cuban and was referred to by his football-playing colleagues as "Mollie" or "Lou") by the Frankford Yellow Jackets— the team that eventually became the Chicago Bears—Latinos have participated at the highest levels of American football.

Molinet played his collegiate ball at Cornell and is in their athletic Hall of Fame, as is his brother. Among some of the most recognizable Latinos who have followed in Molinet's wake in more recent decades are professional players such as George Mira (playing for the University of Miami and various professional teams), Joe Kapp (with the University of California–Berkeley, in the CFL, and with the Minnesota Vikings), Anthony Calvillo (with Utah State University and in the CFL with the Montreal Alouettes) and Hall of Famers Tom Fears (at UCLA and the Los Angeles Rams) and Anthony Muñoz (at the University of Southern California and with the Cincinnati Bengals), to name just a few.[5] Gabe Rivera's career at Texas Tech, I argue here, was as significant as that of these legendary performers. Unfortunately, he did not have the opportunity to play at the next level long enough to cement his status in the professional ranks.

For some time, the early pioneers of the sport viewed football as being merely for elites; these battles were perceived as a method to toughen the intellectual and physical mettle of future US military, political, and economic leaders ensconced during their youth at places such as Harvard, Yale, and similar institutions. The game would prepare players for the late nineteenth and early twentieth centuries' contests in arenas critical to national development. An example of this attitude can be found in a letter from outdoorsman and author Caspar Whitney to the father of American football, Yale's Walter Camp. As Whitney argued, "What do we care . . . for the men in the Fall River Mills [mostly Portuguese immigrants] or the silk mills in Patterson [mostly Italian immigrants] . . . the only Foot Ball in America is the Inter-College game."[6] Clearly, such an attitude reflected the notion that the game was to be "open" only to certain groups. Unfortunately for those who adhered to this attitude, as the desire by various universities and colleges to win became more and more prevalent (as opposed to simply having "gentlemen" play to prepare them for other endeavors), football ultimately began to open the door—if only a crack initially—to others who did not fit the mold to which Whitney referred in his letter.

Eventually, however, the rough-and-tumble aspect of the sport helped spread the game among blue-collar workers in locales such as western Pennsylvania and Ohio. Another scholar of the early game, Michael Oriard, in his important 2001 work, *King Football*, acknowledged this trend. The gridiron of the late nineteenth and early twentieth centuries, similar to the baseball diamond, often served as an agent of Americanization for immigrants or their offspring. These were youths who hoped for greater acceptance into the broader society; frequently, though not overcoming all obstacles, they found what they were looking for on the football field. Oriard's analysis of this trend is worth noting:

> Sport meant one of two things for immigrant communities: the neighborhood and local sports clubs . . . that both preserved ethnic identities and fostered assimilation into mainstream American culture. . . . To play football, whether at the high school or on a college or professional team, was to be thoroughly American.

> Polish and Italian youths were simply drawn to football in high school as a vehicle for achieving status. . . . Seeing them succeed, their communities celebrated such achievements . . . and more and more youngsters saw an opportunity to make it in America by following this example. Through this more "natural" process football contributed to . . . acculturation over time far more powerfully than such concerted efforts as the Americanization movement during the First World War.[7]

The game ultimately spread into locations that held substantial numbers of Mexican Americans, Cuban Americans, and other Latinos, and some athletes of these backgrounds followed suit with their Polish, Italian, and other ethnic colleagues.

The Johnny Appleseeds of football almost invariably had connections back to Walter Camp and New Haven. Such was the case for James Perkins Richardson (a teacher at Ball High School in Galveston and Yale alum) and John Sealy (though he was a graduate of Princeton). These two individuals are credited with establishing the first clubs in Texas: Richardson at Ball High and Sealy via a team called the Galveston Rugbys, which comprised recent college graduates and young businessmen. The two teams played the first contest within the boundaries of the Lone Star State on Christmas Eve of 1892, the first date of what would become a passionate love affair that continues to the present. As David Barron argued in a 2003 book chapter titled "The Birth of Texas Schoolboy Football," "Over the next decade, Sealy and his athletes played squads (both club and high school) in Dallas, Fort Worth, and San Antonio. By 1900, secondary schools . . . were competing against each other in the increasingly popular sport." Newspapers in the state's areas with the highest concentrations of Mexican Americans, such as El Paso, Laredo, and the Rio Grande Valley, recorded the staging of such contests by high school teams in 1895, the 1900s, and 1911. Thus, the game was known and played in locales with dense Latino populations in Texas; the issue was that the overwhelming majority of such youngsters never made it to high school to line up for local elevens. Further, even for those who did make it to a secondary institution, the economic survival of their families often precluded them from participating in extracurricular activities.[8]

One scholar who has documented significant moments of the early history of Latino (Mexican American) participation on the gridiron in Texas is Greg Selber of the University of Texas–Rio Grande Valley.[9] Initially, even in the locales mentioned in the previous paragraph, there was an almost total lack of participation by such athletes. Selber argues that "there was consistent racial strife . . . and most accounts . . . indicate that the Anglo kids did not exactly welcome their Latino Valley

mates into the [football] fold." This was not hard-and-fast segregation, however, as Selber notes that more light-skinned,
Spanish-surnamed players, such as a youth named Rodolfo
Somano, were able to play for the Brownsville High School
Eagles in the late 1920s. What made Somano different? He was
described as a "blue-eyed, blond-haired Spaniard" as opposed
to a "Mexican." One of the first of the darker-skinned individuals whom Selber discussed in his work was Amador Rodriguez,
who first took the field with his Edinburg High Bobcat teammates in 1927.[10]

Another researcher who has examined aspects of this story
is Joel Huerta in his article, "Friday Night Rights: South Texas
High-School Football and the Struggle for Equality." In this
essay, he quotes a coach from McAllen who wondered why so
few Mexican American boys tried out for his team in the 1930s.
"Was it something cultural? Was there something about football that the Mexican mind did not find conceptually interesting? . . . Finally, it clicked. In the stands and on the field, brown
athletes faced racist, vocal crowds. What attraction did that
hold?"[11]

Another legendary, early player (and later, coach) from the
Kingsville area, Everardo Carlos Lerma, faced teammates who
did not wish to play by his side at the local high school. He
proved his detractors wrong and earned all-district honors in
1933. Lerma was even offered a scholarship to play for Texas
Christian University. Instead, he chose to remain at home and
suited up for the hometown Javelinas of Texas A&I (now Texas
A&M University–Kingsville). Lerma completed his studies,
earning a degree in education in 1938, and eventually became
one of the first Mexican American coaches in the state, making his mark mostly during his years at Benavides High School
(through 1954). One of the men who would later fill this post, in
the early 1960s, was Juan Rivera, Gabriel's father. In his later
years (he passed in 1998), Lerma recalled how difficult it was to
get his first coaching job, noting that it took a lot to convince

"the school board to give him a chance because 'people just couldn't believe that a Mexican American could do as good of a job as an Anglo. Well, I think I proved them wrong.'"

Moving to the other side of the state, specifically to El Paso, we see similar issues. By the early 1930s, football had become an important part of school life in the city's predominantly Mexican American secondary school, Bowie High (Bears). Among some of the most memorable events in these years was a 29–13 victory over the "white" school in town, Austin High in 1933. One participant in the often-intense Bears-Panthers tilts recalled that "each side of town saw the game as a battle between two cultures, one trying to prove their supremacy while the other was trying to prove they were equal." An interesting aspect of this contest was that the winner of the district title was rewarded with a trophy known as the Silver Cup. Austin, which had held this prize previously, refused to surrender it to their rivals in the fall of that year. Not to be deterred, the denizens of Bowie's halls instead "made a 'Pink Teacup' to represent a temporary emblem . . . and it was taken through a ceremony held at the school." The administration of Austin High finally turned over the coveted emblem of citywide dominance to the Bears in January 1934.[12]

The 1940s and 1950s were a period that offered a few more opportunities as well as key historical moments for the participation of Latinos in Texas football at the high school and collegiate levels, though obstacles remained. Juan Rivera was an individual who experienced both aspects of this reality while in Crystal City and at Howard Payne College. A few more Mexican American coaches in addition to Lerma came to prominence during this time. The most notable was Nemo Herrera, who began a successful career in San Antonio during the late 1920s, including winning state titles in basketball for the Sidney Lanier High School Voks, and later moved on to coach baseball and football—the latter sport only temporarily, as the result of the sudden and tragic death of the head coach—and guided Bowie to its first state title in baseball in 1949. To this day, Herrera remains the lone individual in Texas to lead teams from two different schools to state championships in two sports.[13]

One noteworthy game took place in 1941, as the Bowie Bears played the Voks on September 26: one of the first contests to feature two football squads composed almost exclusively of Mexican American athletes. A paper from El Paso took note of the event, stating that "the game is a natural, in that the players are largely of Spanish American extraction; but Bowie, with its best club in several years, must be rated the heavy favorite." The local scribe did not prove to be prescient, as the tilt ended in a scoreless draw. The writer in the next day's edition of the *El Paso Times* praised the athleticism of both sides but could not help but make snide remarks about the "tricky" nature of the players, as well as the fact that the game ended with the mostly Latino crowd dissolving into "hysteria" (while providing no particulars of what this meant or what caused the mania).[14]

Among some of the important players and coaches during this era, we see a few who, like Juan Rivera, managed to parlay athletic abilities into collegiate football and postathletic professional careers. For example, Gonzalo Garcia played at Brownsville High and earned Little All-American status at Southwest Texas State (now Texas State University) in 1949. He later returned to coach at his high school alma mater. Garcia followed Juan Rivera as head coach at Benavides in 1966. R. C. "Tito" Flores played for five years at Edinburg High School, actually starting on varsity as an eighth grader due to the shortage of players during World War II. He would later go on to play at the University of Colorado and serve in the Air Force. Finally, Chipper Zamora was the first Mexican American to fill the quarterback slot at Harlingen High School in 1957 and then went on to a distinguished coaching and administrative career throughout the Valley. When interviewed by Professor Selber, this gridiron legend well summarized what success on the football field meant to him and to other Mexican Americans:

> I think that Harlingen was among the last schools to integrate at that position. . . . We just figured that's the way it is. I do remember wondering what happened to the Mexican American kids who had been successful at the lower levels. I grew up in Harlingen, and when we went to the movies, we had to sit upstairs, while the Anglos sat downstairs. . . . In sports I saw that there was more equality. . . . I know we had discrimination in the Valley in the old days. But at the same time, my older brother was the first Mexican American to be named King Cardinal. . . . Some of us just kept working hard, through the obstacles.[15]

A few Mexican Americans made even more impressive marks during the 1950s, playing for some of the principal universities in the state. One of the legendary players during this era was Carlos Esquivel from Edinburg High School, who demonstrated great skills and leadership both on and off the field. In 1953 he rushed for over 1,100 yards and led the Bobcats to the state semifinals, including defeating a team from San Antonio along the way. Even more uniquely, Esquivel accomplished an almost unheard-of feat in his senior season: being named to the All-State team. This success attracted the attention of Paul "Bear" Bryant, who recruited Carlos to Texas A&M University. Esquivel was one of the athletes who survived the fabled "Junction Boys" training camp. The highlight of his collegiate career came in 1956 when he scored a game-winning touchdown against the LSU Tigers. A fellow Aggie, Heisman Trophy winner John David Crow, noted the significance of Esquivel's career at A&M, stating that his teammate "was the first Hispanic I'd ever been around. . . . He was one of us. He was tough and played through all the injuries. . . . I don't mean to be too corny about it, but we would have fought for each other like brothers." Statements such as this were certainly not commonly articulated in the Texas of the 1950s. Esquivel then went on to a long coaching and administrative career in the Valley, including leading his high school alma mater during the early 1970s. Further, his status helped make it possible for him to assist other Mexican Americans in entering the coaching profession in this part of Texas.[16]

The state's flagship institution also had some prominent Mexican American players during this era. For example, Richard Ochoa of Laredo was a halfback for the Longhorns and earned MVP honors in the 1953 Cotton Bowl. Another individual of note from the 1950s is Rene Ramirez from Hebbronville. When he graduated high school in 1956, Ramirez was not only a star on the football field, he was also his class valedictorian. The Longhorns recruited Rene, who came to the Austin campus just as Darrell Royal arrived to start the 1957 campaign. The team went to the Sugar Bowl after that season in large part due to the efforts of the "Galloping Gaucho," who led the burnt orange in all-purpose yardage from scrimmage. The following season, Ramirez scored three touchdowns against the A&M Aggies in a 27–0 Longhorn romp. Finally, in 1959 Ramirez merited first-team All-Southwest Conference honors as Texas went 9–1 and faced Syracuse in the Cotton Bowl. This scholar-athlete went on to earn a degree in mechanical engineering. Many years later, Ramirez earned induction into the UT Hall of Honor. David McWilliams of the Longhorn Association noted at this august event that "now you find more Mexican Americans playing ... not only for UT, but in the state of Texas and across the nation." No doubt, players such as Rene Ramirez helped to open these opportunities.[17]

Alongside the Latino athletes who played at A&M and UT during the 1950s was one of Texas Tech's own: the great Bobby Cavazos from Kingsville, who suited up for the Red Raiders between 1951 and 1953, highlighting his career with an MVP performance at the 1954 Gator Bowl as Tech defeated Auburn, 35–13. In his senior season, Cavazos led the Red Raider ground game with 757 yards and scored 80 points. That team finished

11–1 as Bobby rushed for 141 yards and three touchdowns in the bowl game against the Tigers. That season helped make the case that Texas Tech belonged in the Southwest Conference, which it joined in May 1956. In addition to his exploits on the field, I've noted elsewhere Cavazos's historical and social importance; here was

> a Spanish-surnamed individual who stood proud, success-ful, and victorious in an endeavor most Texans respected and glorified. Contrast this with the daily life of most of the region's Mexican Americans—segregation, racism, sub-standard schooling for their children, and dominance by Democratic political machines. Unintentionally, the arti-cles on Bobby Cavazos's athletic brilliance provided a form of resistance against Anglo perceptions and dominance.[18]

As we move into the 1960s, several key events concerning Mexican Americans and football in Texas helped shatter per-ceptions of these players' capabilities and the significance of the sport to this particular community throughout the state. First, the 1961 Donna Redskins became the first—and so far, still the only—predominantly Mexican American team from the Valley or elsewhere to win a state title among pub-lic schools competing at the AA level (several teams that play in the parochial and private school league, TAPPS, have gar-nered state titles). Next, two teams comprising a mixture of white, African American, and Mexican American players—the 1962 Brackenridge Eagles and the 1968 Lubbock Estacado Matadors—claimed state titles in higher classifications. A final example of the impact of football on Mexican American con-sciousness comes from another player from the Valley, Robert Cortez of San Benito, who played his collegiate ball at A&M for another legend: Gene Stallings. Finally, as we see in greater detail in a later chapter, events took place on the football field at Crystal City that demonstrate how the Chicano Movement of the 1960s managed to utilize this "All American" event to state its case for equal treatment.

Even though it has been almost sixty years since the Redskins claimed their state title, the story of "the team" remains one of the most powerful symbols of Mexican American pride in the Valley. A former principal of Donna High School recalled in the early 2000s that "I was born in 1963 and heard about that team all of my life. That was the big talk. To be like that team was everybody's dream." Given the importance of that season, it is essential to provide a brief overview of Donna's drive to the title.

At the start of the 1961 season, few fans could have envisioned what this club would accomplish. They were seen as competitors for the district crown, certainly, but no one expected that a team comprising mostly Mexican Americans would achieve much beyond defeating their regional competition. Things did not start off well, as the Redskins lost their first two contests. Then they reeled off eight consecutive victories and made the playoffs. After defeating teams from Refugio and Devine, Donna lined up against a club from Sweeny. Here, one of their foe's coaches mentioned to Redskin coach Earl Scott that his team did not have much to fear; after all, the understanding around Texas was that "pepper bellies" could not hold their own on the gridiron. "I mean, you never hear about any of them in the Southwest Conference." The final score in that game was Donna 32, Sweeny 14.

For the title game, the boys from the Valley drew the Quanah Indians, a team that had scored 483 points over the season while surrendering a mere 56. Things looked grim as a touchdown put the Indians ahead, 21–12, early in the fourth quarter. Then Donna marched down the field and added a two-point conversion to make it 21–20 with around six minutes remaining. After a defensive stand, the Redskins took over on the Quanah 42. They scored again and converted the two-point play to claim an improbable 28–21 victory. A late interception squashed the final Indians drive.

In a 2002 interview, one of the members of that team, Oscar Avila, articulated the significance of that victory for the Mexican American population of the region by telling me about an encounter he had in the late 1990s. During a visit to Donna, an older gentleman approached Avila and asked if he was one of the boys from the 1961 squad. Oscar replied that he was a member of the club. The old man then turned to his wife and said, "*Mira viejita, este es uno de los Avilas que jugó en el equipo del '61 cuando les encellamos a los gringos que nosotros también sabíamos jugar football*" (My dear, this is one of the Avila boys who played for the '61 team when we showed the gringos that we too knew how to play football).[19]

Similar stories of challenging perceptions of Mexican American athletic capabilities can be found in the championship seasons of both the Eagles and the Matadors. In regard to Brackenridge's victory in 1962, Mario Longoria noted in his recent work on Latinos and football,

> As a student . . . at another 1962 San Antonio public school that was also predominantly Mexican American, I recall to this day how proud I felt to be a Mexican American; and more importantly, to see these young men succeed when they were expected to fail. Their success instilled a great sense of pride in their communities, San Antonio, and more importantly, upon countless Mexican Americans . . . both young and old, throughout all of Texas.[20]

Likewise, the author of *Mighty, Mighty Matadors: Estacado High School, Integration, and a Championship Season*, Al Pickett, noted the significance of this interracial team and the impact it had on the city of Lubbock, which was still dealing with integration efforts in the late 1960s. "Now, so many years later, we think nothing of athletic teams and schools with mixed races competing together. It is commonplace. Someone or some team had to be the first to prove that color didn't matter. . . . In Lubbock, that team was the Estacado Matadors." As one of the white players on the team, Joe Rose, recalled of his Latino teammates, "Although fewer in numbers, the Hispanic students were also a big part of our student body and our team. . . . Richard Segura,

Rudy Beltran, Angel Rodriguez, and Enedino Samudio were stalwarts of the football program."[21]

A final example from the 1960s shows, in a very direct way, how Mexican American football players believed they had earned a right to play the sport and to compete straight up with whites. Robert Cortez was initially on the radar of Darrell Royal and the Longhorns, but Cortez chose College Station because, he felt, it would afford him less opportunity to get in trouble. Greg Selber noted that fellow Aggies were in for a surprise if they believed that Cortez would put up with racism on or off the field. During practices, the former San Benito High Greyhound would often be chided for being too aggressive. "They kept saying, 'Damn it, Cortez, take it easy, take it easy!' But I came from a family of 13 kids, most of them had to quit school to work, and I grew up competitive and hard-nosed, that's just the way it was back then." Apparently, this attitude on the field made an impression on Stallings, who, after several players quit his squad in 1965, was heard to say, "Hell, let them all quit, we'll just go out there on the field with Cortez and nobody else!" Robert displayed a similar attitude in the dorms. One evening, another undergrad looked at him and said, "Hey, how's it going, taco-maker?" The result was not what the white student expected.

> I jumped up and socked that guy right in the mouth, I didn't want to hear any of that shit. After that, the teasing tailed off dramatically. . . . "That's one tough Mexican, don't mess with him." I got into several fights right off the bat until I let them know that I wasn't going to stand for being called a taco-bender or a greasy Mexican.[22]

By the time the Rivera family arrived in San Antonio in 1972, as we will see later, Juan was already well established as a high school coach. By these years, E. C. Lerma's son, John, had also begun his coaching career—one that would take him all over southern Texas and, in more recent years, into New

Mexico and see him earn over 200 victories. He was not alone. Other greats such as Alex Leal, who coached successfully at Raymondville, McAllen High, and Harlingen South (finishing with over 200 career victories), and Joe Solis, who led teams in Weslaco, Raymondville, Donna, and Edcouch-Elsa (his 1997 E-E team proceeded all the way to the state quarterfinals) also made their marks as field generals. While not achieving complete equality, the door for Spanish-heritage coaches, at least in some parts of Texas, was certainly open.[23]

On the playing field, many great athletes appear in the Longoria and Iber and Selber books, but one player's story stands out for professional achievements, overcoming of obstacles, and challenging the perception of Mexican Americans as players and coaches. That individual is Juan Castillo, who has had a long and storied NFL coaching career. Juan played his high school football at Port Isabel High and for the A&M–Kingsville Javelinas. His parents had immigrated to Texas from Mexico in their early teens. His father worked as a shrimper and was killed in 1970 as a result of an on-board accident. Overnight, the then-11-year-old Juan started helping his mother, who worked two jobs (as a maid and a waitress), to support and raise his two sisters. Although busy with these duties, Juan found time to play football for the Port Isabel Tarpons as both a linebacker and a tight end (the same positions that Gabe would play for Jefferson). He played well but did not earn a scholarship from a US-based school. This led to a one-year sojourn to his parents' native land to play for Monterrey Tech. After a year south of the border, Juan returned to South Texas, and his high school coach put in a good word for him at Kingsville. He walked on in 1978 and eventually earned a degree in kinesiology.

After graduation, Castillo served as defensive coordinator for Kingsville High and then moved on to coach the offensive line at his collegiate alma mater. Here he established ties with various individuals who worked for the NFL's minority internship program, leading to a job as a quality-control coach for the Eagles under the guidance of a legendary workaholic, Jon Gruden. One of the first things Gruden mentioned to Juan was, "When I did your job, I was always here at four in the morning." Juan, taught a diligent work ethic by his parents, decided he would arrive at the Eagles' facility at 3:30. After four years, Andy Reid named him offensive line coach, and he would also serve as offensive coordinator for Philadelphia.

Juan was fired after the 2012 season but then moved on to guide the offensive line with the Baltimore Ravens, earning a Super Bowl ring in 2013. After three years in Charm City, he moved on to Buffalo but was fired from his post there in early 2019. The Chicago Bears hired him in 2020. Hirings and firings are part of the coaching profession, and Juan has made a name for himself at the highest levels of football, which makes him an important example for other individuals of similar backgrounds. An effective summary of Juan's career, and its significance to Latinos in football, appeared in 2002. He stated, "There's a lot of people in Texas just like me. I want to help pave the way. I want to do a good job for my boss but also for the people of my heritage so that the next time there's an opening, a Hispanic will get a good look."[24]

By the time Gabe Rivera began playing on the high school gridiron in the mid-1970s, he had opportunities that Mexican American football players could not have imagined in previous decades. Without a doubt, he was supremely talented, but many dozens of other athletes and coaches struggled to break down the barriers that allowed him to play the game in the Lone Star State. Rivera would go on to make a mark for himself with the Mustangs and the Red Raiders; indeed, the Steelers saw him as a potential replacement for another Texas legend, the great "Mean" Joe Greene. How Gabe's family came to Texas from Mexico; their own story; the struggles that Mexican Americans confronted in the Crystal City, Zavala County, area; and the role that this community and football played in the Chicano Movement of the 1960s and early 1970s are the subjects of the next chapter.

CHAPTER 2

Setting the Scene for the Rivera Family in South Texas

Mexican American Life and Education in Crystal City, Texas, 1900s–1969

THEY SAY THERE IS NO DISCRIMINATION, BUT WE ONLY HAVE
TO LOOK AROUND US TO KNOW THE TRUTH. WE LOOK AT THE
SCHOOLS . . . THE HOUSES WE LIVE IN . . . THE FEW OPPORTUNI-
TIES . . . THE DIRT IN THE STREETS . . . AND WE KNOW.[1]

THE QUOTATION ABOVE COMES FROM a speech given by one
of the legendary figures of the Chicano Movement in Texas,
Jose Angel Gutierrez, before a group of supporters in Crystal
City on April 1, 1963. This individual is recognized as one of
the catalysts of the overarching effort to gain civil rights for
Mexican Americans not only in his home state but throughout
the nation. The story of Jose Angel has been told numerous
times, including in his autobiographical work, *The Making of a*

Chicano Militant: Lessons from Cristal, which appeared in 1998.[2] One part of Gutierrez's story that is not often discussed, however, is that, for a time, while he attended his hometown high school (he graduated in 1962), Jose Angel donned the green and gold of the Crystal City Javelinas. While circumstances for Mexican Americans were still quite adverse, by the late 1950s, certain social changes had taken place at the school, and Mexican American athletes were becoming a bit more common at the institution.

This did not mean, however, that all or even most barriers to equality had been eliminated. Even more significantly for the purposes of this work, Gutierrez's head coach in the late 1950s and early 1960s—for the B team, similar to a junior varsity squad—was none other than Juan Rivera Jr., Gabriel's father. Some of the bitter lessons that Jose Angel learned by playing football, and how the Javelinas' Mexican American athletes (and cheerleaders and members of the general student body) were treated, helped fuel Gutierrez's fire in the quest for activism and social change. In an interesting twist of fate, after the dramatic political changes of the late 1960s and early 1970s in Crystal City, Juan actually wound up working for his former player, serving briefly as athletic director for the school district for the 1971–1972 school year. This era in the community and region was highly charged politically and, as will be noted, this was not the elder Rivera's main concern in life: he merely wanted to coach football and track and to support his family. Juan's tenure under the leadership of Jose Angel Gutierrez was brief, and the Riveras eventually relocated to San Antonio.

This chapter, then, discusses the establishment of Crystal City in Zavala County, as well as provides an overview of the conditions Mexican Americans faced there during the first decades of the 1900s. I cover topics such as this group's economic and social circumstances, as well as what was happening with the community's youths in the local public schools. Key supporting materials about these early years come from a recent work by Marc Simon Rodriguez and a truly unique source: a federal document generated by Selden Menefee for the Works Progress Administration (WPA) in 1941 that provides insight into the conditions that Mexicans and Mexican Americans faced in Crystal City during the Great Depression.[3]

Other sources buttress the chronology and bring the story up to the years between 1963 and 1972, the year that Gabriel and his family left this area. In that period, several crucial moments in the town's history occurred:

1. The election of Los Cinco Candidatos (The Five Candidates) to the city council in 1963. This marked a dramatic turnaround in which the Mexican American populace, the overwhelming majority in town, began to assert its political power.

2. The response to the victory of Los Cinco and this slate's ultimate political defeat in 1965.

3. The next wave of political action, triggered partly by the process instituted for the selection of cheerleaders and other such leadership and team booster posts at Crystal City High School.

4. The "blowout" (student walkout) in the fall of 1969, the results of these efforts, and the rise of the La Raza Unida (United Race) Party (LRUP).

5. The school board election of 1970 and the administrative changes put in place by this new leadership, including Jose Angel Gutierrez's hiring of Juan Rivera as athletic director.

Given this background information regarding the place where the Riveras lived for many years, the chapter finally notes the arrival of Cresencio Rivera, Gabriel's great-grandfather, to South Texas in the late 1890s after leaving his native San Buenaventura, Coahuila. One of his offspring, Juan Rivera Sr., begat Gabe's father (Juan Rivera Jr.) in 1930. Juan Jr. would begin the family's climb to middle-class status, in large part through his participation in the sport of football. Much of the information that follows comes from interviews with Rivera family members, primarily Gabe's older brother Norbert, and is used throughout the remainder of this work.

Menefee's WPA manuscript provides a brief, overarching account of the establishment of both Crystal City and Zavala County. The first white settlers to the area, about 100 miles southwest of San Antonio, arrived in the 1860s. They were not greeted by lush, verdant pasturages. Instead, they encountered "only a dry, low-lying valley covered with sprawling mesquite trees." The first irrigation efforts started in the nation's centennial year, and later in the 1880s there was a discovery made of a source of artesian water. By the early 1900s, "the building of a branch line of the Missouri Pacific Railroad through Zavala County provided transportation advantages which made irrigated vegetable farming profitable." Subsequently, these early farmers began to grow onions, spinach, and other crops. From a scanty output of four acres in 1917–1918, the spinach harvest increased to more than 100 acres by the following season. By the early years of the 1920s, "913 carlots of spinach were shipped from Crystal City. Two years later, 2,555 carlots shipments were sent to market from the town's loading platform." All of this economic activity helped to establish Crystal City as "the primary urban, commercial and labor center for the district."[4] This pattern of increase continued until the Winter Garden District[5] began to feel the effects of the Great Depression by the end of 1933.[6]

Who would perform the backbreaking labor required to pick this valuable crop? The answer quickly became apparent, given the town's proximity to the international border (around 50 miles): Mexican laborers. Again, Menefee provides some insight into this situation, and his explanation merits a lengthy quote:

> The history of the Mexicans of Crystal City is in large part the history of spinach growing in the Winter Garden

Area. . . . Prior to the development of irrigation the . . . [area] was sparsely populated, and the few Mexicans living there worked principally for cattle and sheep ranchers. One present-day Mexican resident of Crystal City said that when he came . . . in 1914 "they were just colonizing it." There were at that time only a few houses and tents on the site of the town. During the next 15 years widespread irrigation and the resultant increase in growing of spinach and other vegetables were to create a need for quantities of Mexican labor. . . . In the early postwar period south Texas growers . . . opposed all restrictions on Mexican immigration. . . . Migration of Mexicans to Crystal City reached its peak in 1926. . . . By 1930 Crystal City was predominantly a Mexican town in population: 5,166 out of a total of 6,609 persons were classified as members of "other races" (than the white and Negro). Once they had come to Crystal City, the Mexican workers tended to return year after year because the spinach harvest occurred in the winter when employment was lacking in beets and onions.[7]

Menefee conducted interviews with members of approximately 300 families in Crystal City. His investigation provided an extensive amount of detail of the conditions that such individuals endured. The majority of these laborers and their families arrived in the years after 1920, with the peak being between 1923 and 1931 (he estimated around 60 percent). Three other important points to note from Menefee's study focused on why these individuals came to Crystal City. First and not surprisingly, more than 80 percent were induced to come to the area for employment. Second, more than three-quarters of respondents did not go directly to the Zavala County metropolis, but rather lived previously somewhere else in Texas. Approximately 85 percent of arrivals came from one of the four states of northeastern Mexico, and of those, 60 percent came from Coahuila (as in the case of Cresencio Rivera).

In most cases, large families predominated. The average figure in 1938 was 5.5 persons, with more than three workers per household being the norm. Obviously, the larger the unit, the more laborers it could place in the fields. The largest clan interviewed, for example, totaled 18 persons, with one dozen employed in agricultural work. Importantly, more than 80 percent of these families included one or more members who had been born in the United States. Finally, by the time of the publication of Menefee's report, these "Mexicans" were seemingly on their way to viewing themselves as "Mexican Americans." In other words, with the large number of children born north of the border, and the amount of time that those who arrived as adults had spent in South Texas by the start of World War II, these families "consider this south Texas town their permanent home."[8] Certainly, they would travel elsewhere following various crops, but "Cristal" was their home base. As Marc Simon Rodriguez noted, "Even as they settled permanently, however, they remained a migrant laboring people ... [and] planted two dominant crops, onions and spinach. ... In the late fall, they began the labor-intensive period of transplant and harvest work . . . that provided employment through late spring. Summer brought work in cotton and ... migration to find work in the Great Lakes and Great Plains states."[9]

As did the whites who first settled Zavala County in the 1860s, the Mexicans who arrived after World War I did not find wonderful conditions upon making their appearance in this area, although the circumstances they faced were man-made, not environmental. As Menefee noted, the community was divided into two sections: one for whites, the other for the Spanish-surnamed laborers. There was a further subdivision within the "Mexican" section, one part known as "Mexico Grande," the other, as "Mexico Chico." Menefee's summary of this part of Crystal City was as follows:

> These areas are crowded with the houses and shacks of the
> Mexicans in spite of the abundance of open land nearby.
> They have no modern improvements; sewers and street

lights are lacking. The unpaved streets are dusty in summer and muddy in winter.

Within this Mexican section are found social maladjustments that usually accompany poverty. The ramshackle houses are overcrowded, health conditions are bad and medical care is inadequate, school attendance is poor and unenforced, ... and the social life of the Mexicans is hedged about with economic and racial restrictions.[10]

In regard to housing, Menefee described the living quarters as mostly having dirt floors, tin roofs, and no ceilings. This made for appallingly warm conditions in warm weather and the opposite in cold. The windows did not have glass, just cheese cloth or old flour sacks. "Flies, attracted to the Mexican quarter by open toilets and the lack of any system of refuse disposal, find their way in spite of such safeguards." Less than 10 percent of the families interviewed had electricity or running water. Still, many of these subjects owned their domiciles, as local farmers and merchants encouraged the Mexicans to settle down in town, particularly during the peak spinach years of 1924 through 1932. For many, even modest dwellings created a great debt burden (either paying for the property itself or for taxes owed to governmental agencies), which further ossified their ties to the area.[11]

The sphere of health matters also did not present a very positive picture for the Mexicans of Crystal City. In the spring and summer of 1939, for example, there was an epidemic of diarrhea, with over 2,000 individuals affected. Of these patients, sixteen died (fifteen of them in the Mexican sections); all of them (save one) were infants less than one year old. During the same time, twenty-five persons succumbed in Zavala County from tuberculosis, a rate equivalent to about 300 deaths per 100,000 population—more than twice the mortality rate for this disease in the city of San Antonio. The individuals Menefee interviewed "reported great difficulty in gaining admittance to a State institution for the treatment of tuberculosis." Lastly, even for common illnesses, there were not many options available as "many of the families complained that they could not afford the $2 fee charged for each visit by private physicians and that the public health services available to them were inadequate."[12]

Conditions for the children of the Spanish-speaking populace were not much better in the pre–World War II years in the public schools of Crystal City. Menefee's research documented that almost one-quarter of the population of Zavala County was illiterate in 1930, with nearly all of the persons so classified being Mexicans. Less than 20 percent of students between the ages of 7 and 10 and only about 40 percent of those ages 11 to 13 attended school for the entire academic year of 1939, mostly due to their families traveling to follow crops. The most common time for school attendance was during the spinach planting and harvest season, roughly from November to March. "The rest did not go to school at all in spite of a legal requirement that all Texas children 7 to 16 years of age must attend school for at least 120 days each year." Even for those who did attend, relatively few managed to get beyond the fourth grade. "The Crystal City high school is open to Mexican students but few attend. Only the children of the most prosperous families are apt to go beyond grade school, and these are likely to be excluded from most of the high school's social activities." Of course, this lack of education had an impact on the job opportunities for the children of this group, even for those born in the United States. "Because of their poverty and inadequate schooling . . . [such] youth have scant opportunity to find employment except in the migratory agricultural work followed by their parents."[13]

The overall economic picture for these workers and their offspring was bleak indeed, with an average cash income of just $506 in 1938. Since around 96 percent of the Crystal City clans reported doing at least some migratory work that year, the costs incurred for travel further reduced this already meager income figure. The winter months tended to be the most difficult, as many families survived on only a few days of work per week in the spinach harvest. Varied financial levels still existed among the group, though. Menefee noted that the bottom 15 percent earned less than $300, while those further up the economic ladder did better. For example, the top 3 percent earned $1,500 or more per year; this group tended to work as labor contractors or small shop owners, or in the harvesting of sugar beets.

Many of the trends noted above continued even after World War II. For example, tuberculosis remained a concern among this population well into the 1950s. The separation of families caused by traveling to other states to work the fields contributed to a not insignificant rate of abandonment and desertion, and over 80 percent of these clans continued to participate in migratory agricultural labor. In regard to the labor situation, the passage of Public Law 78 in 1951—the creation of the Bracero Program—further limited the opportunities of Mexican Americans living in Crystal City to find winter work.[14]

Marc Simon Rodriguez's research allows a bird's-eye view of the layout of Crystal City in the years after World War II, right up to the time of the election of the Cinco Candidatos and the subsequent events noted above. The community had distinct neighborhoods, with the Anglo-Americans (Rodriguez's term) having their business district on both sides of the railroad tracks on Zavala Street (both east and west) in the southwestern portion of town. From there, this district "expanded eastward . . . along paved roads with modern ranch- and Victorian-style homes served by major utilities." A few blocks north, past West Crocket Street, was located the Mexican business area, which was at the heart of Mexico Grande, "the largest concentration of Mexican ancestry residents and businesses in the city." This sector was bordered on the east by North First Avenue. Rodriguez described both the positives and negatives of this area, stating that it "was well developed when compared to barrios . . . in other nearby towns but shabby when compared to Zavala Street. . . . [It] provided a full array of Mexican-style shops . . . [including] a medical office." Mexico Chico was to the south and east of the Anglo-American commercial sector below East Lake Street. There was yet another substantive concentration of the Spanish-surnamed in an area known as Campo Santo, which was located close to the Benito Juarez Cemetery in the northwest portion of the town. No matter where one went in Crystal City, however, one trait was certain: wherever the Anglo-American population was not predominant, one found "limited or no street paving, as well as uneven utility service, with some houses lacking running water well into the 1960s." Overall, while there were some signs of success, "the poverty of the Mexican American majority was palpable as one walked the streets of Crystal City."[15]

Relations between Anglos and Spanish speakers began to change somewhat after World War II, as Rodriguez notes. The transformation took place in various facets of life. For example, the arrival of national businesses—such as J. C. Penney, Sears, and Montgomery Ward—to Crystal City opened up a new avenue of employment for some Mexican Americans, high school students and adults. This only made sense, as the town's population was 85 percent Spanish-surnamed by 1960. Some local retailers, such as the Leonard Furniture Company, soon followed this trend. Additionally, a few Mexican-owned businesses began to target whites with English-language ads in the local paper, and a select few even moved into the main commercial sector. The local paper, the *Zavala County Sentinel*, hired a Mexican American scribe, Olga Lopez, to report on events such as weddings, births, deaths, and other happenings in the community. During the Korean War, "Mexican American service members routinely appeared in front-page veterans' profiles."

Still, there were limits. As one resident noted, while some Anglo-owned enterprises wanted the trade of the Spanish-surnamed, there "were several places that you weren't allowed to go." A similar sense of the limitations on interethnic ties existed in regard to the membership rolls of community organizations, such as the Lions Club and the Chamber of Commerce, both of which "had no Spanish-surnamed members well into the postwar period." This pattern helped to stimulate the development of Mexican American–focused organizations, such as the American GI Forum (AGIF) and a Mexican Chamber of Commerce. Even the Catholic Church and other denominations conformed to the pattern of segregation.[16]

In regard to employment in the postwar years, many of the Spanish-surnamed continued to work the fields and do migratory labor, with one major change: the arrival of the California Packing Plant (later to be known as Del Monte), to process and pack primarily spinach, in 1945. As Charles Vale Fitzpatrick noted in his 2004 thesis, this instigated key developments that would help bring about a dramatic transformation of Crystal City.

> The plant and its accompanying fields, centralizing much of the vegetable growing and packaging in the area, was the largest employer of Latinos in Crystal City, with both seasonal and year-round jobs.
>
> With the Del Monte plant came several ideas foreign to Texas. The most important was the plant's decisions to allow unionization. By 1956 the Teamsters Union had established itself at the plant and was recognized as the official collective bargaining agent by the Del Monte Corporation. The Del Monte plant provided large-scale employment for hundreds of workers, paying wages above the norm for Crystal City. The plant's predominantly Latino Teamster union and certain Latino union leaders would play a pivotal role in the attempt to wrest power away from the Anglos.[17]

During the mid-1950s, two other key incidents took place in the town's politics that helped foster the desire for change.

Fitzpatrick notes these occurrences as (1) a veterans' land scandal and (2) the city's application and misuse of federal urban renewal funds. In a nutshell, the first disgrace featured a concerted effort to swindle Mexican American World War II veterans out of land that Texas had set aside for them. The scheme worked like this: appraisers for the program were bribed to buy land from real estate agents at inflated prices. Then speculators enticed the veterans to apply for land grants. The veterans purportedly would pay for the land through long-term, low-interest loans. This, however, was not what the victims were told. Instead, they were supposedly to be granted a $300 "bonus" for having served in the military. In order to get the money, they had to sign some paperwork. What they really signed was a contract to purchase land owned by the speculators. Since the veterans did not pay back the loans, the state was left with the lands the veterans had "bought." In Zavala County, the perpetrators of this diabolical scheme included "the mayor, the county judge, and several prominent lawyers."[18]

The second ignominy involved the city council's application for urban renewal monies, purportedly to increase the number of sewage connections and to pave roads in town. This application was joined to a bond issue to fund further improvements. The result of these efforts did not proceed apace, as "the implementation of the program proceeded slowly . . . [and] what little urban renewal had been accomplished was often at the expense of the Latino community by condemning their houses and businesses to supply room for improvements that benefitted the Anglo, and, seldom, Latino neighborhoods, causing a growing discontent among the Latinos."[19]

For the purposes of this study, it is critical also to have a sense of the historical trends within the Crystal City Independent School District (CCISD)—not simply because of the connections between Jose Angel Gutierrez and Juan Rivera Jr. (on the football field and as administrators) between the late 1950s and 1972, but also to gain an overall perspective of, in general, the treatment of Mexican American pupils in the classroom, on the sidelines, and on the gridiron over the town's history. How did these patterns help bring about the revolt that occurred in the late 1960s? Additionally, as is examined in detail in chapter 3, Juan Rivera Jr. suffered discrimination and indignities attending CCISD, even though his prowess on the football field helped mitigate some negative elements. Indeed, it was a legendary local educator, Sterling H. Fly, who helped Juan onto the field, as well as running interference to provide him with the opportunity to attend Howard Payne College and to continue playing football, and further to earn his undergraduate degree in education. The story of CCISD has been examined on various occasions, and I use these materials to flesh out the community's story and how it intersects with that of the Rivera family.[20]

One of the first researchers to write about this school district was R. C. Tate, who completed a master's thesis titled "A History of Zavala County, Texas" in 1942. At the time of his study, the system included six schools, "two for Anglo-Americans, three for Mexicans, and one for Negroes." The names of the centers for Spanish-speaking children were as follows: the Swindall School, the De Zavala School, and the Mexico Chico School. As did Menefee, Tate noted that the high school was open to pupils of Mexican descent.[21] While Tate detailed the value of the properties and the number of teachers at the institutions, he did not give readers much sense of what was happening inside the schools and how they dealt with Mexican American pupils. For that key information, we need to turn to other, more recent sources.

The 1974 publication of James Staples Shockley's *Chicano Revolt in a Texas Town* gives a clearer sense of conditions inside the classrooms. Shockley summarized that conditions in these schools were far less than "equal." For example, he noted that the valuation of the buildings for the three Mexican American schools (as mentioned in Tate) totaled less than the valuation of the single "Anglo" elementary school. The value of the physical plant of the high school was estimated at three times the amount invested in the three Mexican primary schools combined. Further, and aligning with Menefee's findings, Shockley noted that the year 1931, the first of the new high school's operation, saw not a single Spanish-surnamed graduate earn a diploma. This figure did improve over time, however, as the total was three out of 31 in 1940. By 1950 there were nine Mexican American youths who graduated from CCHS, "and by the late 1950s, a majority of those graduating from high school were Mexican Americans." Juan Rivera Jr. earned his diploma in 1948 and then went on to Howard Payne College. Considering that the community, by the middle decades of the 20th century, had been overwhelmingly Mexican American for some time, the final statistic quoted in Shockley is not necessarily impressive. Further, as leaders of the student revolt in the late 1960s would point out, "Social discrimination was common, and the school system was run by Anglo teachers and Anglo administrators, basically for Anglo children, even as the Mexican American children increasingly began going to school and continuing in school."[22]

In Crystal City, however, as well as in the rest of Texas, change was on the horizon. For example, in 1949 the passage of the Gilmer-Aikin laws "linked state funding to average daily attendance, a move that brought more minority children into the schools even as racial and pedagogical segregation continued."[23] On the negative side of the ledger was the continuing instructional apartheid that occurred with placing the overwhelming majority of Spanish-surnamed students into "lower skilled tracks and most Anglo children in higher skilled tracks." As Jose Angel Gutierrez noted, "'Anglos were not placed in the fourth, fifth, or sixth track' with Mexican American 'slow learners.'"[24] On the other hand, Rodriguez does provide some sense of progress, though still tinged with the need to maintain white control, among the burgeoning number of Mexican American Javelinas within the halls of CCHS:

Changes within school society, politics and sports were mapped in the high school yearbooks, which encapsulated each year's various activities and the ethnic makeup of student life. From the mid-1950s onward, nearly every page is a testament to the growth of Mexican American teen participation in athletics, clubs, and student government and their success in winning those honors that came with full-page photos. After 1955, Mexican Americans won most elective school offices and honors in Crystal City. A small group of Mexican American students also played leading roles in high-prestige nonathletic clubs overwhelmingly populated by middle-class Anglo students, such as band, debate, Future Farmers of America, and the academic honor societies. . . . In reaction to this changed environment, school officials supported the creation of faculty-selected honors and the tailoring of extracurricular activities to appeal to Anglo students and alumni. . . . By placing honors under school control, teachers preserved the school's important place in local Anglo society while also accepting the rise of Mexican American majority politics in other areas of student life.[25]

Another recent study, this one by Baldemar James Barrera in 2007, provides even more insight into the particulars of what was occurring in the Crystal City classrooms in the years before the 1969 walkouts. Barrera argued that, even after the landmark *Brown v. Board of Education* case, educational disparities continued in CCISD. For example, he cited that "only 9% of all Mexican American students who began first grade together graduated from high school in 1951, and only 17% graduated in 1958." For the 1968–1969 school year, 376 whites, twelve African Americans, and 2,966 Mexican American youths constituted the population of the local schools. On the other hand, the roster of teachers remained heavily skewed in the other direction and featured three times as many Anglos (91) as Spanish-surnamed (30).[26] While it is reasonable to assume that some of these instructors worked diligently to teach their charges and better their lives, students in CCHS remembered that a substantial percentage did not. "Certain Anglo teachers at Crystal City High School regarded Mexican students [as] racially, culturally, and intellectually inferior." This sense of inequality was borne out in other ways, such as in recognizing academic excellence. As a 1970 report by the US Commission on Civil Rights noted,

> Generally, it was discovered that the percentage of Mexican American students receiving academic awards was unusually low when compared with the student population. . . . In those cases where the selection is done strictly by the students the recipients are usually Mexican American, but when the teachers or others participate in the selection, the recipients are usually Anglo.[27]

As articulated in chapter 3, the disparity was not limited to academics. Juan Rivera Jr., though playing at a very high level for the Javelinas, did not get the recognition he deserved for his success on the field, according to family lore. Later, in 1969, similar discriminatory practices, this time in the selection of homecoming and festival queens, would help bring about the walkouts by Mexican American students.

In regard to the leadership of the school board and other city offices in Crystal City, limited progress was made during the postwar years. Rodriguez's work details the experiences of E. C. Muñoz, the president of the town's AGIF branch, and the frustration of Mexican Americans who tried to bring about change by working within the system. In 1951, Muñoz, with the assistance of Hector Garcia, the leader of the AGIF, promoted the candidacy of Abbie Guevara, described as a "mild mannered store clerk who was the son of a prominent Mexican American Protestant minister," to become a member of the school board. The reaction was discouraging for the Spanish-surnamed citizens who believed that whites would work with them in order to improve conditions. A smear campaign took place against Guevara, and accusations were made about those working to elect him of attempting "reverse discrimination." This claim by whites generated a surge in voter registration by the powerful minority of Crystal City, and Guevara ultimately went down to defeat. Rodriguez summarized the impact of this school board election by stating that it "demonstrated that the airing of complaints . . . resulted in massive resistance. . . . Though Anglos did not support a single Mexican American candidate for office, Anglo politicians spent the 1950s appealing to the majority . . . for their votes." Muñoz himself ran for a school board seat in 1960, meeting the same fate as Guevara had a decade earlier. In 1961, however, "two prominent Mexican Americans with close ties of dependency and family relationships with the Anglo establishment were elected with the majority of the Anglo vote to serve on the school board."[28]

A further example of intransigence on the part of the white minority concerning schooling can be found in the case of a Protestant minister, the Reverend Arnold Lopez, newly arrived in town in 1960. Rev. Lopez tried to enroll his child in school, only to have his offspring relegated to one of the "Mexican" schools. Once again, the AGIF took action, and soon more than 100 Spanish-surnamed individuals raised an outcry at a CCISD board meeting. Ultimately, the board determined that some Mexican American students could attend the "regular" (white) schools, though the majority (in the lower grades) remained in class with other "migrants." These events, Rodriguez argues, "failed to alter the structure of ethnic and class segregation . . . [but] everyday people learned how to organize . . . as they grew increasingly wary . . . of hardened formal and informal Anglo opposition to even limited . . . participation in the social life of the city."[29] Given the extensive list of incidents and long-standing trends described here, that a major upheaval would ultimately take place in Crystal City is not surprising. This would come in 1969. One of the individuals at the center of the events was a young lady named Severita Lara.

Severita, whose life is detailed in a 2005 book by Jose Angel Gutierrez, was born in Crystal City in February 1952.[30] In many ways, she was typical of the Mexican American youths in the community before the blowout of 1969. For early instruction, her parents sent her to a private school, which operated behind a bakery in the Mexico Grande section of town. The goal of this institution was to teach the community's offspring both Spanish and English. This was done because "Mexican parents knew the Anglo teachers would keep Mexican children in first grade until they learned English. . . . In the public schools, a child could be ten or eleven years old and only in first grade. . . . Spanish-speaking children who already knew English were still retained in first grade to help the teacher with those who needed help with the language." When she did start in the CCISD schools, Severita inevitably endured paddling for speaking Spanish on school grounds. Still, she earned good grades and eventually moved on to high school. Severita also participated in another staple of life in Crystal City: heading north to work as a migrant, spending time in Minnesota and South Dakota during the summer of 1968.[31]

The following summer and fall proved momentous to the history of not just this small community in Zavala County, Texas, but to the overall trajectory of the Chicano Movement of the late 1960s and early 1970s. Two particular events, both featuring ties to athletics, were crucial to bringing about the walkout of 1969; Severita was involved in both. First, as Severita traveled to visit relatives in California with some friends, she heard from one of these companions that there had been an ugly incident at the Popeye Baseball Tournament in April. The matter centered around the selection process of the tournament sweetheart. While the majority of the players were Mexican American, the young lady named to this honor was always Anglo. The players protested to the high school principal, John B. Lair, only to be rebuffed, as he claimed that the decision was made exclusively by the baseball coach. In response, "Chicano students demanded a fair election with stated rules of eligibility, or no sweetheart be presented at the conclusion of the tournament. Some of the more informed . . . [were] talking about contacting MAYO, a group of militant Chicano youth based in San Antonio. MAYO stood for the Mexican American Youth Organization . . . [and] it had been involved with many school walkouts in the state." Once the specter of MAYO came on the scene, the administration agreed to have two sweethearts: one Anglo and the other Mexican American.[32] Severita was intrigued by this story, though she had never heard of MAYO or, for that matter, walkouts.

A second noteworthy event took place involving one of the most solemn of Texas's fall rituals: a football game. The homecoming contest for the Javelinas was fast approaching, and all over town discussion was happening around the selection of the homecoming queen. Severita's recollection of the lead-up to this incident was that "Chicano students and football players began asking teachers, coaches . . . and the high school principal about the election. . . . Many a girl, Chicana and Anglo, had private hopes of being a candidate and being chosen." It was then that the school board, influenced by white high school graduates in the community, instituted a change in the selection policy. Instead of a direct vote for the queen by the student body, the new arrangement called for "a football sweetheart chosen from among those girls whose parents had graduated high school [and that this] was better than a homecoming queen chosen by the students." This procedure outraged CCHS students, as they perceived it as a continuation of the pattern described above: a direct effort to keep certain honors out of the hands of the Mexican American majority population in the student body. Ultimately, the principal and the school board both refused to remedy the situation.[33] A further discussion of this episode, how it helped spur the walkout, and how it was instrumental in bringing Juan Rivera Jr. back to Crystal City—and his leaving employment with CCISD for good—appears in chapter 3.

A final voice that provides key information on sports in Crystal City prior to the 1969 blowout comes from Jose Angel Gutierrez himself in an interview I conducted with him in October 2018. While much has been written on his life, times, and activities, very little discussion has taken place on this part of his narrative. Like many youths of the 1940s (he was born in October 1944), Jose Angel was eager to play Little League Baseball and he did, at least until this became impossible after he and his mother had to resort to migrant work following his father's death. The sport was supposed to create a wonderful bond between fathers and sons, but this level of the game was "problematic" due to the ethnic relations extant in Crystal City. Jose Angel recalled that in order for a Mexican American to be able to play, he "had to be truly outstanding." Indeed, one of his other recollections about playing on the diamond was the limited interaction between the Spanish-surnamed and white players on these teams. "The Chicanos always sat at the end of the bench, and if you screwed up, you were to be avoided." Circumstances were similar on the gridiron, particularly before the late 1950s.

As noted in other works on Latinos and football, the issue of economics and educational discrimination played a significant role in keeping many athletes off the field.[34] Jose Angel noted in our interview, for example, that many of the Mexican Americans who wanted to play the sport were forced to give up the game in order to work (both as migrants and in town) to assist in their families' financial survival. Additionally, few of these potential players and their parents had cars, and since the school buses would leave right after school, this further reduced the number of such players who could come out to play for the Javelinas.[35]

While the Gutierrez family, which resided two blocks from the cantinas in the Mexico Grande neighborhood, did have a more privileged situation than most, the death of Jose Angel's father in 1957 was traumatic and transforming, personally, economically, and socially. Although Jose Angel's father practiced medicine, he was not given the respect and treatment usually afforded a medical professional. "My father was a doctor for Mexicans, without hospital privileges or referrals to use of equipment such as x-ray machines. . . . He took care of all, with or without money, for decades. He had to buy all of these items over time to have a full-service medical office in the barrio." Things got worse after his passing. "The annual Christmas baskets of fruit from Anglo employers my dad had cured stopped coming. . . . Our economic world also turned upside down. The local banker refused to lend my mother any money, even for the remaining funeral and medical expenses related to his death."[36] Shortly thereafter, Gutierrez and his mother began their time as migrants in Wisconsin. Jose Angel eventually returned to Crystal City in 1958 to live with his grandmother, while his mother moved on to California. At first he attended Sterling Fly Junior High School, which had a substantial population of migrant children. Later he played under the guidance of Juan Rivera Jr. at the high school.

Gabe's father was the coach of the B team, which, Gutierrez argued, was more akin to a "farm team" than an actual junior varsity. Jose Angel noted that the B squad comprised exclusively Mexican Americans. Practices, he stated, had the B team mostly serving as "tackling dummies" for the improvement of techniques by whites on the varsity. While a few of the Spanish-surnamed did make the jump to the "big club," the majority did not. Juan would sometimes be allowed on the sidelines with the other football coaches for varsity contests, but not always. Like the situation with Little League Baseball, the Spanish-surnamed players who toiled under Rivera Jr. had to be truly extraordinary in order to get "the call."

Additionally, when a Mexican American did make it to the pinnacle of athletics at CCHS, local social mores still had to be observed. For example, Jose Angel recalled that a player named Mike Trevino actually started at quarterback for the green and gold in 1961. "Mike was the big man on campus, and he even dated a white girl." Of course, Gutierrez added, this did not sit well with many in the minority population of Crystal City. According to Jose Angel, Trevino paid the price for this indiscretion on two occasions: once by being beaten up by some of his classmates, and a second time by not being selected for an award by the local Quarterback Club.[37] While there is no evidence that Juan Rivera Jr. ever suffered a beating, as did Trevino, according to family lore, he was shortchanged by the same booster organization in 1948 by not receiving a deserved award. Of course, it was presented to a white player.

The information provided in this chapter sought to furnish readers with a sense of the social, economic, educational, and sporting context that existed in Crystal City between the early 1900s and the year of the walkout, 1969. Into the early years of this milieu, Gabe's great-grandfather Cresencio arrived when he moved to a portion of town known as El Swiche in the early 1900s. There, he and his wife, Valeriana Lerma, raised eight children. Marc Simon Rodriguez, whose family is also from Crystal City, indicated that this sector "was not in town, but was about two to three miles southeast, next to the Nueces River." This section of town was located near an onion and spinach processing plant (not the one that becomes Del Monte). "The area was called 'El Swiche' because the railroad had a switch between the processing facilities and the main line that went into town and out to market." Norbert Rivera stated that this was a railroad spur and that his grandfather, granduncles, and grandaunts all lived in that vicinity. We now turn to the story of Gabriel's father and his interactions with the local schools, both on and off the gridiron.[38]

CHAPTER 3

THE MAKING OF A FOOTBALL COACH

JUAN RIVERA AND HIS ATHLETIC AND COACHING CAREER IN SOUTH TEXAS, 1930–1972

THE WORKS PROGRESS ADMINISTRATION STUDY by Selden Menefee referenced in the previous chapter provided a contemporary overview of the circumstances of daily life confronted by Mexicans who came to Zavala County, and particularly Crystal City, in the early decades of the twentieth century. Several key points raised in that work tie directly to the story of the Riveras: (1) the overwhelming presence of families from Coahuila in the community, (2) the prevalence of migratory labor among the group, and (3) the existence of income-level distinctions.

The first point should not be a surprise. A quick perusal of a map of Coahuila and Texas shows that the distance from a major community in that Mexican state, Piedras Negras, to Crystal City is but 50 miles. Given the availability of work, there was certainly bound to be a connection between the municipalities. Next, although work was plentiful in Zavala County, it was overwhelmingly seasonal in nature and necessitated the exodus of families from the county at specific times of the year. While working directly in the fields was the fate of most Coahuiltecans, not all of the Spanish-surnamed individuals performed that type of labor. Tasks were associated with keeping the agricultural machinery going, such as working as contractors (*contratistas*), those whose job was to move laborers from point A to point B. While not highly paid, the endeavor allowed some individuals to make a slightly better living than others, as well as not having to migrate north. All of the elements listed above are part of the Rivera clan's story. The majority of the information that follows in the next few paragraphs comes from the author's interviews with Gabe's older brother, Norbert Rivera, and is based on his genealogical research.

The first forebear to arrive in the area was Gabe's great-grandfather Cresencio Rivera, who hailed from San Buenaventura, Coahuila, where he was born on October 27, 1872. He married Valeriana Lerma (born in 1876, no information on her specific date of birth) on his birthday in 1894. The couple had eight children, all but one of whom lived into adulthood. Some were delivered in Texas, others back in Coahuila. One of the most interesting aspects of Cresencio's story is that, by the late 1910s, well into his 40s, he was required to register for the draft during World War I. He dutifully complied, and his card is available in the Mexican National Archives.[1]

Juan Rivera Sr. was the couple's first child. He was born in 1897 and died on March 16, 1984. Gabe's grandfather was born in Hacienda de Guadalupe, in the municipality of Guerrero. The remaining offspring were as follows: Maria De Los Angeles (no dates of birth or death available); Rafael, who was the couple's first child to be delivered in the United States, in Crystal City (October 24, 1907–August 1, 1981); Guadalupe (no information on where she was born and died; she lived between 1905 and 1930); Margarita, who was born in Piedras Negras and lived from November 22, 1905 to 1978; Anastacio, the only child to not reach adulthood (died in 1908); Dolores, who ultimately moved to and raised her family in California (March 30, 1912–May 16, 2002); and Maria Felicita (February 22, 1915–January 1983), both of whom were born in Crystal City. Maria Felicita remained in her hometown with her family (her married name was Dominguez) living in El Swiche.

While the birth places of the scions show that the family did move, Norbert indicated that the Riveras at no time endured the hardships faced by migrant workers. Rather, sons Juan and Rafael helped Cresencio in his work as a *contratista*. The family operated trucks (no information on whether they owned the vehicles or merely drove them) that were used to shuttle workers from location to location under contract to area farmers. When Cresencio died from a heart attack in Carrizo Springs in January 1934, his obituary described him as being a "laborer." Norbert stressed, however, that his ancestor did not work the fields, nor did he or his children migrate. When asked if this meant that the Riveras were "better off" than most, Norbert stipulated that they were, but added then that that was "a relative term."[2] Cresencio and Valeriana owned a house and some land, but the description of such properties in the "Mexican sections" of Crystal City mentioned in Menefee clarifies that most such domiciles were neither spacious nor had modern amenities such as indoor toilets or electricity. As noted in the story of Jose Angel Gutierrez in the previous chapter, even those Mexican Americans who did not labor directly in the fields were not perceived as equals by the local whites.

Juan Rivera Sr. would work for his father shuttling workers to farms in the Winter Garden area. He married Ricarda Cabral in August 1914. She was born in April 1901 and passed away in October 1968, the result of a long battle with hypertension. This union produced a total of nine children, eight of whom lived to adulthood.

An important fact that Menefee discussed in his work is evident in this second generation of the Rivera family. Unlike

Cresencio and Valeriana, Juan and Ricarda did not shuttle back and forth across the border, and all of their offspring were born in Texas. Additionally, the third cohort of the family also sought opportunities outside of the Lone Star State. The first child, Jose Maria, was born in Cline and lived from July 1916 until December 2004. He followed the path carved out by his grandfather and father, working as a contractor in Eagle Pass. Next came Refugio, also known as "Cuca," who was born in the Uvalde County town of Knippa and lived from July 1920 until November 2008. She married and raised her family in the community of her birth, though they lived for some time in San Antonio. Elegia, known as "Cona," was born in December 1923 and passed away in August 2007. She left Crystal City and joined her younger brother, Pedro, in Illinois. The next two children, Barbara (born in December 1925 and died in March 1945) and Nieves (born and died in 1927) did not live long. Barbara's demise came about due to an infection after surgery for a ruptured appendix. Pedro, who lived from January 1928 until July 1995, was the first member of the family to bolt for a job in the industrial Midwest, working as a warehouse foreman in Chicago until his retirement. His domicile in the Windy City served as a base for family members at different times. Juan Rivera Jr. was next. He was born in May 1930 and lived until 1990; the rest of this chapter focuses on his family and his athletic and coaching careers. Vicenta was the next child of Juan Sr. and Ricarda. She was born in July 1934 and died in September 2002. She married, moved to Colorado, and raised her children there. The last sister in this family is Maria de Jesus, who was born in January 1937 and still lives in San Antonio. By the time this youngest child turned 10, Ricarda had moved the youngest children of the family to San Antonio, with Juan Jr. and Pedro having bucked the educational odds noted previously and completed studies at Crystal City High School.

Maria de Jesus also graduated from high school, although she completed her studies at an institution in San Antonio. She finished in 1957. During our interview, she proudly stated that she graduated on May 30 of that year, and the very next day, her brother Juan Jr. received his undergraduate degree from Howard Payne College. The reason the family moved to the Alamo City, she noted, was that her parents had separated. Shortly after the war, Ricarda, already suffering from the issue that would claim her life two decades hence, moved to Chicago to be with her older brother and receive better medical treatment than was available to her in Crystal City. While she was away, Juan Sr. broke his marital covenant. As a result, upon her return to Texas, Ricarda took her youngest children to live with Refugio and her husband. The couple never divorced and reconciled in 1960. After Ricarda's passing, Juan Sr. also made the trip to Chicago, as he sought treatment for problems with his eyesight.[3]

As previous historians have articulated, circumstances in the Zavala County schools were not ideal for Mexican American students throughout most of the twentieth century. A 1986 publication by the Zavala County Historical Commission sought to portray as positive a picture as possible for this sordid story. The contributors provided extensive details about the number of buildings constructed, when the edifices were built, and the financial commitments involved. The history did not mention, however, any issues concerning how the majority of the students in the system, those of Mexican background, were mistreated. Only toward the final paragraphs of the essay in this manuscript was any mention made of the "great changes" that took place in 1969 and beyond.[4] Clearly, things were difficult for such students in Crystal City; most educational and sporting opportunities were simply denied to them. Juan Rivera Jr.'s experiences within the system, however, were both in line with and different from those of the majority of his co-ethnics. His athletic talent, though, obviously opened doors and helped bring him to the attention of one of the most important men in the community, an individual synonymous with the early history of CCISD: Sterling Harper Fly.

Fly and his wife, Mary (née Sutherland), arrived in Crystal City in 1925, and he served as superintendent of CCISD until 1953, when he would go on to become president of Southwest Texas Junior College in Uvalde. Given the poignant realities of CCISD detailed previously, the Zavala County Historical Commission's description of Fly may be a bit buoyant in its praise: "Long before the civil rights movement, Sterling insisted on quality education for all. Fully bilingual himself and recognizing the value of a bilingual citizenry, he instituted the teaching of Spanish from the lower grades through High School."[5] In response, Jose Angel Gutierrez indicated to me that this statement was "blatantly not true. I was punished for speaking Spanish while attending Fly Jr. High in 1957. Severita Lara, walkout leader in 1969, also mentions being spanked by Principal Harbin" for speaking Spanish.[6]

Fly took an interest in Juan because of his athletic and classroom abilities. Given CCHS's less-than-sterling gridiron record, the team needed all the help it could get, even if it meant having to line up Mexican Americans on the field from time to time. Over its first three seasons, 1920 to 1922, the Javelinas' squad tallied just one victory. The program was briefly discontinued between 1923 and 1925. In Fly's second year at the administrative helm, the sport resurfaced with Clyde Tate serving as head coach between 1926 and 1940. During that span, the team had but four winning seasons. By the middle of the 1940s, talent such as Rivera, a strapping youth who could play effectively on both sides of the line, could help improve results on the field. Juan played for two coaches during his tenure: Reagan Nesbitt and Jerome Davis. The team was slightly less than mediocre during the 1946 to 1948 campaigns, finishing with an overall mark of 12–14–3.[7]

Juan's most important accomplishment during his time on the CCHS gridiron was earning a spot on the All-District second team his senior year.[8] Norbert indicated during one of our interviews that his father mentioned that an award presented by the local Quarterback Club, which Juan felt he had earned, was instead bestowed upon a white teammate.[9] There is evidence, however, that at least one other entity in town rewarded Juan for his play on the field in one midseason game: the Lions Club. In a regular feature of the *Zavala County Sentinel* titled "This Was the News," the September 26, 1958, issue hearkened back to a story from October 1948 in which Juan was feted for his play. The local paper was glowing in its praise of his performance:

> Juan Rivera was guest of the Lions Club Monday on being selected as the most outstanding player on the Javelina eleven. His work on offense and defense was something to see. The fans who saw the game know that he is the spark that the team needs and when he went out during the last half due to an injury, our team showed the result.[10]

Perhaps, in line with the arguments Jose Angel Gutierrez presented in the previous chapter, it is possible to provide more narrowly focused examples of in-season appreciation for a Mexican American athlete, but not recognition for an entire campaign's worth of work.

Helping direct Juan toward the team would be just the first of several times Fly would play an active role on Rivera's behalf and help move him toward professional success. Indeed, Fly would be of great importance in allowing Juan Rivera Jr. the opportunity to continue to play football, as well as eventually opening up avenues to earn the collegiate education that would catapult his family into middle-class status.

Before moving on to discuss Juan's collegiate playing and, later, his coaching career, it is necessary to better contextualize the relationship between Gabe's father and Sterling Fly. In 1993, in an article titled "Our *Gringo Amigos*: Anglo Americans and the Tejano Experience," Arnoldo De Leon articulated a position that was controversial in some quarters of the historical profession that focused on Mexican American history: that is, that not all whites in Texas stood in the way of this minority population.[11] As De Leon argued,

> What I propose in this essay, therefore, is to move away from the common depiction of Anglos as tormentors ... and chronicle cases where sympathetic whites have spoken out on behalf of Mexican American interests. These examples do not derive from new research; they have always been part of the general literature which shows that, indeed, there have ever existed "*gringos*" who for one reason or another proved to be "*amigos*" of *Tejanos.*[12]

De Leon then proceeds to provide a series of instances where there were "positive" interactions between specific Spanish-surnamed persons and whites over the years. The author adroitly notes that in many such cases, there was, of course, "something" of benefit to the gringo involved: be it access to land, marriage partners (in the early years of the nineteenth century), political alliances, or in the twentieth century, votes to be gained (such as with the various political machines operating in parts of the state). Perhaps it was that way between Fly and Juan Rivera Jr. By helping him succeed and graduate, however, the Javelinas had a good player on their side who could help improve results on the field.[13] Still, Fly may have simply been a truly progressive educator genuinely concerned with helping a particular Mexican American youth with promise on the field and in the classroom. Fly subsequently helped Juan move on to the next level of athletic competition, running interference to get him a scholarship at Howard Payne College (HPC).

Juan graduated from Crystal City High School in 1948, and Sterling Fly had helped to bring his athletic skills to the attention of then Yellowjackets' coach, Felton Wright. Juan first lined up for HPC in the 1950 season. The HPC yearbook, the *Lasso,* showed that he took part in several activities on campus. In addition to the football team, Juan also was a member of the track team (shot-putter) and the Spanish Club. Interestingly, a total of four Mexican Americans were listed on the roster of that gridiron team. Other Spanish-surnamed athletes included Mike Gonzalez from Uvalde, Aureliano Ortiz from Brady, and Tom Valdez from Eagle Pass. In 1951, the yearbook showed that Rivera was part of an exclusive club on campus: the H Club, reserved for lettermen. Here, he was joined by his aforementioned teammates. It is interesting to note that several Latinos at HPC at this time were members of a prominent on-campus organization charged with the goal of promoting "good sportsmanship and to uphold the traditions of Howard Payne in all athletic contests."[14]

After the 1951–1952 academic year, Juan interrupted his studies and athletic career and volunteered to serve in the Air Force during the Korean War. He was stationed in Greenland, and after finishing his commitment, his Veterans Administration benefits helped him return to HPC and complete his undergraduate degree in education. Not surprisingly, the Yellowjackets were happy to have him back. An article in the local paper, the *Brownwood Bulletin*, gushed with anticipation of having "the Chief" be part of the 1955–1956 squad. Sportswriter Tom Penn noted,

> Juan Rivera . . . was a sideline visitor at the Jackets' scrimmage session Tuesday afternoon. The Chief . . . plans to return here soon after Christmas and enroll at HP for the spring semester. Rivera, one of the nice guys in the trade, as the saying goes, looks just as trim and hard as he did in 1950, when he was handling the guard slots with "mucho gusto." Anywhere there was leather popping, Chief could always be found. Rivera could be a valuable addition to Coach Guy Gardner's plans for 1955. The 200-pounder, who hails from Crystal City, and who is only 24 years of age, would fit in very nicely in that sophomore-loaded line that just might become the toughest outfit in Texas small college circles.[15]

A return to civilian life, the football field, and the classroom were not the only changes for Juan Rivera Jr. in the autumn of 1954; he also married Maria Antonia Garcia, who hailed from

San Antonio, on October 24. The couple would go on to have five children, all boys.

Juan would play for the Yellowjackets during the 1955 and 1956 campaigns. While there were highlights, he was often injured over the two seasons. An overview of his performance on the field shows that he was regularly listed as the starter at either guard or center, but a series of injuries repeatedly kept him out of the lineup. One high point came in late October 1955 when Juan intercepted a pass against Northwestern State of Louisiana and helped the Yellowjackets defeat the Demons, 12–7. Unfortunately, later in that game, he injured his back.[16] Although he was not expected to play, Juan took the field with his teammates the following contest, only to suffer another injury when he was clipped by a McMurry Cowboys player. It was at the following contest, against rival Abilene Christian College, when Juan's replacement, Don Dendy, entered as his substitute (after Rivera hurt his leg). The Yellowjackets had a successful year, finishing 9–1 and claiming the Texas Conference title.[17]

The following season brought Juan more frustration on the field, though there certainly was a reason for joy off of it. As noted previously, the Riveras would have five boys, four of whom would reach adulthood. While Juan was working on his undergraduate degree, the couple had two offspring: Oscar, who was born and died in 1955, and then Bernardo, who arrived on September 4, 1956.[18] On the gridiron, the spring practice period revealed that Juan was still considered the starter, but that Dendy was right on his heels. "Juan Rivera . . . gained a starting spot at the end of last season and should remain there if an old leg injury is healed. Don Dendy . . . starred in the final game of the year when he came off the bench at a crucial point." Unfortunately, Juan then suffered a cut on his arm that kept him out of practice for a few days. Later, as training wrapped up for the semester, he was still unable to participate and was forced to sit out an annual contest against former

Yellowjackets.[19] By the start of the fall term, the local paper was expressing doubt as to his ability to remain on the field. "The Jackets appear quite strong at end, tackle, and fullback. The team will also be adequate at center if Rivera, a regular part of last season although hampered with injuries, can stay on the active list." It would not be so, and by the first games of the season, the local scribes waxed eloquently on the continuing issues with Juan's legs:

> The threat of a knee injury also dangles blackly over the important center position where spirited Juan Rivera holds forth with gusto. Juan appeared last season to have the same attraction for misfortune that molasses has for flies. It was a knee injury to Juan which put Dendy on the sport in last year's final game. Dendy came through in tremendous style, and probably can do so again if necessary. . . . Rivera's leg appears to be whole now, and we hope the big fellow is able to play every minute of all 10 scheduled games. But the air of uncertainty remains.[20]

Interestingly, after this particular item there is no further mention in the local papers about Juan's performance during this season. His picture does show up in the *Lasso* as being part of the team, unlike in the 1955 version of the publication. The 1956 squad finished its campaign with a mark of 6–2–2 and was runner-up in the Texas Conference.

Juan graduated with his degree in education at the end of the 1956–1957 academic year. He still had the football bug, however, and, according to Norbert, went to Chicago to try out for the Cardinals. He prepared for this endeavor by running in muddy fields around Brownwood in an attempt to strengthen his injured leg and back. While in the Windy City, Juan stayed with his older brother, Pedro. The assay at a professional playing career did not work out, and then it was time for Rivera to hang up his cleats—as an on-field participant, at least. Then, with his degree in hand and a family to support, Juan sought work as a teacher and coach. His first job, not surprisingly, entailed a return to his hometown of Crystal City in order to lead the B team for the Javelinas. Norbert noted that his father had opportunities elsewhere but was asked directly by Sterling Fly to return to his hometown. Given the connection that existed between the two men, Rivera cast his lot in Crystal City.[21]

The *Zavala County Sentinel* noted the arrival of the former football star to work at CCHS as the community approached the start of the 1957–1958 academic year.[22] A bit later in the year, the paper gave more background information on Juan's duties when it observed that he had "graduated from Crystal High, where he was a football star, received his degree from Howard Payne College. He helps coach the High School B team and teaches in Junior High." It is interesting to note that there was also another Spanish-surnamed individual, Mary Medellin, teaching physical education (as well as Spanish and junior high school science) in the district. A quick perusal of the teachers' roster for CCISD does support the information presented previously: though the majority of students were of Spanish-speaking descent, the vast plurality of educators were not of that background. There was also documentation in the local paper concerning some of Juan's other activities in town— for example, he joined the Catholic Men's Club at Sacred Heart Parish.[23]

Before proceeding with more information on Coach Rivera's tenure at Crystal City, we should note the presence of a few Latino athletes on the Javelinas' roster during these years. As Jose Angel Gutierrez stipulated earlier, the majority of the Mexican American players for CCHS remained at the B-team level. Still, the starting lineups for some games during the late 1950s did include a few players of this background on the Crystal City varsity. For example, in the November 15, 1957, issue of the paper, the starting lineup for the local eleven included Ray Villegas, Sam Guevara, and Rey Perez in the backfield, and Amador Acosta was the first-string split end.

The 1958 edition of the club featured even more such players listed as starters for the first game of the year: Lalo Martinez at left guard, Joe Talamantes at left tackle, Joe Lopez at right tackle, Raul Flores at right end, and Eusebio Salinas at left end. A late-season 1958 game had even more Spanish-surnamed players listed as starters: Aurelio Ramirez at left end, Eusebio Salinas at left tackle, Hector Navarez at left guard, Joe Lopez at right tackle, and Ray Villegas at right halfback. Similarly, in the senior page of the 1958 edition of the *Javelin*, several other Mexican Americans were listed as participating (though not necessarily starters) in the football program: Dionicio Avila, Tigero Guajardo, Robert Gamez, Robert Diaz, Encarnacion Rios Mata, Salvador Menchaca, and Rosario Muñoz. While discriminatory practices were certainly in place, at least a few Latino players were making it onto the CCHS varsity by the end of the 1950s.[24]

Juan Rivera's professional, personal, and family life continued to blossom during his time in Crystal City. He earned his master's in education in the summer of 1959, and he and Maria Antonia celebrated the birth of their final three children. In addition to Bernardo, who had been born in Brownwood, the couple welcomed Norbert in September 1957, Gabe in April 1961, and finally Adrian in February 1963. Shortly after Adrian's birth, Juan Rivera's athletic and educational mentor, Sterling Fly, succumbed from an illness soon after his retirement from the presidency of Southwest Texas Junior College in Uvalde.[25]

Coach Rivera worked in his hometown from 1957 through 1963. He continued to coach the B team and even saw some of his players make it to the varsity. He was able to work with the head coaches of the big club, George Mabe (who was the Javelinas' leader between 1952 and 1960) and Frank Rutledge (head coach between 1961 and 1964), and even spent time on the sidelines on some Friday nights. Neither of these white field generals had much success at the CCHS helm. The highlight of the Mabe tenure came in 1953, when the team finished

9–2–1 and were district champions. Overall, he concluded with a mark of 34–51–8. Rutledge had one winning campaign, a 6–4–0 record in 1961, and never claimed a district title. His overall mark at Crystal City was 16–21–2. Given these two individuals' lack of success, it raises a question about whether an individual of the same ethnic background as the majority of the student body might not have merited an opportunity to take over as head coach. The answer to this question is multifaceted and involves events outside the school and beyond the gridiron.

It is not surprising that Juan Rivera took leave of his high school alma mater when he did. A confluence of circumstances was involved. First, as Norbert Rivera indicated in one of our interviews, his father was absolutely and resolutely nonpolitical. He wanted to coach, teach, and take care of his family. Given that the first phase of the Crystal City revolts commenced in 1963, the tumultuous changes taking place in the community likely helped prompt his decision to seek employment elsewhere. Second, in the midst of all the uncertainty surrounding the election of Los Cinco, there was little hope that Coach Rivera would have been called upon to take over a key position in the community from the struggling Frank Rutledge.[26] Finally, again according to Norbert's recollection, the then-current coach of Benavides High School (in nearby Duval County), Isaac Gonzales (who coached at BHS between 1957 and 1963 and had an overall mark of 34–26–7), invited Juan to succeed him as head coach of the Eagles. Juan served as an assistant to Gonzales during the 1963 campaign. The Eagles finished with a mark of 4–3–2.

At this point in time, there were simply not many places in Texas that would hire a Mexican American to lead an important institution such as the local high school's football team. Fortunately for Juan, the hiring of a "Mexican" to lead a gridiron squad was not perceived as a major issue in Benavides. Indeed, Gonzales (with the exception of two years, 1955 and

1956 with Frank Schneider) was not the first Spanish-surnamed field general for BHS. He followed in the footsteps of a southern Texas coaching legend, Everardo Carlos (E. C.) Lerma, who had guided the Eagles to great success on the gridiron (including two regional titles and two perfect seasons), on the basketball court, and on the track between the years of 1938 and 1954.

Given the small size of the Mexican American head football coaching fraternity in the early 1960s, it seems reasonable that Coach Gonzalez would reach out to a co-ethnic to help lead a school that, like Crystal City, overwhelmingly comprised Spanish-surnamed student-athletes.[27] Juan took over as head coach for the 1964 season, and his promotion merited a brief, factual mention in the Crystal City paper. While the squad eked out a winning record the previous year, the new field general was less sanguine about the prospects of his first season at the helm. "Juan Rivera, Jr., former assistant coach of the Crystal City Javelins, is the head coach this year of the Benavides Eagles. . . . According to the new head coach, the team will be smaller and slower than last year." The regional paper, the *Alice Daily Echo*, sounded an optimistic tone at the start of the season, indicating that there were thirty-seven returning players from the previous season, including eight two-year veterans. Additionally, the new field general was assisted by another South Texas football legend, Carlos Esquivel, who had not only run wild at Edinburg High School during a legendary career but also played football at the highest levels: during 1955 and 1956 for the Texas A&M University Aggies. Certainly the leadership of the team would be good, but Coach Rivera was quite prescient in his assessment of his team's talent (or lack thereof) as his charges finished 0–10 and were outscored by a 262–14 margin.[28]

Things did improve for the Eagles in 1965, as they ended with a mark of 3–4–3 and were tied with two other teams for the district title. For 1966 BHS hoped to be even stronger, as the *Echo* noted at the start of the season that they were "for the first time a definite threat in preseason guessing by some 'experts." Although they did not finish with a winning mark, the team was improved, turning in a 4–6 record and only being outscored 116–102. For 1967 Rivera again had a substantial number of returning veterans, a total of six on each side of the ball, but the Eagles struggled to a 2–6–1 mark. As do most coaches, Rivera "talked a good game" for 1968, but prognosticators did not see much hope for BHS. At least there were increased numbers of athletes turning out. Juan noted, "We have 50 players out for football this year, and that is more than we have had during my six years with the Eagles." While certainly having more material to work with, the paper also stated that "only 21 players of 50 on both the varsity and B-team have ever played football before. A number of those out for the sport for the first time are several of the 12 who this year are seniors."[29] The 1968 season saw another mediocre campaign, as the Eagles finished 3–6–1. Juan's final season at the helm proved to be his least successful since the winless campaign of 1964. The Eagles finished 1–9 and were outscored by a 213–36 tally. Overall, Coach Rivera was never able to turn the Eagles around, and his overall record was a less-than-stellar tally of 13–41–5.[30] His next position would be to follow Esquivel to Edinburg and serve as an assistant coach of the offensive line as well as head coach of the Bobcats' track team.[31]

Although things did not go very well on the field, Benavides proved to be a wonderful place for the Rivera youths to spend part of their childhood. Gabe and his siblings attended the local elementary and middle schools, and he and his brothers often played tackle football in the family's driveway and in an open field across the street. Eventually, all of the boys wound up participating in some type of athletic activities. Norbert played football (when the family moved to San Antonio) but did not care for the contact. His brother Bernie (who is now an engineer) played football at Eastern New Mexico University, and brother Adrian also played, briefly as will be noted, at

Texas Tech. As Norbert indicated in one of our interviews, "Football was the family business."[32] Gabe would also eventually play baseball and basketball and be on the track team (not surprisingly, he was a shot-putter) during his high school years in San Antonio.

After one year working with the Bobcats, Juan Rivera Jr. once again heard the siren call that he could not resist: that of his alma mater. He moved his family back to his hometown in early 1971. To say that things were not as they had been in the 1940s and 1950s was most certainly an understatement. Juan may have spent several years in the school's halls as a student, teacher, and coach, but by the start of the 1970s the political and social settings in the community were radically different from the days of his youth and early career. On the football field, however, things remained pretty much the same, if they had not actually become worse. The years of 1964 to 1970 consisted of the last year of Frank Rutledge's tenure, three seasons under Gerald Riley, two under T. W. Harvey, and for 1970, one campaign with John Ladner at the helm. The combined record for these seven teams was a miserable 13–53–2. As early as 1964 there was already some grumbling in the *Sentinel* that the community was not supporting the team and that it was a civic and institutional duty to do so, even with its abysmal results. In the midst of all the turmoil happening on campus and in town, there was a call to rally around the football team as a unifying force (hopefully) for the entire community; obviously, though, by this stage of the game, it was way too late for that possibility to come to fruition.

> You will agree that in order for our schools to succeed in all encounters, we must be UNITED or we will FAIL. . . .
> For at no time in life will anything be accomplished that is not derived by hard work and cooperation. Therefore, our enthusiasm should be so great that our leaders should feel it without having to look for it to see whether it is there. BUT WE fall or will we rise above all obstacles? That is up to

YOU. . . . I am not sure whether my yells are audible on the field, BUT I do know the boys are definitely aware of the backing and the enthusiasm that is there or not.[33]

The fervor of the fans and the efforts of the athletes helped generate only two victories that season. In 1965 the Javelinas actually had a winning mark, finishing at 5–4. The final two years of the Gerald Riley era and the first season under T. W. Harvey proved to be the absolute nadir of Javelinas football, as the team went 0–30 and was outscored by a combined margin of 1224–123 over the three years. In 1969, the season of the December blowout, the team showed some spunk and won two games, finishing 2–8. This was the last season for Coach Harvey, who closed out his career with a 2–18 mark and never again served as a head coach in Texas. John Ladner actually managed to guide the team to a respectable season, with a 4–5–1 mark (and they were only outscored by a margin of 202–132) during the 1970 campaign.[34]

As mentioned in chapter 2, one of the seminal events in the 1969 revolt that took place at CCHS occurred in the lead-up to the Javelinas' homecoming game. As had been done in the past, the Ex-Students' Association met to select the homecoming court. In that year, however, the school board reneged on the association's right to use the football field. While there was Mexican American representation on the board at this time, they were still in the minority; the transformation of the board to Spanish-surnamed majority control took place with the election of 1970. The local paper noted that the administrators had

voted to deny the use of school facilities last week following a stormy protest by a group of Mexican American parents, students, and friends. The controversy developed over the ex-students' method of electing the homecoming court which required that a girl must be the daughter of a CCHS ex-student in order to be eligible. The Mexican American group charged that this was discriminatory since not many of them had graduated from the school.[35]

A quick perusal of the court's composition demonstrates why the Mexican American protesters expressed outrage and frustration. For a student body that comprised at least 85 to 90 percent Spanish-surnamed youths, the court consisted exclusively of whites. A few Latinas were eligible, according to the *Sentinel*—Patricia Muñoz, Maria Avila, Rita Avila, Diana Serna, and Yolanda Flores—but none of those candidates were selected. Additionally, the football sweetheart for this season, Sandra Moore, was also non-Latina.[36] Further documentation of this inequitable situation comes from Jose Angel Gutierrez's book on the Crystal City revolt. As to the selection process for the court and the cheerleading squad, he reported,

> Without regard for how many girls had parents that had graduated from the high school, the school board approved the plan [noted above]. Chicana students were outraged at being disenfranchised simply because their parents had quit and not graduated from the high school; only six of 280 Chicanas were eligible. The school board had also ignored the student demand that the cheerleading squad be comprised of more than one token Chicana, with the rest Anglos.[37]

Building upon the success and the publicity created by the blowout, the burgeoning leadership (featuring the establishment of the LRUP, La Raza Unida Party) among the Mexican American community in Crystal City next set its sights on taking complete control of the school board. As Shockley argued in his 1974 work, *Chicano Revolt in a Texas Town*, "With school policies so much in the forefront . . . Mexican representation on the board became totally inadequate. Control of the school system and redirection toward Chicano needs became the goal. . . . Gutierrez headed a slate running for the three positions . . . vacant on the seven-man board." In April 1970, Jose Angel and two other LRUP candidates swept to victory. Once a previously appointed Mexican American member (Eddie Trevino) aligned himself with the LRUP adherents, the takeover of the board was complete. After some wrangling, Gutierrez became president.[38]

It was now his duty to fill key academic and administrative positions. As Gutierrez stated during our interview, his goal was to "have as many Mexicans in positions of power" as possible.[39] He eventually replaced the superintendent and the athletic director (Coach Ladner), as well as people in other posts. Given that he was familiar with Juan Rivera Jr. from his playing days, and given the dearth of available candidates, Gutierrez turned to his old coach. Gutierrez indicated in our interview that another individual considered, Jimmy Valdez, had been a very successful baseball player at CCHS, but by the 1970s Valdez was blind and felt he was not up to the task of operating an athletic department. Thus, the call went out to Edinburg for Juan to come home.[40]

Although Rivera was a well-known and appreciated personage in Crystal City, the atmosphere was simply too tense to permit his hiring to be anything but contentious. For a man who did not care for political shenanigans and who merely wanted to do his job, taking this leadership post with CCISD in 1971 was certainly problematic. An article from the *Sentinel* dated February 11 of that year provided readers with a blow-by-blow account of the process. The Anglo members of the board, Ed Mayer and M. A. Maedgen Jr., voted against Rivera's hiring; another non–Mexican American trustee, Wayne Hamilton, abstained. All four Spanish-surnamed individuals on the board voted in the affirmative. Amid all of the tumult, it was an example of the respect that Juan Rivera had earned over his time at CCHS that Mayer and Maedgen argued that their negative votes were not cast because they felt that Juan could not do the job, but rather "against the method in which the position was filled." Hamilton added,

> I consider that a vote on Mr. Rivera at this time is a grave procedural impropriety on the part of this board. It is grossly unfair to board members who had no previous knowledge

of any applicants for the position and no opportunity to see, hear from, or consider in an adequate manner any other applicants. It is mostly unfair to Mr. Rivera who has lost the opportunity to know that this district's governing body has selected him not only as the only applicant available, but after due and careful consideration by all board members of all applicants.[41]

Ultimately Juan was hired, and he took control of the program. In his memoir, Jose Angel Gutierrez discussed the method he employed to ram through his various decisions, and the implications that came from them. He stated, "If you have the votes, you don't have to explain, convince or argue . . . in support of your position—just vote. . . . In this case the people loved my machismo because here was a young Chicano . . . not only facing down the older gringo board . . . but also putting them in their place, at his will."[42] Thus, a staunchly apolitical individual took over a job he wanted to do at his alma mater as a part of a highly charged partisan process. The results would not be what Juan wanted, on the field and off, which partially led to his truncated second stay at CCISD.

One of the key jobs of any incoming athletic director in any state is to hire the school's football coach. Rivera took a chance on Juan Salinas, an individual who had never led a program. This Juan, like his boss, was stepping onto a gridiron that was actually a minefield. In 1970 the Javelinas had a respectable season, but 1971 would not be a satisfactory follow-up to that positive—by Crystal City standards—campaign. Once the LRUP leadership took over the school board, many teachers quit, and numerous parents transferred students and student-athletes out of CCHS. A 1973 article in the publication *Texas Coach* sheds light on this exodus of athletic talent. The essay documents the transfer of two players who played for the Javelinas in 1970— tight end Ruben Alcorta and quarterback Lynn Leonard—to Uvalde High School in part to get away from the turbulence at CCHS. As reporter Charlie Robinson noted, "So in this area of

South Texas where so much is blown out of proportion about racial strife, the same segment [of the population] . . . has said very little about a Mexican and a gringo who teamed up to bring harmony . . . [and] produced a state championship" for the Coyotes.[43] Both players went on to compete at the collegiate level at Angelo State University from 1973 until 1976. Certainly, the always-thin Crystal City roster would have benefited from having two such talented players on their sideline.

The result was a winless campaign with the local eleven being pummeled by a combined 391–21 margin. Gutierrez indicated that the roster that suited up as the 1971 varsity was almost completely the B team from 1970. Though the young men and the coaching staff worked hard to improve, the athletes were mostly what Gutierrez termed "runts" who simply could not stand up physically to the opponents on the schedule. The year 1972 was not much better, though the squad did claim one victory to finish 1–9. Still, they were outscored 262–76. Although Salinas did eventually have some decent seasons over his last three years, with his best being 4–6 in 1973, he left Crystal City with an overall mark of 11–36.[44] Jose Angel stated during our interview that the issues discussed previously continued to beleaguer the Javelinas: namely, a lack of funds for facility improvement and potential student-athletes not being able to participate due to needing to work to help support their families.[45]

As the 1971 academic year came to an end, Juan—no doubt encouraged by Maria Antonia, who wanted to return to her hometown—looked for a way out of Crystal City. That opportunity came in a position at Fox Technical High School in the Alamo City. There, Juan would serve as an assistant in football as well as head track coach. He would eventually be promoted to head coach for the Buffaloes' grid squad in September 1972. By the time the family arrived in town, Gabe was getting ready to enter fourth grade. He would begin his scholastic football career in seventh grade at Horace Mann Middle School. Prior to that, once the family settled in the neighborhood, the Rivera siblings continued playing football on the street and in nearby parks, just as they had done in Benavides. Though Gabe was only about 10 or 11, many of the neighborhood players were surprised at the size, speed, and agility of Norbert's "little" brother. It was not long before many in the area came to realize that Gabe had a great deal of innate talent to go along with his developing, and impressive, bulk. Soon, if Norbert wanted to play football on a particular side, his teammates insisted that he bring Gabe along. Gabe would continue to make his mark on the sport.[46]

Chapter 4

"He Did Not Realize How Good He Was"

Gabe Rivera's High School Athletic Career, His Arrival and First Year at Texas Tech, 1972–1979

AS DISCUSSED IN CHAPTER I, by the time that Gabe Rivera began his football-playing career in the middle of the 1970s, he and his brothers benefited from the efforts that other competitors and coaches had performed in breaking down barriers for Latinos on the gridiron. Gabe did not have to look far, as certainly his father was a role model who had used his athletic abilities to help fashion a middle-class life for his family as well as a professional career for himself.

In Benavides, Edinburg, and Crystal City, the Rivera brothers were able to interact with high school field generals and players of their own background. Additionally, some participants in the sport had made it to the highest levels of competition and served as exemplars of achievement for the younger generation. One such person was the former quarterback of the British Columbia Lions and the Minnesota Vikings, the legendary Joe Kapp.[1] In a 1970 article in *Sports Illustrated* titled "A Man of Machismo," Kapp detailed his rise to glory at the University of California and in the Canadian Football League (CFL), and finally the NFL. In many ways, Kapp personified the self-assured mindset that many Latino players and coaches had to have in order to prove themselves in football. Kapp recalled that when he was in fifth grade a fellow student called him a "dirty Mexican":

> At first, I didn't challenge him. But when I got home, I brooded on what he had said. . . . My sense of justice was outraged. . . . So I went back and found him and really whaled on him. I didn't win the fight, but I got in some licks. That was machismo, not backing down, acting like a man. . . . I've never backed down since. . . . I would look around me and say to myself, "Well, if I'm gonna win this game I'm gonna have to kick somebody's butt!" That was valuable training for NFL football.[2]

Not surprisingly, given the changes that took place in Crystal City as a result of the takeover of the school board by La Raza Unida Party (LRUP) in 1970, this individual who epitomized the essence of "Chicanismo"[3] was invited to visit the high school. Kapp spoke before the assembled crowd of Javelina faithful. Later he visited nearby Asherton High (mostly Mexican American as well), which was, at the time, suffering through a 40-game gridiron losing streak. This was all part of an effort "to improve the image of Chicano young people and serve as a motivation factor for them."[4] The message Kapp presented was simple, yet revolutionary. Circumstances might have been difficult in Texas and elsewhere—in a social setting as well as on the football field—but Mexican Americans needed to continue to fight to improve their situations. What had happened in Zavala County under the leadership of Jose Angel Gutierrez and the LRUP was just the beginning of a new (and, hopefully, better) era for the school as well as for its overwhelmingly Spanish-surnamed student body.

While the Riveras were not in town to witness these events in Crystal City, they undoubtedly served as motivation for all the football players and coaches of this background that men such as Kapp, Jim Plunkett (who is also Mexican American), Danny Villanueva, and Tom Flores, among others, were making names for themselves and their ethnic group on the grand stage of the NFL by the early 1970s. Perhaps, with luck and training, some if not all of the Rivera boys might be able, like their father, to play football not only in high school but also at the collegiate level. Who knew, it could even be possible that one of the boys might get a look by an NFL or CFL squad, just as Juan Jr. did, ever so briefly, back in the 1950s. Norbert Rivera was correct when he indicated during one of our interviews that "football was the family's business," as all of the offspring of Juan Jr. and Maria Antonia played the sport, in addition to other athletic endeavors. Before moving on to discuss Gabe's career as an athlete, we should consider some of the achievements of his brothers, Bernie, Norbert, and Adrian.

Bernie, born in 1956, was the first of the boys to take to the gridiron for San Antonio's Jefferson High Mustangs. In his senior year of 1973, these horses were, pun intended, merely also-rans in the District 31-AAAA race, finishing with a less-than-stellar mark of 3–5–2. One of the few newspaper items that documented Bernie's play that year appeared in the description of a late-season tangle versus San Antonio's Lee High, a 21–0 defeat for Jefferson. The Mustangs' offensive output that game was absolutely anemic, as they generated a mere 43 yards of total offense and two first downs. The contest was close until the fourth quarter when the Volunteers scored twice to account for the fairly lopsided final tally. The *Express/News* took note of the valiant effort by the losing side's defense to keep the game close and mentioned Bernie's contribution to the cause. "The Mustangs' defense was equally impressive in repeatedly restraining Lee drives during the first three quarters before the floodgates opened.... Linebackers Tom Pollard and Bernie Rivera . . . gave Lee headaches all night."[5] While his team did not do particularly well, Bernie attracted the attention of coaches at Eastern New Mexico University (ENM) located in Portales (an NAIA institution at that time)[6] and continued his gridiron and educational careers there. As the first son to leave the nest, Bernie had to deal with Maria Antonia's concerns about his well-being and ability to survive in the hinterlands of New Mexico. Norbert noted that Maria Antonia went "overboard" in packing suitcases full of San Antonio's delicacies for her son's move to the Land of Enchantment. This pattern was repeated as each of the boys left home to go to college.

By the time Bernie became a Greyhound with Eastern New Mexico, he bore some of the physical traits that would define the Riveras: they were quite big and athletic, though, of course, Gabe turned out to be the largest and most gifted of the progeny. An article from 1975 noted that Bernie was over six feet tall and weighed in at (for the time) an impressive 210 pounds. He started as a freshman defensive lineman for a 1974 ENM team that finished the season 7–4. A year later, he was still a starter and was now listed at 220 pounds. This team finished the campaign with a mark of 8–3. Finally, for the US bicentennial year, coaches selected Bernie as one of the most impressive players in spring training. That year's version of the Greyhounds went 7–3–1. Bernie, having finished his eligibility, then moved on to the University of Houston, where he graduated in 1979 with a degree in electrical engineering.[7]

Norbert Rivera, born in 1957, had a more varied athletic career, though he also played football for the Mustangs, if for only one year. The first mention of his sporting success comes from a San Antonio Independent School District junior high track meet, where he finished in sixth place in the 70-meter hurdles for Horace Mann Middle School. Later he asked Maria Antonia, who was always much attached to her faith, if he could enroll at a Catholic, instead of a public, institution. Norbert subsequently attended St. Anthony's and made the Texas Catholic

Interscholastic League (TCIL) 3-AA All-District Team in 1975. He was also a star on the Yellowjackets' basketball team. In his senior year, 1976–1977, he was listed as being one of the leaders for the Jackets and was described by his coach as "a pleasant surprise after not playing last year. He has good strength on the boards and is our best 'big man' in defense." Norbert also played football at Jefferson in 1974, at the position that his younger brother would fill in subsequent seasons: tight end.[8]

Norbert decided to hang up his cleats after graduating from high school and attended Southern Methodist University. After two years at the private institution, he transferred to the University of Texas at Arlington and earned his degree in mechanical engineering in 1981. One interesting story from Norbert's football career occurred when Gabe was first spotted by coaches on the Jefferson football field. When varsity coach Mike Honeycutt noticed the size difference between Norbert and his younger brother, his reaction was similar to that of the Riveras' playground buddies. He wanted Gabe on his side. Honeycutt asked Norbert, "What the heck happened to you?" By this point in time, although Norbert stood six-feet-two and weighed about 200 pounds in his senior year, Gabe already towered in at six-feet-three and weighed around 225 pounds as a 14-year-old.[9]

Adrian, who was born in 1963, was an offensive lineman for the Mustangs, though he did not garner the same citywide praise as his brothers. He graduated from Jefferson in 1981 and then traveled to join Gabe in the Hub City. Adrian tried out for the Red Raiders as a walk-on and made the team. According to Norbert, Adrian was extremely proud of this accomplishment, but unfortunately, "he forgot to go to class," and was in serious academic trouble after his first year in Lubbock. He decided not to return to Texas Tech and did not finish his degree. Eventually, he settled into a position with the *San Antonio Express* newspaper. He gained acclaim throughout the city as the "Wingoman." Wingo was a type of bingo-based contest that awarded cash prizes to contestants, and it was Adrian's job to determine the winners. As an article from 1990 in the paper noted, he was both the "most popular, and most hated" individual in the building. He continued to work for the paper until his passing in 2016.[10]

Gabe was born in 1961. Having been a successful athlete himself, as well as a coach, Juan noted his fourth son's athleticism from a relatively young age. "As early as middle school, he simply overpowered everyone around him," brother Norbert recalled. "He had excellent hand–eye coordination and was great at baseball, basketball, and track (discus and shot put) as well." He began playing organized football at Horace Mann Middle School in seventh grade in the 1973–1974 school year. When he got to Jefferson he was recovering from a ruptured appendix that caused him to miss much of his sophomore season. The Mustangs were coming off a .500 year in 1975, and Coach Honeycutt hoped for better results in the following campaign. As the *Express* noted in September, "Honeycutt broke even . . . in his debut at Jeff last year. The team has a good chance of finishing on the plus side . . . and should be a pennant contender in the all-San Antonio School District league." Gabe contributed to this squad on both sides of the ball.[11]

Several games this season highlighted Rivera's abilities. For example, in a 49–14 victory against San Antonio's Wheatley High, Gabe had an interception. This triumph raised the team's mark to 5–2, and they remained undefeated in district play.[12] The following week, against Edison High of San Antonio, Gabe showed his abilities on the offensive side of the line of scrimmage, catching a couple of passes to help secure a 14–12 victory. Watching on the Bears sideline, no doubt with both a sense of joy and one of trepidation, was Juan, now serving as an assistant at Edison, as well as head track coach.[13] The following week, Gabe scored a touchdown on a pass reception as Jefferson defeated the Fox Tech Buffaloes by a score of 35–6

A cartoon highlighting Gabe's versatility and athleticism while he was playing for Jefferson High School in San Antonio (Southwest Collection, TTU University Archives)

to claim a share of the 31-AAAA title, the team's first district crown since 1961.[14]

After beating Tech, Jefferson played Highland High of San Antonio in the first round of the playoffs. The local scribes anticipated a high-scoring affair between the foes, but it was not to be, as Highland's Rudy Sanchez kicked a field goal with just over six minutes left in the final quarter—the only scoring in a 3–0 victory for the Owls.[15] Although certainly disappointed to lose in the football playoffs, Gabe then turned his attention to track and baseball. Toward the end of the 1976–1977 school year, he won the district's discus throw with a mark of 141 feet, 8 inches, besting his nearest competitor by almost 11 inches. He then took to the diamond where he hit over .400 as a designated hitter. That team, after a 3–2–1 start to the season, won 21 consecutive contests to claim the district title. Overall, it was a memorable sophomore year for Gabe as part of the Mustangs' athletics program, just the start of his legend at Jefferson High.[16]

The 1977 campaign began with a stern test, as the Mustangs faced San Antonio's MacArthur High Brahmas, a team that trounced them 42–8 in the first game of the previous season. The cupboard was certainly not bare for Coach Honeycutt, as his squad returned eight starters on offense and six on defense from a side that finished 7–3 in his second season at the helm. Gabe was one of the returning players noted in a preseason article. The Mustangs lost the opening contest to the Brahmas, but only by a score of 13–12. They then defeated Lee High of San Antonio, 21–6, for their first victory over the Volunteers since 1968. A local sports reporter noted that Gabe would continue to play on both sides of the ball: an imposing figure at tight end (now weighing in at 225 pounds) and as a linebacker. Overall, with senior leadership and talented underclassmen (such as Gabe) there was hope that Jefferson would make a repeat appearance in the state playoffs.[17]

Gabe notched many highlights that junior season, but undoubtedly his most impressive contest, one that best displayed his versatility and athleticism, was a performance against the Burbank Bulldogs, a clash where Jefferson triumphed, 35–7. That evening, Rivera intercepted a pass and returned it 25 yards to the opponent's 4-yard line, setting up a score that put the Mustangs up, 14–0. Later, quarterback Bobby Flores hit Gabe for a 12-yard touchdown. He then capped his evening by catching a pass that covered 51 yards, the last 45 of which came after the reception. Early the following week, Gabe received extensive coverage for (though he did not win) "Player of the Week" honors as determined by the *Express-News*. All told, he was a one-player wrecking crew, even contributing on special teams. As the article noted, "Rivera did nearly everything. He caught four passes for 76 yards—two for TDs . . . set up another score by returning an interception . . . and made a touchdown saving tackle on a kickoff return."[18] Later that season, Juan got a bit of revenge against his son; even though Gabe contributed to the offense by catching a fourth-down pass at a critical juncture in the contest, the Bears managed to hold off the Mustangs, 23–20. This defeat left Jefferson at 5–3 and dropped them from the ranks of the district's unbeaten. It certainly must have been an interesting evening and weekend at the Rivera household! As Norbert noted in one of our interviews, while Maria Antonia always wanted her husband's teams to do well, she loyally cheered for her sons, even when they played against their father's team.[19]

Jefferson did not make the playoffs in 1977, finishing with a pedestrian 6–4 mark. This was Coach Honeycutt's final season as the school's field general. Once the campaign ended, however, Gabe earned a very important accolade from the *Express-News* when he was one of only two juniors (the other being Mike Langford from Highlands) named to the paper's All-City Team. Rivera came within one vote of being a unanimous selection for the star-studded group. He was joined on the All-City squad by fellow Mustangs Bobby Flores at quarterback and defensive back Darryl Hemphill. After that season Gabe transitioned to play basketball, once again, for a Mustang team that was one of the most highly regarded squads in the city, having garnered district titles every year since 1971 in addition to two regional crowns. Coach Will Williamson most likely was referring to his sizable (although not necessarily towering by basketball standards) multisport athlete when he stipulated that "we are not tall but are physical and have a lot of strength inside."[20]

Playing at a high level (in various athletic endeavors), in a large metropolitan area, in the football-mad state of Texas soon generated a plethora of letters and materials from recruiters filling the family's mailbox. These items represented interest from programs at the upper echelons of competition, with some institutions reaching out in Gabe's junior year. Norbert indicated that he saw and read much of the correspondence, though none survived to become part of the Rivera Collection now housed at the Southwest Collection Archive at Texas Tech University. There would be phone calls and visits by coaches to the Rivera domicile, particularly after the impressive award Gabe earned in his senior season during the fall of 1978.

A preseason article by Johnny Campos of the *San Antonio Light* provides documentation concerning Gabe's status as a legitimate recruit to compete at the stratosphere of collegiate football. The article also notes a key issue that would play a significant role in the remainder of his football career. The essay, which featured a photo of Gabe alongside his new head coach, Stuart McBirnie, not only prognosticated on the Mustangs' upcoming season, it also provided background on Gabe's overall importance to the Jefferson squad, as well as noting, for the first time in print, the developing concerns about his weight.

The Mustangs faced several major obstacles going into the 1978 season. First, they had lost the services of an All-District performer at quarterback and linebacker (though he also lined up as a fullback in his final season), Tom Lyda, to the rival Lee Volunteers. That, plus graduation, meant that all of the starters but one on the offensive squad would have to be replaced. Gabe was the one returning starter on this side of the line of scrimmage—a player who "was going to be a vital part of our offense anyway" would have to carry an even heavier load. McBirnie argued that "it'll just put a little more pressure on him." Given that Gabe was now a senior and had proven himself as a prime target for the Jefferson offense (he caught 21 passes for 370 yards and five scores), even more was expected of him by the new coaching staff. With greater responsibilities for the team's scoring output on his broad shoulders, it was also problematic that Jefferson's star athlete experienced issues with his back during preseason practices. "Rivera reported for his senior season about 15–20 pounds heavier than his 240–245 playing weight last year, but so far the additional weight hasn't been a problem. His back, however, has."

Three key points to note here are that, first, this article contradicted what reports had indicated in the fall of 1977, wherein Gabe was presented as having weighed only 225 pounds at the start of that season. In this *Light* article, Gabe argued that "as a sophomore I weighed around 250 pounds." This is in line with Norbert's recollection of his brother's girth. Second, Gabe stipulated as to why he started to gain weight: as a result of his appendectomy. "When I came back from the operation, I started eating a lot." This would not be the last time that this issue would be mentioned during his football career. Last, even with the extra bulk, his physical abilities continued to impress, and not just on the gridiron.

> The added weight has not been a hindrance to Rivera's speed—which is considerable. He has been timed in the 40-yard dash at 04.7 and 04.65. At his current weight, however, he has probably "slowed down" to a 04.8 or so. Rivera participated on the Jefferson track team last year, competing in the obvious events, the shot put and the discus, and in the not-so-obvious events, like the sprints. "The coaches just wanted to see how fast I was," he explained. Rivera responded by running a 10.3 in the 100 and 23.3 in the 220. And although Rivera never won any races, he did surprise a few people on the track. "Especially my dad . . . He didn't know I was that fast."

Such freakish athleticism meant that Southwest Conference (SWC) schools, and other elite programs from elsewhere in the nation, were salivating at the prospect of having Rivera line up for them. As the Mustangs headed into their season, Gabe remained noncommittal about his collegiate destination, though he did believe that, most likely, he would wind up playing for an SWC team.

Even with the team's youth, the 1978 version of the Mustangs managed a 6–4 overall mark and went 5–2 in the district, finishing in third place. During preseason drills, Gabe argued that one of the games he was most looking forward to would be the final one: a contest against the Edison Golden Bears. "I try extra hard when we play Edison, because I want to look good for my dad." In addition to having one last crack at Juan's team as a senior, an added incentive was that Adrian (listed at five-feet-eleven and 220 pounds) would also line up on the Jefferson offensive line. With barely a .500 mark going into his final high school gridiron action, the Mustang's 19–14 victory over Edison must have been very gratifying indeed.

Of course, the Jefferson yearbook, appropriately named the *Monticello*, also noted that Rivera was All-District, along with three teammates. Additionally, he was named to the All-City High School Football Team by KMOL.[21] While the honors of making the All-District and All-City teams were impressive accomplishments, Gabe's performance on the field merited not just local but nationwide recognition. First, he earned acclaim as the best individual player in the city (presented annually by the *Light*), known as the Thom McAn Award. Then, even more impressively, he was named part of the *Parade* All-American Team (Honorable Mention) for 1978.

Another Texan named to that squad was the legendary Eric Dickerson of Sealy High School. These two titans of Lone Star football would have a very memorable and consequential run-in just a couple of years later when Texas Tech played against the Mustangs of Southern Methodist University. Norbert recalls that Juan, a man of few words, could only shake his head and argue that his fourth son "did not really know how good he was." After the fall of 1978, Juan walked around with the newspaper clippings about his son's accomplishments for a long time.[22]

In an article in the *Light* dated January 7, 1979, Gabe expressed his gratitude for his selection as *Parade* All-American and indicated that the quest to land his services at the collegiate level was proceeding apace. "Notre Dame is trying to contact me. . . . They called at home, but I haven't been there. I've been kind of busy." The total number of suitors reached as high as 15, but the article stated that "the final decision will rest on which school can offer him the best education in architecture, which will be his major." As of the time of this interview, he indicated that, so far, he planned to look in on Arizona, Baylor, and Texas Tech for official visits. The date for a final decision was February 14. While seeking to make his selection, Gabe also continued to play baseball, basketball, and track. His reaction to the acclaim was very much in line with the way that Norbert described his younger brother: he was very laid back and did not necessarily think of himself as a star. Campos's article described Gabe as follows: "Rivera didn't seem too excited about all the publicity he had received lately, but his father Juan . . . and his mother 'are pretty happy about it. I care about it [publicity] a little, but I kind of want to stay in the background.'" Anonymity would prove elusive as Gabe continued to develop as a player with the Red Raiders.[23]

The recruitment process for this star athlete featured all of the usual trappings: phone calls, mailed materials, and eventually home visits by position and head coaches. Two of the most memorable individuals to grace the Rivera household were the legendary Baylor field general Grant Teaff and the ill-fated Texas Tech head man Rex Dockery. Norbert's recollections of these meetings center around two key topics: what opportunity would Gabe have to play, and how did Maria Antonia feel about the schools' representatives? In further support of Juan's argument that Gabe did not really understand how special he was, these visits provide evidence.

The Baylor Bears finished the 1978 season with a mark of 3–8. It stands to reason that Coach Teaff would have argued that Gabe would get a chance to play early in his career if he committed to attend the Waco-based institution. Dockery, on the other hand, was coming off of a fine first year at the helm, a season in which he guided the Red Raiders to a 7–4 mark. He'd served as Texas Tech offensive coordinator between 1975 and 1977 and had replaced Steve Sloan, who left Tech to become head coach at the University of Mississippi. Dockery's 1978 record helped earn him SWC Coach of the Year honors. Although Tech completed a much better season than did the

Bears, Dockery also stressed that Gabe would play a great deal if he decided to come to Lubbock. Certainly, whichever school he selected, the depth chart would be easier to navigate than if Gabe chose to become either a Longhorn or an Aggie.

A final aspect of the selection process came down, not surprisingly, to how Mom felt about the men recruiting her boy. Norbert's assessment and recollection of the situation were that, although Maria Antonia insisted that it was ultimately Gabe's decision, "Mom liked the [Tech] folks." For some reason, the person Maria Antonia felt most comfortable with was the man who would be Gabe's position coach in Lubbock, Donnie Laurence, who had previously served as a successful high school coach at Mount Pleasant High School.[24] In the days just before the signing deadline, Gabe made his decision. The *Light* noted that Texas Tech had successfully mined the San Antonio area for new talent to help Coach Dockery continue to build his squad. The Red Raiders signed Gabe and also landed a commitment from San Antonio John Jay's Anthony Hutchinson (who would go on to generate almost 2,000 career yards from scrimmage for the Red Raiders).[25]

Shortly after Gabe put pen to paper, Juan and Maria Antonia received letters directly from Texas Tech personnel to help reassure the Riveras that their son would not only get the finest possible education but also the finest training and medical care available. Rob Thomas, the academic coordinator for athletics, wrote to remind the family that the institution had "an excellent athletic program but equally important, a young man can receive a great education here. An education is a part of life that can never be lost and will be useful to you in the near future." Given that Bernie was almost done with his degree, Gabe was expected to continue the family tradition in attending, and being successful in, collegiate classrooms. To this end, Norbert brought Gabe up to the Dallas area so that he could visit and learn the time management and studying ropes from him while he attended SMU. The family firmly believed that athletics and football were paths to a better life. It was presumed that Gabe would fulfill his part of the plan in his academics as well as on the gridiron. While he indicated previously a desire to pursue architecture as a major, Norbert stated that, ultimately, Gabe decided to major in kinesiology.[26]

Ken Murray, head athletic trainer, chimed in as well, concerning the top-flight facilities available to meet medical and rehabilitation needs. "We have a well-equipped training room. . . . Our team physician is Dr. Wallace Hess. . . . Our orthopedic surgeon is Dr. Emmett Shannon. . . . Both are tremendous doctors and really do us an excellent job. We have a fine student clinic . . . that also gives us good service and takes good care of us." The following note is interesting because it provided a hint that Tech had concerns about Gabe's weight. "It is the feeling by our coaches . . . that 'prevention' of injuries is the best thing we can do. . . . Your son will be receiving a workout program from us to do this summer. Encourage him to get himself in top physical shape so he will be ready to play."[27]

Being cognizant of Gabe's weight issue, San Antonio–based papers continued to focus on the subject. The *San Antonio Light* published an essay with the unflattering title of "Did Tech Recruit Rivera or the 'Burger King'?" It started off in a light-hearted manner, mentioning that Coach Dockery asked Gabe whether it was factual that he had consumed 14 Whataburgers in a 30-minute time frame. The new Red Raider responded, "Oh, no. It was 14 Big Macs." To this humorous quote the field general added a serious note by intoning, "'One of these days, when he gets that weight down,' Dockery continued, letting the writers use their imaginations as to what he had in mind." Dockery believed that if Gabe could get down to 270, he would be of help to Tech on both sides of the ball, just as he had done with the Mustangs at Jefferson High. "What is surprising is that he really can catch the ball." Early in the 1979 practice season Gabe had ballooned up to as much 315 pounds, after reporting to campus at an already hefty 280. Coaches were apprehensive but were also simply incredulous as to Gabe's innate athletic ability. On the first day of freshman drills, all present were astonished to see that the big man ran the 40-yard dash in 4.9 seconds. Further, at another practice, Tech's James Hadnot had the unfortunate luck of running into Gabe's back as the defender was being blocked by an offensive lineman. The 230-pound running back "went down hard." Gabe's recollection of the play was simply that "Yeah, I felt something."[28]

As the end of the summer of 1979 approached, with two-a-days just on the horizon (in mid-August), Gabe had certainly attracted the attention of Coach Dockery, as well as the local media. In late July the Tech field general noted, "People like Rivera . . . who have been here and been working out this summer—I've seen them play—and it's easier to judge them. But I think we can be playing some freshman this fall." Thus, what Gabe had done in team activities so far demonstrated that he could contribute to the Raiders' cause immediately. Shortly after the positive piece noting his coach's praise, however, there was another article in the *Avalanche-Journal* that, once again, brought up the touchy subject of Gabe's heft. Norval Pollard, one of the paper's Tech beat reporters, recalled his meeting with the crop of incoming freshmen as follows: "Here comes Gabe Rivera . . . the Tech press guide has Rivera listed as 6 3 , 264, with 4.8 in the 40, no less. [After one practice session] Rivera tipped the scales at 306." Still, Gabe was not concerned, as he knew he would regain his playing shape quickly. "In this heat, it should only take a couple of days, the coaches will have it off me in a couple of days."[29]

Overall, Tech's players were optimistic going into the season after finishing 7–4 in 1978. Running back Hadnot indicated that he was looking forward to getting back to a bowl game; Tech had played Florida State and lost by a score of 40–17 in the Tangerine Bowl in December 1977. Hopefully, the addition of talented freshmen such as Rivera pointed toward an even brighter future for the Red Raiders.[30] Prior to the start of the season, Gabe was listed as second on the depth chart (to Hans Bischof) at the noseguard position. But, "all indications are he will be spelling [the] starter ... once the season gets going."[31]

Unfortunately, the 1979 season proved a dud, with the Red Raiders skidding to 3–6–2. Rivera, however, proved his worth on the defensive line, leading that unit in tackles. He also picked up the moniker by which he would be known for the rest of his time at Tech: "Señor Sack." His first test at the collegiate level would come against one of the elite programs in the nation: the defending national champion University of Southern California (USC). Although not starting, Rivera did not disappoint and began to gain notoriety, local and statewide, as a force to be reckoned with in collegiate football.

The Red Raiders had played against the Trojans in the fabled Los Angeles Memorial Coliseum in their first contest of 1978. Tech's performance that day was more than respectable, losing only by a score of 17–9. The mighty cardinal and gold then made the trip to the hinterlands of West Texas for the second leg of the home-and-home arrangement. They no doubt expected a tough contest—and were not disappointed in that regard. Keeping an eye on San Antonio's native son, the *Express News* had its reporter Barry Robinson attend Jones Stadium for the tilt. The final score of the game was 21–7 in favor of the Californians, but, Robinson noted, the victory was hard won. One particular play by Gabe helped to squelch a Trojan drive:

> Early in the second the Trojans marched to the TT 22 before being stopped by 300-pound freshman Gabe "Señor Sack" Rivera. On third down on the 22, [USC quarterback Paul] McDonald dropped back to pass but the hungry Rivera ... was right on his heels. Rivera hurled McDonald out of bounds at the 29, for a loss of seven, and before going down the USC quarterback intentionally grounded the ball, resulting in a five yard penalty.[32]

A few days later, Robinson, in an article specifically focused on Gabe's play in his first collegiate contest, was even more effusive in his praise of the freshman's performance. Robinson, once again, cited the play when USC was threatening on the Tech 22-yard line. His commentary merits an extensive quote:

> For a really big play, you turn to a real big man and Texas Tech has the biggest of them all in freshman Gabe Rivera, the 300 pound freshman who was tilting football fields here while playing for Jefferson a year ago. . . . Two yards before McDonald reached the sidelines, Señor Sack reached out, grabbed the quarterback by the jersey and, with one hand, tossed him several yards through the air and out of bounds. . . . Big Gabe waved a clenched fist. Hugged his defensive teammates and trotted to the sidelines as thousands of Tech fans stood and cheered. . . . Although a sub who played only sparingly, Rivera was credited with five key tackles against the nation's No. 1 team. . . . "He'll be starting by midseason," said one press box helper. . . . "One thing is certain," another scribe said later in the hospitality room. "In the near future, Texas Tech is going to have an All American on defense. Señor Sack is a stud."[33]

Although his first game was impressive, an even more extraordinary performance would take place in a contest against Arkansas on October 13. Gabe had played well in limited action against New Mexico, Arizona, Baylor, and Texas A&M. Going into the contest versus the Aggies on October 6, the Tech game-day program noted that "Gabe is the leading tackler among Raider linemen through four games. He has been in on 27 tackles, and his 17 assists is a current team high."[34] Still, Bischof was listed as the starter at noseguard before the contest versus A&M.

By this point in the campaign, some, particularly in the Mexican American community, were wondering openly why Gabe had not yet been given an opportunity to start. Roberto Delgado, writing in Lubbock's "Mexican" paper, *El Editor*, brought up this very issue just before a clash versus the Rice University Owls on October 20. "Gabriel has not started for the Raiders, but has done a lot of damage and SWC teams are beginning to feel his presence. . . . Why Rivera doesn't start is a mystery question that's still not answered by Tech Coach Dockery." Delgado and the denizens of the Lubbock *comunidad* (community), who no doubt were quite interested in seeing a player of their ethnic background do well at the local university, did not have to wait much longer, as Gabe's performance on October 13 would be so noteworthy that it finally merited him a collegiate start.[35] In this contest, he totaled thirteen individual tackles. Coach Dockery, in his commentary after the game against Arkansas, "praised freshman nose guard Gabe Rivera . . . for . . . excellent defensive play against the Hogs."[36]

In total, Gabe led the Red Raider down linemen in stops for the season with a total of 67. While gaining more playing time was of course important, Norbert stated in one of our interviews that some even more significant ideas took root in Gabe's mind during his freshman year. First, he came to the understanding that he was more than "good enough" to play at the SWC level—one of the premier conferences in the land. Second, Gabe realized that it was imperative to attend classes in order to remain eligible. The advice he received from Norbert and Bernie made it abundantly clear that this part of the equation needed more than just a modicum of interest and effort. Last, Norbert recalled that Gabe was intrigued by the talk that he might be considered for "postseason honors," as noted in the 1980 media guide. There were even some whisperings on campus about the possibility that Gabe might have the potential to play at the "next level," particularly if he could maintain some control over his weight. As Norval Pollard argued in one of his columns before the start of the season, "One thing is certain, Rivera has the potential to be a great player in the Southwest Conference and he's got four years of eligibility at Tech. If Red Raider coaches have to order an Acme tent and awnings, they'll find a jersey to fit Gabe."[37]

The remainder of Rivera's career at Texas Tech featured many more defeats by his team than victories. Over the next three seasons, however (with the nadir coming in 1981—Jerry Moore's first season—with a 1–9–1 mark), he would come to national notoriety (particularly in 1982) all the while playing for squads that were seldom in the national spotlight. Even in the midst of these doldrums, there would be memorable moments that highlighted the uniqueness of his talents, particularly against the Arkansas Razorbacks, in one memorable tackle of Eric Dickerson, and of course, his monstrous game against another team ranked No. 1 in the country, the Washington Huskies. While his career on the field was taking off, there would be some problematic moments where Gabe did not exhibit the best judgment and nearly lost the opportunity to take his playing to the next level. We now turn to this part of his story.

CHAPTER 5

SEÑOR SACK MAKES HIS MARK

WITH BUMPS ALONG THE WAY, 1980–1982

THE 1979 SEASON WAS A major disappointment for the football fans of West Texas. After TTU had finished 7–4, and with Coach Rex Dockery earning Southwest Conference (SWC) Coach of the Year honors for 1978, aficionados in Lubbock and surrounding areas certainly anticipated continued improvement in victory totals. It was not to be, as Texas Tech struggled to finish 3–6–2, with a 2–5–1 mark in the SWC—beating out only the Horned Frogs of Texas Christian University (who finished 2–8–1 and 1–6–1 in conference) and a Rice University Owls squad that ended the campaign 1–10 and went winless in SWC play.

There were some stars on the field at Jones Stadium that season: for example, running back James Hadnot led the conference in touches from scrimmage (combined rushing attempts and pass receptions) with 283 and total yards from scrimmage with 1,464 (for an impressive average of almost 5.2 yards gained per attempt). Hadnot was chosen as the SWC Offensive Player of the Year his final two seasons at Tech. Leading up to the

1980 NFL draft, Hadnot's name was the most prominently mentioned among former Tech players. He was chosen in the third round and went on to play for the Kansas City Chiefs and, later, the San Antonio Gunslingers of the USFL between the years 1980 and 1985.[1]

On the defensive side of the ball, in addition to Gabe's impressive freshman play with 67 tackles from the noseguard position, cornerback Ted Watts tied for the conference lead in interceptions with six. Watts would be a preseason All-American candidate for Tech going into the 1980 season. Eventually, he would go on to play in the NFL for the Oakland Raiders (appropriately enough), New York Giants, and San Diego Chargers between 1981 and 1987.[2] Overall, the team's defense surrendered a respectable 16.5 points per contest (which placed them sixth in the SWC). Given the statistics that the Tech defense has produced over the past decade or so, these results hearken back to an era when the Red Raiders were better known for stopping opponents from reaching the end zone than the highlight reels generated by the team's offense in more recent times. In 1979, the primary weakness was that Tech notched a mere 12.8 points per game, outscoring only the two teams below them in the final standings.[3]

Going into the 1980 campaign, Coach Dockery was determined to right his ship and once again make Tech relevant in the SWC. One of the principal contributors to that effort would be the prized, now sophomore noseguard who had acquitted himself so well as a freshman. As the Red Raiders moved toward the start of the spring practice schedule, once again, the pesky question concerning Gabe's weight percolated into the public's discussion about the squad. Something had changed, however. While reporters still marveled at his size, the coaching staff appeared more comfortable concerning Rivera's bulk. After all, he had run two 40-yard sprints at 4.9 seconds while weighing 300 pounds early in the year. Subsequently, he had more than proved his mettle, agility, and strength against offensive lines from the likes of Texas, Arkansas, and most impressively, the no. 1 team in the nation, the USC Trojans. Perhaps Gabe could be effective at a weight that was almost unheard of for players in the early 1980s.

In March 1980, Barry Robinson from the *San Antonio Express* had made the trek to Lubbock to check out the progress of the former Jefferson High School standout. In keeping with the theme from 1979, the first part of his story focused on the weight issue and the enormity of Gabe's appetite, as well as how much attention he was generating. Once again, we heard stories about his superhuman consumption of Big Macs. Robinson even quoted quarterback Ron Reeves, noting how exciting it was to go to the nearest greasy spoon and watch his teammate perform his magic devouring burgers. When asked about visits to the Golden Arches specifically, Reeves argued that to him, "It's fun going to McDonald's with Gabe and watching the [count of burgers served by the firm's restaurants] numbers change."

By the time of the start of the spring 1980 term in January, Gabe had, again, moved above 300 pounds, tipping the scales at 313. As a result, his coaches "increased his off-season workout and . . . [he was] down to 303" before the start of spring practice. Robinson then mentioned that the consensus was that "as long as Gabe stays around 300 coaches are happy because most of his weight is bulk, bone and muscle from the waist up. Gabe's back and shoulders are so huge that the Tech equipment manager had to put in a special order for a jersey big enough to fit him."

Robinson's final paragraphs in this article relayed a comical story from Gabe's freshman year that demonstrated his athletic abilities and sense of humor. In the contest against USC, Rivera made a tackle on his first play from scrimmage by beating the opposing center, making a stop for no gain. Then,

> the teams lined up again, the veteran center gave Gabe a
> cold stare, gritted his teeth and grunted a few obscenities,

trying to put a psych job on the inexperienced opponent. Just before the ball was snapped, Señor Sack looked up at the center and with a wide grin said, "If I were you, I'd be ashamed of myself. You can't even block a freshman." A few plays later, Rivera tossed the center aside and sacked the USC quarterback for a seven-yard loss.[4]

One other important event took place in Gabe's life and career during the spring practice season of 1980: he became involved with a public relations effort by Tech Athletics that involved Lubbock-area children. The effort was known as the Junior Red Raider Program, and the intent was to provide affordable tickets and access to players and Jones Stadium for kids under the age of 15. One would think that this type of role would be handled by offensive stars. In this case, one of the honorary leadership positions of the undertaking was assigned to "Ron Reeves, who operates out of the tradition-ally glamorous quarterback spot." Gabe was the other titular head of this booster association. "They called me for that, and I didn't know what it was about. Usually stuff like that is just for quarterbacks and running backs." Maybe Rivera was a totally new type of athlete at his position, and Tech certainly used his growing notoriety and personality to its benefit. As Gabe indicated in another interview in August 1980, "I don't know if I'm changing the image of a lineman. But I've thought about all that and I just want to keep preparing for each season as it goes along. Otherwise, people forget you." In late July 1980, the *Avalanche-Journal* announced that local youngsters had the opportunity to visit with Gabe and Ron at Jones Stadium on August 14. While Gabe's final three campaigns in Lubbock did not generate memorable seasons for the Red Raiders (they would finish 5–6, 1–9–1, and 4–7), his play on the field certainly, and his work with kids, eventually made it impossible for fans in West Texas, and in time the rest of the country, to overlook the giant presence of Señor Sack. These endeavors prior to his sophomore campaign demonstrated and foreshadowed Gabe's

Gabe with a young fan—a future Chair of the TTU Department of History (courtesy of Dr. Sean Cunningham)

ability and desire to work with youths, and his genuine care for them. This aspect of his personality would be an integral part of the final years of his life.[5]

Going into the 1980 academic year, there was a great deal of consternation about the Red Raiders' overall athletic program. The football team had certainly regressed from the successful 1978 season, which placed Rex Dockery squarely on the hot seat. As Norval Pollard noted in late July of that year, Dockery was just one of several SWC field generals whose positions were less than secure. "Starting right here in Lubbock, Dockery could be at the crossroads of his tenure. . . . Last fall's 3–6–2 record was the worst by a Tech squad since Jim Carlen's 4–7 mark in 1971." Still, ever the optimistic homer, the scribe thought that the conditions and available talent were present for a quick return to glory, or at least a minor bowl game. "With a little luck, something Tech didn't have much of at all in 1979, the

Raiders might even take seven or eight [wins]."[6] Simultaneously, over that summer the school's administration faced the need to replace the top slot in the Athletics Department as Dick Tamburo, the entity's head (himself a former All-American center at Michigan State), decided to leave Lubbock for the same post with Arizona State University. Before Tamburo's departing for Tempe, however, President Lauro Cavazos (due to a contractual stipulation) was forced to allow the athletics administrator to remain at the helm for another 60 days. Tamburo's lame-duck status, in turn, upset fans who felt that an essentially rudderless Tech sports program was falling even further behind in competition for elite athletes, particularly against bitter in-state rivals Texas and Texas A&M.[7]

As the calendar turned from summer to autumn, fearless prognosticators began to make predictions as to where Texas Tech would finish in the first season of the new decade. Pollard quoted SMU head man Ron Meyer (who would field the legendary "Pony Express" backfield of Eric Dickerson and Craig James) disparaging the gridders from Lubbock, lumping them into a category even below the also-rans of the SWC. Meyer pontificated, "You have Houston and Texas A&M on top. The next category is Texas and Arkansas. Baylor and SMU are the next level. Then you have Tech, TCU, and Rice." Well, that statement certainly raised the hair on the back of some necks around the South Plains! Pollard countered, "And just in case you've forgotten, Ron, you and the Mustangs have to visit the quiet little community of Lubbock, Texas later this year. I give you my word I'll not tell a soul of what you really think of the Red Raiders."[8] The contest with the Mustangs turned out to be one of the highlights of 1980 for Tech and featured one of Gabe's most memorable games and hits. Another reporter covering the team, Chuck McDonald, agreed with Meyer's assessment concerning the top of the league, but also did his best to inspire at least a modicum of hope among the locals. "If you thought I was gonna predict the hometown team to wind up

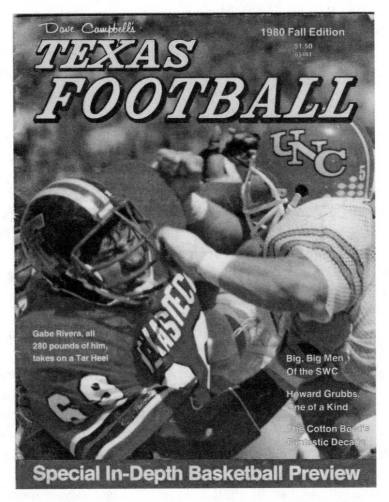

Gabe on the cover of *Dave Campbell's Texas Football*, the "bible" of the sport in the Lone Star State (Southwest Collection, TTU University Archives)

seventh or eighth, like a lot of publications are doing, you're crazy. I live here and have a little boy that I want to see grow up. The Raiders are in a prime position to surprise some folks. . . . While questions abound on offense, the defense could keep this team in a bunch of ball games." McDonald ultimately argued that the Red Raiders would finish in fifth place.[9]

As the offensive side of the ball searched for consistency and success during spring and fall drills, there was no doubt that the Red Raiders' best athletes resided on the defensive side of the line of scrimmage. Pollard even argued that some experts believed Tech's defense "may be the best in the conference." In addition to a secondary that featured preseason All-American candidate Ted Watts, the line was perceived as being the unit's anchor, with one article stating that "the five-man front should have both talent and depth." Not surprisingly, the young San Antonian was at the core of this assessment. "Texas Tech sophomore noseguard Gabe Rivera, who delighted Tech fans last season as a freshman with the ability to run down the quickest of quarterbacks and running backs despite his 300-pound-plus frame, has reportedly dropped down to 275 pounds."[10] Thus, with tempered hopes, the Tech football team took the field for the first time on September 6, 1980, against a nearby school that they had not played since 1963, the University of Texas at El Paso (UTEP).[11]

The Red Raiders had no difficulty in dispatching their foes from the borderland, drubbing the Miners, perennial cellar-dwellers of the Western Athletic Conference (WAC), 35–7. Worth mentioning are some postgame comments regarding Gabe by the head coach of the Miners, Bill Michael, who was awestruck by his abilities. "I was really impressed with Rivera. We had to double block him most of the time. We had a lot of respect for him, he's a good football player. We just felt we had to double him all night."[12] After playing a weak opponent, Dockery's squad moved on to challenge better competition, as the fifteenth-ranked University of North Carolina of the Atlantic Coast Conference (ACC) visited Lubbock the following week. Facing a stiff defense led by the legendary linebacker Lawrence Taylor, the local's offense had no answers, losing by a score of 9–3. Coach Dockery complimented his defenders, stating that "they gave us every chance they could to win for us." The game's summary by the Lubbock reporters was that "the defense deserved better" than to lose the contest against the Tar Heels.[13]

The *Avalanche-Journal* also noted that there appeared to have been some critical lapses by the coaching staff when sending in offensive signals. Coach Dockery denied that such miscues had occurred and instead chose to focus on the positives from the hard-fought game. "The players are not down at all. They saw films that they were only a step away from breaking it on a number of plays. This team knows that it has a chance to be very good." The following week, Tech once again returned to the victory column, notching a 28–17 triumph against another nearby rival, the University of New Mexico Lobos, also of the WAC. Although sporting a 2–1 mark heading into conference play, there were concerns about the season's ultimate outcome, as the Raiders tallied both victories against also-rans from a weak conference and fared poorly (at least on offense) against a higher-quality foe. Also of concern was a substantial downturn in support by aficionados. Over their first three home contests, the Red Raiders did not crack the 40,000 mark in attendance at Jones Stadium. Indeed, they would only top that figure at home twice in 1980—not surprisingly against longtime SWC rivals, the Texas Longhorns (with 50,132) and eventual conference champion, Baylor (with 48,539).[14]

The tilt against the Bears on September 27 showed, once again, that the Tech defense could keep the team in games, but that the other half of the platoon simply could not hold up its end of the bargain. In a truly sluggish effort, the offense let yet another excellent performance by Gabe and his teammates go for naught, losing 11–3. The reports by Pollard and McDonald recounted the ineptitude of the Tech attack, while documenting the extraordinary exertion of the defenders. In the second half, the Red Raiders held the Bears without a first down until midway through the fourth quarter, forcing punt after punt. Tech's offense sputtered throughout, with the line surrendering a total of a dozen sacks, ten of which came in the final two quarters. The total rushing output for the contest was a pathetic negative 36 yards. "Texas Tech's offensive line was slightly suspect before the start of the 1980 season. . . . But after Tech's dismal showing against Baylor, the Raiders' offensive line has won back the suspect tag." Without much help from their teammates, the defense held on to keep Tech within striking distance, assuming that the offense could manage to move toward the Bears' goal line. "To their credit, the Tech defense gave the Bears nothing until the final minutes of the game when Baylor drove for its lone touchdown."[15]

Next up on the schedule were the Texas A&M Aggies, and Tech's hopes rested on the assumption that the defense could keep the score close until (really, in case) the offense came around. Going into the October 4 contest, the *Avalanche-Journal* heaped praise on the team's defenders and chastised the offense. "While Tech's offense struggled against Baylor, the defense sparkled. . . . The defense, which seems to get better week-by-week, is led by tackle Jaime Giles, noseguard Gabriel Rivera, free safety Ted Watts and inside linebacker Terry Baer."[16] There was some success in scoring by the red and black during this contest in College Station, but this time it was the defense that failed, allowing the Aggies to run wild in a 41–21 defeat. Five weeks into the 1980 season, the team stood at 2–3 and looked to be on a path similar to that of the 1979 squad. While Rice and TCU remained on tap, the schedule also featured tilts versus heavyweights in the SWC: Texas, SMU, and Houston. It appeared that Dockery's seat was getting warmer and warmer with about one half of the campaign still to go. A victory over Rice—which, by the way, finished with a respectable 5–6 mark in 1980—again highlighted Tech's offensive ineptitude as the Owls, who finished the year surrendering almost 20 points per contest, permitted the Red Raiders to score only half of that total. Again, the defense came to the rescue and Tech triumphed, 10–3, in Houston.[17]

Next the mighty Longhorns, ranked twelfth in the country, rolled into Lubbock on November 1. Uncharacteristically, Tech got off to a quick start, with the offense striking for 10 points in the first quarter on a 66-yard drive that culminated with a two-yard touchdown by Ron Reeves, and then a short field goal. Ted Watts then returned an interception 34 yards for the final score of the quarter. Just like that, the locals led, 17–0. The rout appeared to be on early in the second stanza, as a one-yard touchdown run by Wes Hightower, culminating a 59-yard drive, increased the margin to 24–0. Texas then scored the next 20 points in the quarter on a touchdown run and pass, plus two field goals. As quickly as Tech jumped to a seemingly insurmountable lead, the Austinites charged back and made it a contest, trailing only by four points at intermission. As wild and woolly as the first half was, the second saw no scoring at all (though Texas did miss on a field goal attempt), and Tech defeated its old rival, 24–20. The statistics of the contest showed how impressively the Red Raiders' defense played that afternoon. While the Longhorns outgained their opponents by a slight margin (300 to 273 yards), the Tech defense was on the field for almost two-thirds of the contest (the final time of possession was 39:53 to 20:07). Though the scoreboard showed a more substantial point tally than usual for Tech, it was, again, the defense that saved the day.[18] Suddenly, after consecutive victories in the SWC, the Red Raiders were looking at a turnaround. The woeful Horned Frogs were next on the schedule, so a third consecutive triumph was in the bag, right? Well, not quite. The up-and-down character of the 1980 season for Tech was best exemplified by losing a game to a truly woeful TCU squad (in fact, it was their only victory of the season). In this surprising defeat, however, Gabe had one of his most productive and noteworthy performances of this season.

Tech came into the contest at Amon G. Carter Stadium in Fort Worth with a mediocre 4–3 mark, but on a high note from having defeated Texas the preceding Saturday. The Horned Frogs, on the other hand, were 0–8 and licking their wounds after a 37–5 drubbing by the University of Houston Cougars the previous week. TCU had played a couple of close games over the season, for example, losing to 18th-ranked Auburn in the first game of the campaign, 14–7, then to SMU, 17–14, and later to Rice, 28–24. Most of their contests, however, had been lopsided affairs, such as when they lost to the 10th-ranked Georgia Bulldogs, 34–3, and to the 14th-ranked Arkansas Razorbacks, 44–7. Overall, TCU tallied only 143 points in 1980, finishing 123rd out of 138 teams in the country (an average of 13.0 per contest) in scoring. On the defensive side of the ball, TCU surrendered an average of 26.8 points per game, ranking them 122nd in the nation in that category.[19] If ever there was a chance for the 1980 Red Raiders to win easily, the game on November 8 should have been it.

The final score, however, was 24–17 in favor of the purple and white. Gabe certainly did his part to bring a victory back to Lubbock. Late in the contest, with the score knotted at 17, he seemingly produced the break Tech needed in order to pull out the victory. Commenting on the game at the start of the following week, "one particular play remained etched in Dockery's mind. It came with three minutes remaining. . . . Gabriel Rivera . . . intercepted a deflected . . . pass at the TCU 35. [Unfortunately] Rivera's turnover went up in smoke on third down when Reeves was intercepted by TCU linebacker Kelvin Newton."[20] For his efforts, the *Avalanche-Journal* named Rivera its MVP of the contest and provided a substantial summary of his dominance on the field. This would not be the last time he would garner these—and even more impressive—honors for his prowess.

> For a couple of minutes last Saturday in Fort Worth, Gabriel Rivera had his Texas Tech teammates overjoyed. The 6-3, 280-pound sophomore noseguard, known as Señor Sack, intercepted a . . . pass at the TCU 35-yard line to give the Red Raiders new life. . . . For Rivera's big-play performance . . . [he] is the *Avalanche-Journal*'s Tech player of the week. Rivera made one of his strongest games of the year against TCU. In addition to making the first interception of

his career, he thwarted a Frog scoring drive late in the third quarter when he reached down high to bat down an 18-yard field goal attempt. . . . He made two unassisted tackles and helped bring down TCU backs on four other occasions.[21]

After this disappointing result against a previously winless foe, the Red Raiders had to regroup quickly as the 18th-ranked SMU Mustangs, featuring the Pony Express, was headed into Lubbock on November 15.

As mentioned previously, there had already been some jawing by SMU coach Ron Meyer about the Red Raider football team. Further, the Mustangs were playing well and coming into Jones Stadium with a mark of 7–2, riding a three-game winning streak. Among those triumphs were impressive conquests of Texas (then ranked second in the nation going into the October 25 contest), 20–6, in Austin, as well as against Texas A&M, 27–0, in College Station. As game day approached, local reporters described the offensive talent on the SMU sideline, noting that "SMU's offense revolves around high-powered tailbacks Craig James and Eric Dickerson, a pair of outstanding sophomores. . . . Dickerson doesn't do a bad job in relief. He is fourth in the conference in rushing with 730 yards and 4 TDs on 156 tries for a 4.7-yard average."[22] After the debacle against the Horned Frogs the previous Saturday, it seemed logical to assume that Tech was likely to get run out of Jones Stadium, courtesy of the Pony Express.

Given the helter-skelter nature of this season, exactly the opposite happened. The Tech offense did just enough, while the defense turned in the only shutout the Mustangs endured during the James and Dickerson era. The final was 14–0. Not surprisingly, Gabe Rivera was a key player in this effort as he, along with Dane Kerns, contributed a total of 17 tackles (Gabe made 10 unassisted) to stymie the fabled backfield duo. Gabe said, "We felt like going into the game that we could hold them to three to six points. It feels great to shut them out." As a result of his performance, Gabe garnered more extensive recognition than winning the local paper's praise. This time, the acknowledgment came from the Associated Press and the SWC, which named him Defensive Player of the Week. Other highlights of his performance included:

> He personally stopped a Mustang drive late in the second period on third and fourth downs from the Tech one-yard line. The first time he tackled SMU quarterback Lance McIlherry on a sneak then blocked out the middle as Eric Dickerson tried to charge through on fourth down.... On one particularly impressive tackle, Rivera blasted SMU's Dickerson and sent his helmet flying three yards into the air.... [As Coach Dockery said,] "This was Gabe's best game ever in a Tech uniform. He made people aware of his presence all over the field.... He was much more dominating than he had been. Sometimes, noseguards go unnoticed because they attract so much blocking, but people haven't been able to run inside on us consistently this season and one reason is because of Gabe's ability."[23]

The exhilaration of such a momentous victory was tempered by the fact that Tech coaches and administrators were informed shortly after the contest that the team, currently sitting at a 5–4 mark, would not be bound for a bowl game. Coach Dockery, perhaps feeling less pressure about his status, was philosophical, particularly considering that the Red Raiders has been picked to finish in the lower echelons of the SWC. There was still something to play for over the final two contests versus Houston and Arkansas. The field general argued that "we can't worry about the bowl situation now. There's nothing we can do about it. But we were picked to finish seventh in the conference and have a chance to finish second. We can do something about that. That's what we're playing for now."[24]

Of course, as fate would have it, this angered the football gods and Dockery's statement proved the kiss of death over the last two contests: Tech lost both, 34–7 to the Cougars and 22–16 to the Razorbacks. In the contest at Little Rock, Gabe and his

defensive comrades, several of them seniors playing their last
game for the red and black, did the best they could to keep
Tech in a game for one last time in 1980. Of particular note
were the performances of Terry Baer and Stan Williams, two
linebackers who combined for 29 tackles. Not to be left behind,
Gabe chipped in with 11 solo stops, two of them behind the line
of scrimmage, and a fumble recovery. While an improvement
over 1979, a 5–6 mark left a bad taste in Tech's collective mouths
and precipitated further chatter about Dockery's job status.

Afterward, the coach and his regular quarterback put on a
brave face regarding the unsatisfactory culmination of 1980.
The day after the loss to Arkansas, Ron Reeves proclaimed
that the season would serve as a stepping-stone to better things.
"This year will help us. . . . We had excellent leadership from the
coaches and seniors, and when you have that I think it means
a great deal. Never once did this team get down and quit. We
have the people to win. . . . We're going to be good." For his part,
Coach Dockery recommitted himself to scouring the hinterlands surrounding Lubbock in search of fresh talent to complete the turnaround. "We're real excited about the number
of talented players in West Texas. The prospects are excellent
players and excellent individuals. We're going to spend a lot of
time recruiting them because they are the type of players who
can help our program."[25]

There was some actual positive postseason news for the program at this time, as well as platitudes from an embattled coach.
Defensive back Ted Watts and wide receiver Renie Baker (who
tallied 40 receptions for 625 yards, a 15.6-yard-per-catch average) were both named to the first team All-SWC squad. Gabe
was named to the second-team roster. Additionally, he made
his first appearance on the national scene by garnering an
honorable-mention spot on the All-America team for his sophomore campaign.[26] Rivera's statistics from 1980 were about on
par with those of his freshman season: 50 unassisted stops and
20 assists, for a total of 70 tackles. Of these, 12 were behind the

line of scrimmage; he had four sacks and the same number of forced fumbles.[27]

In early December, President Lauro Cavazos provided Dockery with a statement of support, indicating that he would be back for 1981. Now came the time for the coach and his surrogates to scour the countryside in search of new bodies to help put Tech back into the thick of the SWC race. By the end of the fall term, the *Lubbock Avalanche-Journal* made known the staff's wish list for the upcoming recruiting class: more linemen on both sides of the ball, so as to replace departing seniors from the defense (James Giles, Dane Kerns, Jim Verden, and linebacker Jeff McKinney), as well as adding reinforcements to what had proven to be a porous offensive front. The final figures for the season clearly pointed out the weaknesses and strengths of this edition of the Red Raiders. The defense allowed 17.1 points per game, finishing 42nd out of 138 teams in the country. The offense, on the other hand, managed an improved (from 12.8 in 1979) 16.2 points per contest, ranking 105th in the nation.[28]

Shortly after hitting the recruiting trail, however, Dockery shocked Tech administrators by resigning his position and taking a post in his home state of Tennessee with the Memphis State Tigers. He resigned on December 16, and the next morning's *Avalanche-Journal* spent a significant amount of print space discussing the circumstances surrounding this dramatic decision:

> "I feel at this time it's the best thing for my family and its future. I feel like the most important thing you go by is your heart. I feel like that's what you go by in life. That's the way I've always made my decisions." Tech athletic director John Conley met with President Lauro Cavazos immediately following Dockery's announcement. It was decided then that no timetable would be established in selecting a new coach. . . . Dockery would not substantiate rumors that the Tech Board of Regents placed additional pressure on him

with a "win-or-else" ultimatum at its last meeting two weeks ago. . . . Dockery's announcement ended two days of speculation that began Sunday night when he contacted Conley seeking permission to talk to MSU officials concerning the coaching vacancy.[29]

Tragically, this move led to the coach's death, as he was on board a small jet that crashed on the way to an MSU boosters' meeting in Lawrenceburg, Tennessee, almost three years to the day of his resignation from Tech: December 12, 1983. He was 41 years old. While he struggled his first two years with the Tigers, finishing 1–10 both in 1981 and 1982, it seemed that the program was in the midst of a resurgence, as MSU finished 6–4–1 in 1983.[30]

Now the search was on to replace Rex Dockery, as well as continuing to recruit new players for Tech and holding on to the ones the team had. In discussions with Gabe's family, there was never a mention that he ever considered leaving Tech. After two years in Lubbock, he was beginning to gain recognition at the national and conference level and hoped that the defense would continue to play to the relatively high standards of his first two campaigns. A final reason he might not have considered leaving was that Rivera had developed a close relationship with Tech's defensive coordinator, Jim Bates (who served in that capacity between 1980 and 1983), who was one of the finalists to replace the departed field general. Only two members of the Tech staff, Al Tanara (in charge of the offensive line) and Rocky Felker (running backs coach) made the trip with their boss to Tennessee.[31]

I had an opportunity to interview Coach Bates—now retired and living in Florida after having served in the USFL (with the San Antonio Gunslingers); other colleges (including his alma mater, the University of Tennessee); and with various NFL franchises (mostly as a defensive coordinator), including the Miami Dolphins (where he served as interim head coach in 2004, finishing with a record of 3–4) and the Tampa Bay

Buccaneers (working as defensive coordinator until November 2009)—to discuss his recollections of the process of hiring Dockery's replacement. Bates confirmed that he did interview with the Tech administration about the head coaching position and would have gladly accepted it, had the job been offered. He noted that, since he came to Lubbock in 1979 to serve as coach of the secondary, the Bates family had fallen in love with the area. "It reminded me of the place where I grew up [Oxford, Michigan]. I would have gladly stayed at Tech." When asked as to why he did not get the post, Bates contended that, given the problems the Red Raiders had experienced on the offensive side of the line of scrimmage over the past two years, the university's leadership felt it was imperative to bring in someone who had a track record as a head coach, as well as expertise on that side of ball.[32]

The final two weeks of December 1980 featured a plethora of articles in the *Avalanche-Journal* that detailed the many rumors swirling around the Red Raiders' post. At various times, some of the other names mentioned included Bobby Layne, John Mackovic (then at Wake Forest), former Tech assistant Richard Bell, and West Texas State head coach Bill Yung. One interesting facet of this search is that the name of the individual who ultimately got the job, North Texas State University (NTSU) head coach Jerry Moore, whose offensive scheme was the I-formation, did not appear in print until relatively late in the process.

The first mention of Moore in the local paper surfaced on January 4, 1981, and the title of the article, "Mackovic Emerges as Top Candidate," did not seem to bode well for the other applicants. Still, shortly thereafter, the *Avalanche-Journal* reported that Athletic Director John Conley had offered Moore the position. As confirmation of what Coach Bates shared during his interview, a story by Chuck McDonald quoted the new field general laying out his plan to improve Tech's offensive output. "Moore said a) the Raiders would run and THROW out of an

Gabe on the cover of the Texas Tech media guide, with Coach Jerry Moore and quarterback Ron Reeves

I formation, b) that he planned to build his recruiting base in West Texas, and c) that he'd like to live in Lubbock 'for the rest of my life.'" The fact that Moore sported only a mediocre 11–11 record with the NTSU Mean Green (during 1979 and 1980) adds further support to the contention that Tech's management was primarily concerned with getting someone whom they felt could improve the Raiders' scoring output. Jerry Moore seemed to fit that bill. To his credit, Jim Bates remained in Lubbock through the 1983 season, and Gabe rewarded him with All-Conference and All-American performances for his final year of eligibility on a team that finished well below the .500 mark. While the offense improved under Moore in 1981 (finishing at 18.0 points per contest, 89th in the nation), it reverted to its sluggish form in 1982 (14.3 per game and 102nd in the country). The defensive results regressed in those two seasons, and Tech finished ranked 122nd in 1981 (surrendering 27.1 points per game) and 63rd in 1982 (allowing 21.3 points per contest) despite Rivera's outstanding play.[33]

As with most honeymoon periods, all appeared to be proceeding swimmingly under Coach Moore's steady leadership during the Red Raiders' spring practices in 1981. A string of articles offered effusive praise of the offense in the local paper's headlines and made the I-formation seem almost like a scheme out of the Mike Leach or Kliff Kingsbury eras. Stories noted that the "Raider Offense Coils, Strikes," "Tech Offense Shapes Up," "Tech Offense Shines Again," "Raiders Click Along," and "Reeves Explodes in Scrimmage."[34] Reading these passages, one would think that Ron Reeves had morphed into a 1980s version of Patrick Mahomes and was ready to lead Tech to 40-plus points per contest. As the squad moved toward the end of the semester and camp, a new offensive era appeared to have dawned on the South Plains. Still, Moore made sure to moderate expectations about a team that had finished below .500 the previous season:

> Moore's reaction to the improvement of the offense has been
> one of quiet excitement. His eyes light up when the Raiders

perfectly execute the trap play or complete a long pass of a play-action fake, but he's not trying to kid anyone at this stage of the season. "I think we have a chance to be a good football team, but we still have a long way to go. I'm encouraged by the fact that we have improved this spring and players have done exactly what we've asked of them. These players will work hard to be good, and that's a big part of the battle."[35]

As is traditional, the spring practice season ended with the Red and Black Game, and in this go-round Gabe played for the latter team. While the majority of the ink regarding the Tech football program during this period was used to focus on the new offensive scheme, it was now Rivera's turn to take the spotlight, as he would do so often during his junior and senior campaigns. The report on his performance in this glorified scrimmage showed how dominant he could be. He had five sacks (totaling 52 yards lost for the Red offense), plus several stops of running backs behind the line of scrimmage. Norval Pollard summarized his performance this way: "What it [the game] turned out to be was the Red against Gabe Rivera. And Gabe won hands down. Seldom does a defensive player completely control the tempo of a football game like Tech's 6-3, 280-pound standout did Saturday." Gabe argued that he and his defensive mates were just doing their jobs, though the fact that there was some motivation to do well beyond locker-room boasting certainly helped. "The defense was just doing basic stuff, and I was fortunate to play good. . . . I was fired up at first because of the steaks promised to the winning players." After suffering the ignominy of defeat, the Red squad's dinner that evening consisted of hot dogs.[36]

As the Red Raiders moved into the late summer and the start of the fall term, Coach Moore welcomed a total of 62 freshmen and walk-ons to begin preparation for the 1981 season. Once the upperclassmen arrived on the scene a few days later, again there were words of praise for Gabe, who had clearly established himself as a key cog in the defensive unit in his coach's estimation. Tech's field general, in summarizing the strengths of his team, pointed specifically to Rivera's importance to the overall effort. "'Up front we're in pretty good shape.' Obviously, the Raider defensive line revolves around Rivera . . . who will be at left tackle. 'You've almost got to see Gabe to believe him. . . . He's got a huge upper body, is small from the waist down, the pros have him clocked at a 4.76 40, and he can slam dunk a basketball. . . . Our offensive linemen can't handle him. . . . I hope nobody else can, either."[37]

Heading into September, concerns were expressed about other elements of the squad, a lack of depth on the offensive line cited as the most prevalent. Still, Moore had folks on the South Plains believing in the possibility of a turnaround. Since his hire, things seemed to be moving in the right direction. "The first eight months of the relationship have been total bliss. Much like love-struck newlyweds, Moore and the Red Raiders have toiled hand-in-hand to overcome their apparent shortcomings . . . and loved every minute of it." Norval Pollard was among those sufficiently enthused about the possibilities of the upcoming season, though he was also realistic in not wanting to make reservations for New Year's Day in Dallas for the Cotton Bowl. "The 1981 Red Raiders have a chance to finish higher than the eighth-place spot in the SWC standings reserved for them by some. . . . College football is going to be fun again in Lubbock."[38]

An additional aspect of the optimistic tone surrounding the hiring of Coach Moore can be found in an article from the *Austin American-Statesman*, wherein was found some negative commentary about the previous regime straight from the mouths of Tech players. The criticism focused on the prior offensive schema as well as the personality of Coach Dockery. "'I'm enjoying playing football for the first time since I've been in college,' said junior fullback Wes Hightower. 'Everything is so positive around here. This is the first time it's been like this since I've been here.'" Quarterback Reeves agreed with his backfield mate's assertion, noting that "We're a lot better suited for the 'I' . . . Especially me. When you somehow break into the open and then see your down linemen running past you to block, you know it's time to do something else." In support of this contention, the article noted that in 1980 Tech finished eighth of nine teams in the SWC in total offense, averaging slightly less than 290 yards per game.

The scribe who wrote this story, Randy Riggs, encapsulated the feelings he got from the Red Raider clubhouse: "The distinct impression from talking to Tech players is that few tears were shed when Dockery departed. . . . While the Raiders are reluctant to come out and publicly air dirty linen, they constantly allude to pressure, negativism, and a defeatist attitude that seemed to exist when things began going bad." Lastly, Reeves, while not taking any direct shots at his previous mentor, summarized the mood going into 1981 by stating,

> Even if I didn't feel good about this team, I'd probably say I did because that's what you're supposed to say at these things . . . but I do feel good about us. People are willing to make sacrifices to improve the team. Lots of times, people talk about self-sacrifice, but doing it is something else. I've watched these guys sacrifice all spring and so far, this fall. We are excited.[39]

After two years of proving his mettle on the fields of the SWC, plus a tremendous performance at the Red and Black Game in the spring, Gabe merited substantial discussion (along with Ron Reeves) in the Tech 1981 media guide (as well as gracing the cover with his quarterback and head coach). In this article, both Moore and Bates gushed about Rivera and his potential on the football field. One key point noted was that, by 1981, Gabe's 40-yard-dash time actually improved over that of his freshman year, down to 4.77. "'He's a bona fide player,' says head coach Jerry Moore. 'He wasn't the hardest working guy this spring, but he came on real good at the end. He has amazing strength and quickness for a big man. That 40 time he ran is a good indication of his uniqueness.'" Coach Bates argued that part of Gabe's improvement, now as a junior, had been the betterment of his work ethic, which, in turn, led to greater dependability of performance week-in and week-out. "His biggest problem in the past has been inconsistency. But he really came on and started dominating during the second half of last season. He has learned what commitments you have to make to become a truly great player."[40] In one of our interviews, older brother Norbert commented that part of this process included constant visits and discussions with Gabe, to make sure that he was also keeping up the educational end of the bargain. "He was a free spirit and had to stay focused. He assured us that he was going to all of his classes and that he was passing."[41] Therefore, all seemed to be in place for Gabe personally, as well as for a turnaround season for the Red Raiders. It was not to be, however, as dreams of success imploded, and Tech finished 1–9–1. This was the team's fewest victories since another one-victory campaign in 1961 under J. T. King.[42]

Things started to go off kilter for the Red Raiders right from the first afternoon of the 1981 season, as they lost to the Colorado Buffaloes, 45–27. On September 12, what was supposed to be the team's strength, the defense, was shredded for 564 total yards of offense. "Tech's pass rush was nonexistent during last week's fiasco in Boulder." Almost 400 of those yards came via the pass.[43] Moore stated that it was necessary for Gabe and his mates to turn up the heat on the New Mexico quarterback the following week, lest Tech endure a similar fate to that of week number one. The coach of the Lobos, Joe Morrison, although having watched film of the debacle versus Colorado, was certainly focused on doing whatever he could to neutralize Gabe. "I'm still impressed with Rivera. He may be the best defensive lineman we play against all year. We've got to figure out a way to keep him away from our quarterback (Robin Gabriel, son of former NFL star Roman Gabriel)."[44] Fortunately, as is usually the case, the Red Raiders managed to tame the wolves from Albuquerque, winning 28–21. Although Morrison's charges were keyed to stop him, Rivera made his presence felt all game: totaling 13 stops, four of them for negative yards. Additionally, Gabe helped to stuff the UNM running game (47 total yards in 34 attempts) in addition to giving Gabriel fits whenever he dropped back to pass (two of the negative plays were sacks).[45] This would be Tech's lone victory for 1981.

A 28–15 loss to Baylor followed on September 26, and even the ever reliable homer, Norval Pollard, took notice of the failures on the defensive side of the ball, bemoaning that "Tech built a reputation around the conference with its aggressive, hard-nosed, sure-tackling brand of defense over the course of many seasons. That reputation has been set back on its haunches." The defeats and poor performances in keeping opponents off the scoreboard continued. Tech's next three contests played out this way: a loss to A&M, 24–23; defeated by Arkansas, 26–14; and finally an embarrassing setback to the Rice Owls, 30–23, in mid-October. After six weeks, the team's mark stood at 1–5, and winless in the SWC.[46] On October 24, against the visiting University of Washington of the Pac 10, the defense finally showed some life. Although the Red Raiders fell, 14–7, they held the visitors from Seattle to only 180 yards of total offense and no touchdowns (surrendering only four field goals, with the Huskies trapping a Tech runner in the end zone for a safety to account for their final points). The following weekend brought another disastrous offensive effort, as Tech lost to Texas, 26–9. Here, once again, Ron Reeves was running for his life most of the contest and was sacked several times.[47]

As the calendar turned to November, all Tech had left to play for was pride. Since, of the three games remaining, two were road tilts against contenders SMU and Houston, the last "real" opportunity to add a notch to the win column would come against the Raiders' fellow denizens of the SWC nether region, the TCU Horned Frogs. The game would take place in Lubbock and was Tech's homecoming contest. Prior to that game, Pollard tried to put a positive spin on circumstances by noting that the unpleasant current reality would someday certainly lead to a sunnier tomorrow. With the team standing at 1–7, and 0–5 in the conference, the beat writer praised the recruiting work of Coach Moore and his staff:

> The future looks good for the Raiders. In addition to those freshmen, solid players such as Anthony Hutchinson, David Joeckle, Wes Hightower, Gabe Rivera, Brad White, Stan Williams and Greg Iseral return next season. . . . Moore's 1981 crop is a good one. Those rookies have played with poise and pride. They have suffered adversity right along with the juniors and seniors. But they don't have to keep suffering. Losing has made them hungry for victory. Now all they need is the experiences it takes to secure those wins.[48]

Now, a golden opportunity to have at least some positive results on the field in 1981 was hopping into Jones Stadium in the form of the purple-and-white-clad invaders from Fort Worth who staggered into Lubbock with an unimpressive 2–5–2 record, just barely ahead of the last-place Red Raiders. Given the recent improvement by the Tech defense, having surrendered only an average of 280 yards of total offense over their last four games, the time seemed ripe for the victory bells to ring out again for the first time since September 19.[49] It was not to be.

Of all the defeats and near misses of this dreadful campaign, the game against TCU, a 39–39 tie, had to have been far and away the most frustrating. At one point in the second half, Tech led 32–9. Then, several miscues on the part of special teams allowed the Frogs to mount a furious comeback to knot the score. With six seconds to go, Tech had a chance to snatch victory from the jaws of a tie by kicking a field goal. Of course, usually reliable placekicker John Greve missed. To make matters worse, Gabe sprained his ankle, and his participation was in doubt going into a contest against the SMU Mustangs, out to avenge the 14–0 embarrassment of the previous year.[50]

After the collapse against TCU, the last two contests were anticlimactic. Tech lost to the Ponies, 30–6, in Dallas, then succumbed to the Cougars in Houston, 15–7. In the penultimate contest, Dickerson and James ran wild, combining for more than 260 yards on the ground. This defeat assured the Red Raiders of a last-place finish in the SWC. The game displayed the Red Raiders' offensive ineptitude in spades: with a total of seven Tech turnovers, four in the first half, SMU raced to a 24–0 lead and never looked back. In the Astrodome, the Lubbockites showed some spunk, taking a quick 7–0 lead, only to have Reeves suffer torn ligaments in his left knee during his final game in red and black. The offense mounted no further threats, and the Cougars held on for the victory.[51] Once again, in the fading twilight of a horrid season, Norval Pollard complimented both the Raiders' fans (the team finished averaging around 41,000 per home contest) and Coach Moore, indicating that it would not be long before things improved. "Moore has said over and over this season that he's been proud of the way his team has played—never throwing in the towel, always giving it everything—in defeat this season. . . . During a season when the Raiders won only one time, he said, 'Better times are comin'.'"[52]

In the midst of this debacle, Gabe remained a significant presence on the field. His total tackles increased to 79 (37 unassisted), marking the second consecutive increase in this figure over his career. He had six tackles behind the line of scrimmage, three sacks, and a forced fumble. His biography in the College Football Hall of Fame notes that, even with Tech's poor record, it was not possible to overlook his contributions and hustle at the regional or national level. Thus, although he played for a last-place team, Rivera once again earned honorable mention All-America as well as second-team All-Southwest Conference designations, as did safety Tate Randle. In addition, punter

Maury Buford earned a spot on the first-team All-SWC. Considering Tech's offensive ineptitude that year, Buford certainly had plenty of chances to punt away the football to the Red Raiders' opponents.[53]

The post-1981 campaign period was, to an extent, much quieter than that of the previous year. Tech's football program did not have to endure rumors of a leadership change or undergo the endless speculation that surrounds a typical coaching search. One of the few things that occupied Pollard's articles (concerning football) during this off-season was to complain about how linebacker Terry Baer was shortchanged by not earning even an honorable mention among the SWC All-Stars after leading Tech in tackles (a total of 84 unassisted), including 15 solos against the Arkansas Razorbacks. About the only other discussion concerning the football team during basketball and baseball season dealt with how Tech's recruitment efforts were proceeding during early 1982.[54]

Certainly, Red Raider aficionados were dismayed by a 1–9–1 mark, but there was optimism. Gabe, for example, would be back the next year, and hopefully he and his teammates would improve the on-field results in short order. Then, out of the blue, came a thunderbolt that clouded many of the hopes for a better 1982: Rivera, one of the seniors expected to provide leadership for the turnaround, was suspended for violating team rules in early February. Coach Moore kicked Gabe and three teammates (kicker Jesse Garcia and linemen Rene Reyes and Mark Rothblatt) out of the athletic dorm due to suspicion that they had smoked marijuana. The immediate consequences of this were quite severe: the players were kicked off the team, their scholarships were revoked, and of course, they were not eligible to practice during the spring.[55]

Two interesting sidelights to this story come from the pages of the *Avalanche-Journal* and the recollections of this period by Gabe's brother, Norbert. As noted, the San Antonio papers clearly stated that Gabe and his teammates were suspended specifically due to there being evidence that they had smoked pot in their dorm rooms. The Lubbock periodical, however, never makes this point unambiguously for its readers. The reason for the suspension was always posited as being that the four "violated team rules," not that they were caught using marijuana. Pollard quoted Coach Moore as saying that "'the four players broke team rules so disciplinary action has been taken.' Moore declined to elaborate on the specific rule or rules broken by the four."[56]

My discussions with Norbert Rivera, Gabe's older brother, provided a substantial amount of background information concerning events surrounding the suspension. First, he confirmed that Gabe was indeed smoking pot in his dorm. Next, he also stated that Gabe "liked to take chances" and that this was not the first time he had used the illicit substance. There is also evidence that the family was aware of his use. In the *Express-News* article cited earlier, Juan Rivera indicated that he was surprised that Gabe had been accused of using pot. "I'm real proud of Gabriel. . . . [He] is going to be 21 in April and I've never heard anything negative about him. If there had been some earlier incidents, I guess I wouldn't be so shocked." Norbert argued that this was not accurate. Maria Antonia was aware that Gabe used and, as had happened on previous occasions, directed Norbert to go to Lubbock to help keep his younger sibling on the right path.[57]

Upon his arrival in the Hub City, Norbert chastised his brother for getting into trouble just as he was on the cusp of moving into his senior year, with an NFL career a distinct possibility. Norbert accused his brother of letting down both his family and teammates. Rivera's reaction to this tongue-lashing was, Norbert confessed, very nonchalant, considering the circumstances. If he were kicked out of Tech, the elder brother asked, what would Gabe do with himself? Gabe appeared to have considered that possibility. "He thought he might go into wrestling if he could no longer play football. He had no real worries that, somehow, he would be OK." Norbert spent an entire weekend with Gabe, and even managed to recruit Tech's president, Dr. Lauro Cavazos, and other prominent Mexican Americans from the area to come and "talk some sense" into the star athlete. Cavazos, in particular (in meeting with Gabe, Norbert, and Maria Antonia), argued that the senior was not only important to the Red Raiders but to the entire Mexican American community as a symbol of what persons of his background could achieve. Eventually, after much cajoling, Gabe came to his senses and realized what he had done. By the summer, he was contrite and ready to get back. Norbert added, however, that Gabe probably continued to smoke pot.[58]

By late March, Coach Moore and the rest of the Red Raiders had moved on with their spring practices, minus their star defender, as well as his line mate Hasson Arbubakrr, who was not allowed to participate due to academic issues. Not surprisingly, there were concerns about whether Gabe would be reinstated and the impact that would have on the team's line play. Additionally, after trying a 4–3 defensive alignment in 1981, Tech's brain trust had decided to install a 5–2 configuration for 1982. Of course, the coaching staff worked with the players they had available, though Coach Bates did allude to Rivera as the squad began its workouts. "On the negative side, we won't be able to see how two fine players fit into the defensive scheme and how much improvement they can make during spring practice."[59]

The rest of the articles during this period were the typical ones to be found in local papers covering a team moving into the next football season: yes, last year was difficult, but the boys and coaches are working hard to move the team in the right direction. Pollard dubbed the spring's efforts as "Operation Get Better." Coach Moore did his part, arguing that the players were coming along and learning to do what was necessary to turn things around. "We're doing the little things so much better, not only on the field but in the classroom . . . and those little things are going to make a big difference. They have already." Heck, the Raiders had even found a possible replacement, we were led to believe, for Rivera and Arbubakrr: a transfer from Bakersfield Junior College named Willie Reyneveld. As far as Moore was concerned, as of early April the newcomer was the starter, and Gabe and Hasson, if they returned, would have to earn their previous status all over again.[60] As usual, the spring session ended with the Red and Black Game, though Moore instituted a twist to the contest in his second year: making the clash not between the members of the current squad, but rather the present-day athletes competing against alumni. The final score was 31–26 in favor of the 1982 Raiders. The score was 21–0 at halftime, but then the current athletes dialed back the effort against their predecessors, some of whom had not donned pads in more than a decade.[61]

Now that the spring semester and its associated football undertakings were completed, it was time to get back to the serious business of whether Gabe Rivera and any of the other three wrongdoers would be allowed to return. In interviews, Norbert and Coach Bates both indicated that it was their belief that Coach Moore would, eventually, allow Gabe to return (ultimately, he and Rothblatt were put back on scholarship; Garcia and Reyes did not come back). Two key reasons made Rivera's reinstatement a near certainty: first, he was a truly unique talent; there was absolutely no doubt about that at this point in his collegiate career.[62] He was the type of athlete who comes along only once or twice in the span of most coaches' tenures. Second, for a field general at any institution, the goodwill generated when hired does not survive too many 1–9–1 campaigns. While Moore and his assistants brought in reinforcements as freshmen recruits and transfers, the fans at Jones Stadium wanted to see improvement—and they wanted it now! Thus, by July 1982, the wayward son of the Tech defensive line was restored to his place on the squad. Arbubakrr also returned, having overcome his academic issues.

Interestingly, there was one not-so-subtle hint that indicated Gabe would be allowed back on the team, and it showed up in the Riveras' home mailbox in San Antonio in late June. Juan and Maria Antonia received a letter on team stationery and dated June 21, from Coach Moore. The document went on and on about "how hard your son has worked" and that "All of us [coaches] will be contacting him during the summer." Moore, additionally, wanted Mom and Dad to perform a "special favor" for him, by keeping an eye on Gabe's eating and workout habits while in the Alamo City. It turns out they did more than that. Rivera did go on a diet over the summer (eating mostly tuna), and also did hard manual labor working for a construction company.[63]

Moore admitted in a July interview that, even while on suspension over the spring term, Gabe had been permitted to work out on weights in a Tech rec room (not tied to Athletics). Additionally, the field general asked assistants to keep tabs on the senior defensive lineman. "Naturally, the football coaches kept an eye on him. That last time I saw him, he was in great shape." The official word of the termination of Gabe's suspension came in July. Juan was ecstatic about the turn of events. "I am thrilled that the reinstatement is official. I got my hopes up in . . . June when we received a letter saying that Gabe's football scholarship had been renewed." Moore also came out of the whole mess seen as an able leader who would not shortchange West Texas standards and coddle athletes, even extraordinary ones, in order to win football games. "When this happened, everybody was sitting back to see what I would do. . . . A lot of players thought nothing would be done because Gabe was the star of the team. I had nothing but support from the community and alumni on my decision."[64]

As the summer gave way to fall, the Red Raiders once again geared up to begin practice for the season's first game against a familiar foe: the New Mexico Lobos. As usual, the *Avalanche-Journal* sounded a fairly optimistic tone with the arrival of freshmen and walk-ons starting in the middle of August. Late that month, Gabe was held out of practice due to a sore back but ultimately proved his value to the defensive line once again and soon regained first-string status. To start the campaign, he would be flanked by Brad White and Hasson Arbubakrr.[65]

Given his prominence, papers in Lubbock and elsewhere indicated that Rivera had much to prove in his senior season. It was widely acknowledged that he had tremendous talent, and it was also conceded that he had done severe damage to his reputation by being suspended. Now it was time for Gabe to stake his claim to the status many expected him to achieve: to be an all-time great for the red and black. Given the discussions he had with Norbert, Maria Antonia, President Cavazos, and others, he appeared ready to make amends on the field and off. The fact that Rivera had one last season to prove himself to the NFL also figured into the mix. "I had a lot of time to think about what I had done and about my future. It was hard on me, but real hard on my parents as well. Now I have something to prove and I want to prove it to them." Even his teammates noticed the transformation in his demeanor. "'He doesn't joke around as much,' said strong safety Greg Iseral. 'He's more serious, more of a leader now.'"[66] In the local paper, Norval Pollard struck a similar tone:

> Jerry Moore made only one request of Gabriel Rivera following his return to the Texas Tech football team in early August: that he utilize his awesome natural ability to the utmost and have a great senior year. At that time, following Rivera's well-publicized six-month suspension... Moore sensed that Gabe wanted to finish his off-and-on career with a stellar 1982 showing: the type of season that would confirm a theory... that started three years ago... that Rivera could be one of the best to ever play for the Red Raiders.[67]

All appeared ready to go for what would, hopefully, be a turnaround season for Texas Tech from a nightmarish 1981.

Gabe making short work of an attempted block by a fullback from the Air Force Academy (Southwest Collection, TTU University Archives)

Given all of these positives, of course, the Red Raiders promptly fell flat on their faces offensively and lost to the Lobos, 14–0, in Albuquerque. Gabe contributed to the defensive effort, totaling eight tackles (two unassisted) in this game. Still, it was a great disappointment as what had usually been an annual victory went awry. Going into the second contest of the season, against the Air Force Academy (AFA), Pollard was already expressing apprehension about the direction for the season, particularly on the offensive side of the ball. "The Raiders were mediocre at best in a 14–0 blitz by New Mexico, while the Falcons soared to their most productive offensive day in 10 years [the previous week]."[68] The outcome was in doubt against AFA on September 18, too, as the Red Raiders fell behind, 27–17, in the second half. Fortunately, they managed to score two touchdowns in the final quarter and held off the Coloradoans,

31–30. Gabe totaled 14 tackles, one sack, and a forced fumble in this contest. Additionally, the *Lubbock Avalanche-Journal*'s photographer managed to capture another iconic photo of him in action. The snapshot features a picture of Gabe overwhelming AFA back Mark Melcher and ripping his helmet off. This picture was very reminiscent of the confrontation Rivera had with Eric Dickerson in 1980.[69]

Tech split its next two contests, losing to Baylor at home, 24–23 (on September 25), and then surprising Texas A&M, 24–15 (on October 2). The game in College Station was a stellar one for Rivera. Here, he had five tackles, three of these for losses, and two pass break-ups. "Defensively, senior tackle-nose guard Gabriel Rivera put on a show that the Aggies won't soon forget. . . . [He] was constantly hopping on A&M quarterback Gary Kubiak and led a fierce charge that held the Aggies to a paltry 36 yards rushing." Overall, A&M converted only three of 17 third downs. Coach Moore noted, "He's playing extremely well. . . . This might have been the best game of his career. It couldn't have come at a better time."[70] The best was yet to come, however, starting the following week against Arkansas.

Gabe's performances against the Razorbacks (at that point, ranked ninth in the nation) and the Owls, measured purely by statistics on paper, were effective, but not overwhelming. Combined, he totaled 13 individual tackles, assisted on four more, had one pass break-up and quarterback sack, and two stops for losses. Tech lost in Little Rock, 21–3, and edged Rice, 23–21, in Houston. There was one play in the defeat, however, that astonished the press and helped to make the moniker "Señor Sack" known to many more individuals across the nation. Going into the contest, there was already discussion that Rivera was playing at "an all-conference clip from both the nose and tackle positions."[71] Further, this game would feature another potential All-American, Billy Ray Smith Jr., at defensive end for the home team (he would be so honored both in 1981 and 1982). How would Gabe, from an also-ran squad, measure up against this great talent and a nationally ranked opponent? Quite well, indeed. One play in particular led Norval Pollard to comment, "There haven't been too many days in Billy Ray Smith's illustrious career . . . when the All-American has had to take a back seat to anyone. Saturday was one of those few, but Gabe Rivera isn't just anyone. For the fifth straight week, Texas Tech's do-it-all defensive lineman played like there's no tomorrow." Just what did Gabe do to merit this praise? Only perform one of the most memorable defensive plays in Texas Tech history:

> One play in particular stands as a tribute to both the athletic ability and competitive spirit of the San Antonio native. Late in the third quarter with the Hogs holding the football at their 29, quarterback Tom Jones broke a tackle at the line of scrimmage and slapped it into fourth gear on his way to the goal line. At the midfield stripe, Rivera was a good 10 yards behind Jones. It didn't matter, though, as he passed one of his own defensive backs and slammed Jones out of bounds at the Tech 17. That was it for Jones. He never returned to action. Gabe? He kept right on playing. "I guess if I'm going to run that far to catch him, I might as well hit him hard. . . . I guess I took a little frustration out on him."[72]

It was this play, and the totality of his efforts so far in 1982, that led Coach Jim Bates to utter the "AA" term in reference to Gabe for the first time in an interview. "He's the football-playingest guy you've ever seen. . . . If he isn't an All-America lineman this year then something is wrong."[73] If this contest and play were impressive, even more was to come on October 23 as the Red Raiders traveled to the Pacific Northwest to challenge the top-ranked team in the country: the University of Washington Huskies.

The contests against the Huskies were an unusual setup for the Red Raiders. Not only were they part of a home-and-home series, they also took place in the middle of the conference slate. By the time of the 1982 tilt, Tech had already completed half of its SWC schedule, standing at an unimpressive 2–2 in conference and 3–3 overall. As noted earlier, Gabe and his defensive teammates had put up a tremendous effort in Lubbock against Washington in 1981, losing 14–7, and had not allowed a touchdown. Now it was time for Tech to visit Seattle. Coach Moore indicated that his squad welcomed the challenge, and that they had confidence, given their performance (at least on the defensive side of the ball) the previous year.[74] The task seemed even more daunting as the Huskies had plowed through their previous six opponents while averaging more than 40 points per outing. If there was any hope of pulling off a major upset, it would require yet another titanic effort to keep the Pac 10 foes from lighting up the scoreboard. Gabe, it was expected, would play a major role in this endeavor. "Tech's defensive fortunes rest on the ability of its linemen to put heat on [Steve] Pelluer. That line is supercharged by the play of senior All-America candidate Gabe Rivera . . . who leads the team in tackles, sacks, and tackles for losses."[75] His performance would be all of this, and much, much more.

While he had put up impressive numbers in games in previous years and had also done well in other contests in 1982, Gabe saved his best for the biggest stage. Tech lost, 10–3, in part on a controversial call during an onside kick. While, as usual, the offense struggled, the defense shined, and Tech led 3–0 until late. Against the Huskies Rivera was seemingly everywhere. His stat sheet was worthy of an All-American: 10 tackles (five unassisted), four pass break-ups, one sack, one tackle for loss, and four quarterback rushes. The Raiders' defense also had four interceptions. Washington's legendary head coach, Don James, summarized the performance he witnessed this way: "I've seen a lot of quarterbacks and running backs have outstanding games, but I don't think I've ever seen a defensive player play so well against us. . . . He's the most dominating defensive player, from start to finish, I've ever seen."

Coach Moore echoed his counterpart's assessment and hearkened back to the suspension from early in the year as a motivating factor. "He's just a terrific player. . . . He's done so much since last spring to improve himself, to make himself a complete football player. I'd say this was his best game . . . and it came against the No. 1 team in the country." Not to be outdone by the field generals, several of the Huskies' players, from both sides of the ball, also chimed in with compliments. Don Dow, an offensive lineman who faced Gabe, argued, "He's a load, he's going to make someone a tremendous NFL nose guard." Another member of the Washington line, Eric Moran, agreed, stating, "Rivera is a big Herschel Walker. He has awesome physical strength and balance. Rivera is the best football player I have ever played against, or even seen on film, in intercollegiate football." Finally, watching from the sidelines, linebacker Mark Stewart acknowledged, "He should be on somebody's All-America team somewhere, if not all of them. We joked about his nickname, but I've never seen anybody his size who could run like that."[76]

The words of acclaim came not just from the Lubbock press. The Seattle papers also expressed amazement at Gabe's play, and even christened him with a new moniker, one more familiar to the denizens of the Pacific Northwest: "Big Foot." Steve Rudman, writing for the *Post-Intelligencer*, noted that "Rivera, whose 4.7 footspeed over 40 yards must make professional scouts drool in anticipation, completely terrorized the interior of Washington's offensive line, discarding blockers as if they were mere tinker toys—and Rivera wrought this havoc against tinker toys which weighed upwards of 280 pounds." John Owen, in the same paper, pitied the poor Huskies, who had just played against a foe their coach called "Superman," and next had to face John Elway, also known as "Captain Marvel," and the Stanford Cardinal. Finally, Gil Lyons, in the *Seattle Times*, was even more effusive in his admiration. "The Washington Huskies would be excused if they thought the legendary 'Big Foot' was masquerading yesterday in a uniform worn by a member of the Texas Tech Red Raiders. Gabriel

Rivera almost single-handedly threw Washington's offense into reverse before the Huskies managed to scratch out a 10–3 victory before a Homecoming crowd in Husky Stadium." As a final tribute, Lyons quoted lineman Eric Moran, and he stated, ironically given what would happen to Gabe in Pittsburgh, that Rivera was "the closest thing I've seen to Joe Greene, when Greene could move that well."[77]

After making his way back to Lubbock, Norval Pollard picked up on the sobriquet and noted that for Tech's version of the fabled creature, "there were more inches [of newspaper print] dedicated to . . . Rivera than on the game and Husky features." Pollard then went on to summarize how well Gabe had played over the course of the first seven contests of 1982. "In the big-play department, where All Americans are made, Gabe has 39. That's 30 more than his closest challenger [on the team]. Yes, he is a load." Pollard then turned to an extensive discussion of what he perceived to be the driving factor behind such outstanding work on the field.

> There is another side to Rivera's story. One that he acknowledges but still is embarrassed by: last spring's suspension for breaking team rules. But like a real winner in a desperate situation, the good natured . . . Rivera didn't let the episode whip him and ruin what has been a fine career through three seasons and is now a great career at Tech. The true mark of an All-American is to beat all odds and still be great. Gabe had done that. . . . "He's playing better than I ever thought he could," Moore revealed. "I've never seen a guy dominate the line of scrimmage like he does week after week. . . . I'd like to see him make the All-American team. He certainly deserves it."[78]

The acclaim did not just appear in Lubbock and Seattle papers, as by the middle of the following week, Gabe's achievements generated national headlines. He earned top defensive honors from the SWC, as well as being named Associated Press top lineman of the week. He merited the same honors from

Sports Illustrated, in addition to a segment on him on ESPN *SportsCenter* the Monday following the contest.

Of course, all this publicity was seen as a great bonus for Tech's football program. Although the Raiders had not defeated the Huskies, the nationwide attention helped Coach Moore and his colleagues with recruiting and, it was hoped, would produce a bumper crop in February 1983. "'The response we've received from recruits and their families has been fantastic,' Moore admitted before Tuesday's practice. 'It's much more positive than it was a year ago, and more of the top prospects in the state are taking a genuine interest in Texas Tech.'"[79] Even Gabe's hometown newspaper pushed the notion that he was now a candidate for All-American, having overcome the disadvantage caused by his suspension. "Since Rivera missed spring training . . . he did not have the advantage of preseason billing that is so often vital in getting post-season recognition. . . . The Washington game could have been the boost he needed. . . . Gabe is certainly making up for lost time."[80] A final opportunity for Gabe arrived on campus just after the Washington game in the form of a letter from the sponsors of the Blue–Gray All-Star Football Classic. Coach Frank Howard, the head coach at Clemson and the recruiter for the southern schools participating in the event, contacted Coach Moore asking him to list "your good boys" to participate in the annual event in Montgomery, Alabama. At the bottom of the document, in Howard's own handwriting, he asked his Tech counterpart to "invite Gabe Rivera for me and we may need some more."[81] It was at this event that Gabe came to the attention of Pittsburgh Steelers scouts, who were there to scout hometown hero Dan Marino as a possible heir to Terry Bradshaw.

Then, just as quickly as Tech garnered a plethora of national (and positive) publicity, it all came crashing down. After taking the number-one-ranked team in the nation down to the wire, the following game was against a Texas Longhorns team that had lost consecutive tilts versus Oklahoma and SMU. The hated rivals seemed ripe for the picking in the hostile confines of Jones Stadium on October 30. It was not to be as, once again, the Tech offense was stymied, and the Red Raiders lost, 27–0. In total, the home team generated a paltry 134 total yards and a measly 61 through the air. The visitors from Austin were in complete control, holding on to the ball for almost 41 minutes. To make matters worse, Gabe suffered a knee injury early in the third quarter and left with only eight tackles to his credit (four unassisted). Coach Moore recognized the impact that this had on the Raiders' defense. "Gabe was having a good game even though they were giving him a lot of double-team attention. There probably was more mental harm on our team after he left the game (Tech trailed, 7–0) than there was physical. He's such a great inspiration for everybody when he's in there."[82]

The final three games of the season featured one victory, against TCU (on November 6), and provided a measure of revenge against the Horned Frogs after the embarrassing tie in Lubbock the previous year. On that same day, Coach Moore sent a letter to Juan and Maria Antonia indicating how proud he was of their son, and how far he had come from the suspension at the start of the year. "Words cannot express how I feel about your son and what he has accomplished. I think I am even prouder because of the situation that came up in the spring. He has fought back in such a way that it makes me proud and knowing that he is doing an excellent job both on the field and off."[83]

The last two contests featured one of the most heartbreaking moments in Tech football history. After coming close to defeating the No. 1 team in the nation, the Raiders played the No. 2 squad, the Mustangs, to a 27–27 tie with 17 seconds to go on November 13. Then the unthinkable happened: after SMU fumbled the kickoff, a lateral pass to Bobby Leach produced a 91-yard touchdown that sealed the victory for the visitors. Final score, SMU 34, Tech 27. In these two games, Gabe, probably slowed by his knee injury, had a modest 18 tackles. Then, on November 20, Rivera and the seniors played their final game for the red and black at home against the Houston Cougars. While Tech lost, 24–7, Gabe did not disappoint the 33,000 fans in the stands. He had 19 tackles, one sack, and a pass deflection. Although he expressed disappointment at not leaving Lubbock with a victory in his last game, Rivera seemed content (and redeemed?) with the final year of his career. "I'm satisfied with my play. . . . But going out losing makes it harder. I can't really say how I feel about Tech. Playing in my last game really hit me when I woke up about 6:30 this morning."[84]

In the following week there were several other tributes to Gabriel Rivera's stellar collegiate performance: he earned first-team Kodak All-America as well as United Press International All-SWC first team status. Additionally, he was a member of the Newspaper Enterprise Association (NEA) second team, having been beaten out for the first team by George Achica of the University of Southern California. When asked his reaction by Norval Pollard, Gabe expressed a sense of exoneration, particularly after the issues he confronted in the spring. "My reaction was one of relief. . . . It was one of my goals since coming to college four years ago. I'm happy that I could finish my career with such an honor."[85]

While Gabe did not complete his degree at Texas Tech in the spring of 1983, he looked forward to the upcoming NFL draft in April. Certainly there would be time to finish his studies down the road, as the family stressed. Given all of the on-field accolades, Gabe would likely be a high draft choice, and that would mean more money than he, or Juan, or any of their ancestors from Coahuila could have ever imagined. Yes, the time was now to reset the trajectory of the entire Rivera clan toward horizons previously unimaginable while they lived in Crystal City, Benavides, or San Antonio. Not surprisingly, as the year drew to a close, letters began arriving indicating the wonderful possibilities that lay ahead. In addition to the Blue–Gray Game,

Gabe would participate in the *Bob Hope Christmas Show*, as well as events feting the All-America squad in Orlando. There would also be celebrations in the Alamo City. Moreover, the former Red Raider had an opportunity to hear from important personages "at the next level" of football. One noteworthy letter came from the desk of an NFL legend: Chuck Knox, then serving as the vice president of operations and head coach of the Buffalo Bills. This document serves as an excellent culmination to the story of Gabe's collegiate career. The document, dated December 14, 1982, reads,

> I would like to take this opportunity to congratulate you on the outstanding contribution you have made to your college and the honors that have come your way throughout your college career. Now you will be looking forward to a new goal in professional football, and our Scouting Department has concluded that you have the abilities to succeed at the professional level. With this in mind, I am looking forward to meeting you during your visit to Seattle the weekend of February 24 to February 26. . . . I am looking forward with great enthusiasm to the Seattle weekend. It will be of great value to the Buffalo Bills and more important to your future in professional football.[86]

In addition, Gabe was now engaged to be married and was soon to have his first child. His fiancée was a young lady named Kimberly Covington. The two met in the spring of 1982. Kim's recollection of their first meeting was that Gabe just "used to hang out" near a building where she was taking classes her freshman year. She was not very much into sports, so she really had no idea who Gabe was. The two began to talk in between classes, and eventually a romance blossomed. The couple moved in together in early 1983.[87] Yes, this was going to be a memorable year for the Riveras—on the fields of the NFL and in the family's life. Indeed it would be, for both good and ill.

CHAPTER 6

FROM FIRST-ROUND SELECTION TO "THE STEELER WHO NEVER WAS"

GABE'S BRIEF TIME IN THE NFL

AFTER COMPLETING HIS ALL-AMERICAN SEASON and career, Gabe finished his years at Tech with a total of 321 tackles. At the time, this was the highest total ever for a Red Raider defender. Subsequently, 10 players have surpassed this figure, with the current record holder being Lawrence Flugence, a linebacker who played between 1999 and 2002, with a total of 500 tackles. As of the start of the 2019 season, however, Rivera still held the mark for most stops in a season by a defensive tackle (105 in 1982).[1] These accomplishments ushered in a new epoch in Gabe's life: he was now a highly sought-after commodity, and the opportunities to play in either the NFL or the newly established USFL meant that he should be able to parlay his athletic gifts into a professional career that would, most likely, earn him a substantial amount of fame and money.

The letter from Coach Knox and the Buffalo Bills was just the beginning of the materials that arrived in Rivera's mailbox over the waning days of 1982 offering a plethora of opportunities. This was not the only franchise that contacted Gabe regarding the upcoming draft. The Pittsburgh Steelers also reached out to him after seeing his play at the Blue–Gray contest in Alabama. The famed Steel Curtain was, by the early 1980s, showing serious rust, and it was time to restock that portion of the club. In his telegram, Vice President Arthur Rooney Jr. congratulated Gabe on his accomplishments at Tech and also reminded him that the best talent in football still resided in the NFL, and not in the upstart league. "Although you will receive a lot of attention from other leagues during the next few months, we hope that you will keep your options open until the conclusion of our draft [which would take place on April 26 and 27, 1983]."[2]

Additionally, Gabe was part of the *Bob Hope Christmas Special* that year, and even received a seasonal card from the famed entertainer and his wife, Dolores; the original resides in the Southwest Collection at Texas Tech. Later, he was feted by the San Antonio Independent School District (SAISD) just before the new year. Among the invitees were principals, football coaches, and players from the various institutions in the district. Of course, Juan and Maria Antonia would also be among the honored guests at the event. The letter the proud parents received from Dr. William Elizondo, president of the SAISD board, indicated how important Gabe's success was to the community and to athletes in the Alamo City: "We are very proud, as I know you are, of Gabriel, He serves as a role model for our youngsters and we hope that he continues to maintain an interest in communicating with our district."[3]

Other San Antonio civic and community entities invited Gabe for recognition. For example, in late January, the Mexican American Sports Association asked him to attend a basketball tournament consisting of teams comprising exclusively

Gabe and other members of the All-America team toured Epcot Center in Florida (Southwest Collection, TTU University Archives)

Hispanic athletes. The organization's goal was to showcase a Spanish-surnamed player who had succeeded at the highest levels in hope of inspiring the next generation of Latino athletes in the city and surrounding areas.[4] On February 2, 1983, Gabe was wined and dined by civic and Texas Tech officials. He had lunch at the Plaza Club with Mayor Henry Cisneros, as well as Texas Tech president Dr. Lauro Cavazos, Athletic Director John Conley, Coach Jerry Moore, and other dignitaries. Later, at City Hall, Cisneros read a proclamation and named Gabe an honorary *alcalde* (mayor) of the city. The culmination of the day's festivities came that evening during halftime of the New York Knicks versus San Antonio Spurs game, when Gabe received his Associated Press All-American plaque.[5]

While the opportunity to rub elbows with stars, politicos, and other elites was no doubt exciting and delightful, it was time to begin thinking about the business and financial aspects of life as a professional athlete. Gabe's mailbox did not lack for letters concerning such matters. Most of these related a basic "pitch." First off, they congratulated Gabe on his accomplishments, then shifted to the key issue of how to monetize his success on the football field in the NFL, the new USFL, or even (though unlikely) the Canadian Football League (CFL).

For a young man who, though certainly not impoverished, grew up in a household supported by the modest salary of a teacher/coach, the possibilities of substantial riches certainly must have been intoxicating. One piece of correspondence, from an agent based in Connecticut, predicted that "hopefully, your professional career will be just as productive . . . and, hopefully, more rewarding." Another letter came from a lawyer in California named Jim Armstrong who distinguished himself by listing his qualifications (as opposed to those of a "mere" agent) and stressing the potential savings in comparison. "Anyone can be an agent—there are no educational requirements. . . . As an attorney representing players, I do not charge a percentage, but rather a nominal rate based on where a player is drafted. . . . You already established your value with professional football clubs based on your performance. . . . If you pay a percentage, to anyone, you will be paying monies unnecessarily." A final letter came from a nationwide agency, Intersports Management Corporation, based in Brooklyn, that proffered a full range of services to its clients:

You are one of the best defensive linemen in the country. We expect that you will be a top NFL draft pick in 1983, and soon thereafter become a starting player, but your options will not be limited to the NFL. A better opportunity may present itself within the CFL or the newly formed USFL. In order to make the most of your opportunities once your college career is over, you will need professional representation. No one person can be an expert in every area in which you might need advice or guidance. We believe that it takes a group of professional advisors working as a team to help you achieve all of your career goals. Our team includes a staff of attorneys, financial advisors, physicians, and business professionals.[6]

When Gabe made his final choice concerning representation, his selection would cause trepidation for Maria Antonia, who felt very uncomfortable with the entire process. From the family's perspective, and based on my discussions with Norbert, Gabe's decision seems to have come as a surprise, almost as much of a shock as when he decided to attend Texas Tech University. Norbert's recollections of the time leading up to the draft concern a flurry of calls from potential agents coming into the clan's domicile in San Antonio. There were also attempts at contact by individual teams indicating interest in drafting Gabe. One of these franchises, Norbert recalled, was the Steelers. Norbert indicated that, at the end of the day, Gabe was quite certain that Pittsburgh was going to be his home for professional football. "When I asked him if that was okay, he said a one-word answer: 'Yeah.'"[7] As late April approached, Gabe huddled with Juan and discussed the pros and cons of the various offers by representatives. Ultimately, he chose to work with Harold "Doc" Daniels and Ray Galindo.

Doc Daniels had been in the agent business since the late 1960s, after briefly having played professional football. He was one of the first African Americans in this profession. He injured his knee in 1965, which ended the athletic part of his career, but not his contact with athletes. After leaving the field, he became part of the ownership of a Los Angeles semipro football team, and from that vantage point, he "started advising Mustang players who were contacted by professional teams. It has since mushroomed into a profitable second job." In addition to his work as an agent, Daniels taught classes (by the early 1990s) at Harbor College in Southern California. In an article from 1992, Duane Plank of the *Los Angeles Times* listed some of the then-current clients of Daniels. Among them were Steve Broussard of the Atlanta Falcons and Rodney Hampton of the New York Giants. Doc also negotiated the first contract for Michael Cooper with the Los Angeles Lakers, though he mostly worked with football players. This article also briefly discussed Daniels' modus operandi when negotiating for athletes with the potential of being drafted in early rounds. "When representing a high draft pick, Daniels tries to get a long-term contract that can be negotiated upward when the player proves his worth to the team. 'Some agents try to get long-term contracts for all their clients, including some players who are not high draft picks.'"[8] It seems that this strategy, given Gabe's high status among pro scouts, would have been very appealing.

While Plank's article presented a positive picture of Daniels, almost one decade after his passing (Doc died in 2001 after a long illness), an article appeared in *Sports Illustrated* that pulled back the curtain concerning the realities of these relationships. Agent Josh Luchs, in the October 17, 2010, issue of the magazine, discussed how he got into the business, as well as how he "trained" under Doc Daniels. At first, Luchs paid some college players, but having provided the amounts requested up front, failed to land clients, who simply took advantage of his naivete. That is where Doc came in. "Doc was a legend. . . . Other agents were afraid of him, and he also had a reputation for paying and giving gifts to college kids. There used to be a joke in the industry that if you saw a college player driving a Datsun 280zx, then you could forget about signing him, as it was widely known Doc had a hookup at a Datsun dealership in Southern California." Gabe did not have such a car during his time at Tech, but his accident in October 1983 occurred behind the wheel of a 280ZX that he'd driven back from California.[9] Given the consternation Gabe endured as a result of his suspension, it is doubtful that he would have done anything, such as accepting a car from an agent, that would have jeopardized his return to the team for his senior season. Finally, Norbert also indicated that Gabe felt comfortable with Ray Galindo, who is also Mexican American, and that this helped in moving his brother into Doc's orbit. Ray "was another Spanish-surnamed individual that he [Gabe] could relate to."[10]

Another critical aspect of the lead-up to the annual conscription event was the family being made aware of Gabe's relationship with a young lady he had met at Tech, Kim Covington. According to Norbert, as recently as the Christmas holidays of 1982, Gabe had been dating someone else.[11] What is clear is that the couple met, and by spring of 1983 Kim was pregnant. The pair soon announced their decision to marry and wedded in July.[12] Although Norbert recalls that Maria Antonia, a staunch and highly devout Catholic, was not necessarily pleased with the circumstances, she looked ahead to the arrival of another grandchild. Clearly, these were momentous months for Gabe: he was feted by elites in Lubbock and San Antonio, had an upcoming marriage, was expecting a child, had selected his representation and financial advice team, and had reasonable expectations of being a high draft choice by an NFL franchise (and, if necessary, Doc and Ray had the new USFL available as a mechanism to provide leverage in contract negotiations).

As the big day approached, Gabe and the rest of his clan looked forward to the draft. The efforts of three generations of Riveras could be summarized as follows: moving north from Mexico; working as recruiters in Crystal City; Juan Jr.'s time in high school and on the gridiron with the Javelinas, and his service in the military; Juan Jr. attending and playing football for Howard Payne College; earning degrees in education; uprooting the family in pursuit of a coaching career; working with Bernie, Norbert, Gabe, and Adrian on their athletic and football skills; and helping the boys get opportunities through sport to pursue higher education. All of these endeavors had led to this auspicious moment wherein Gabe was about to reach the pinnacle of his sport and change his, and the family's, financial trajectory into the foreseeable future.

Even before the draft, however, there were some comments about Gabe that were reminiscent of those heard early in his Tech career: he could not watch his weight, and his level of effort waxed and waned. Particular mention of this caveat appeared in a *Sporting News* article on potential defensive line-men draftees on April 4, 1983. Here, reporter Joe Stein singled Gabe out for criticism, and warned teams who were considering drafting him.

> Will Texas Tech's Gabriel Rivera turn out to be the proto-type nose tackle or only the "before" half of a weight-loss ad. . . . Rivera's weight fluctuations are of a far greater concern. When "Señor Sack" is in shape and revved up, he can be magnificent, providing an excellent inside pass rush. When he's overstuffed, he tends to siesta and content himself with clogging up the middle. The NFL team that drafts him will be gambling, knowing full well that Gabe might eat himself out of the league.[13]

On April 26, 1983, at the New York Sheraton, the (then) Baltimore Colts led off the draft by selecting John Elway, quarterback, from Stanford University. They quickly traded him to the Denver Broncos, where the former Cardinal went on to a Hall of Fame career. This 1983 draft has, as of 2019, been classified as the greatest in NFL history. Among the players selected were seven future Hall of Fame inductees, including Elway, Eric Dickerson, Bruce Matthews, Jim Kelly, Darrell Green, and Richard Dent, and an additional 42 players who participated in Pro Bowls.[14] The career of the final member of this draft to be awarded a gold jacket for his entry into Canton, Dan Marino, is directly intertwined with Gabe's story. Sadly, it has led many fans of the Pittsburgh Steelers, and the Riveras as well, to wonder what might have been.

Ultimately, the decision regarding Gabe's selection boiled down to a determination by Chuck Noll and the Rooney family concerning which area of their club needed to be addressed more quickly. Should they draft to find an heir apparent to Terry Bradshaw, by then in his mid-30s and at the tail end of his athletic career, or should they shore up the defensive line and seek to find an athlete who could begin to fill the large shoes of "Mean" Joe Greene, who retired in 1981? Two books, *Chuck Noll: His Life's Work* by Michael MacCambridge and *Ruanaidh: The Story of Art Rooney and His Clan* by Art Rooney Jr. (with Roy McHugh), provide valuable insight into how the Steelers' brass made their determination concerning their choice of either Marino or Rivera.[15]

In the Rooney work, there is a specific chapter titled "Let's Take Rivera," wherein the scion of the franchise's founder lays out the process by which the team made its final decision with the 21st selection in the first round of the 1983 draft. Right off the bat, it is apparent that the Steelers came to regret having made this choice. The younger Rooney noted, "I don't have much to say about the fourteen players we drafted in 1983. No, the player who stands out in my memory, and I am not alone in feeling this way, is the guy we could have taken but didn't."[16] That one who got away was hometown legend Marino, who went on to play sixteen seasons with Miami.

There were three primary reasons for why Pittsburgh's management decided against selecting the quarterback from their city's namesake university. First, Marino, as a junior, led the Pitt Panthers to within a whisker of the 1981 national championship, losing to the Georgia Bulldogs in the Sugar Bowl, 24–20. His senior campaign, however, clearly was subpar by comparison. In 1981, he threw for almost 2,900 yards

with 37 touchdowns and 23 interceptions. In his final collegiate season, Marino had the same number of turnovers, but
the scoring passes declined to 17. Total yardage generated also
declined by more than 400 yards (to 2,432). Finally, using the
modern rating system for determining the efficacy of quarterbacks, Marino's number skidded from 143.1 to 115.2.[17] Still, he
presented the Steelers with a substantial quandary. Marino
was a local, having grown up in the Oakland neighborhood
and attended Central Catholic High School before moving
on to the Panthers. Further, he sported a prototypical (for the
time) quarterback's physique. "He was 6 feet 4 inches and sol-
idly built, a dropback passer in the NFL mold who didn't move
around much in the pocket. His arm may have been as strong
as Bradshaw's. He could pinpoint his receivers and his passes
were easy to catch."[18]

The second reason for the Steelers' concerns were rumors
that Marino had used recreational drugs—specifically, cocaine.
The team did its due diligence in two ways. For information they
went to someone who knew Dan personally. That individual
was Steve Fedell, who had played with Marino for the Panthers
and who was then on injured reserve with the Steelers. "'Is he
into dope? No,' Steve said. Marino's only fault, he told me, was
excessive loyalty to certain friends of long standing—friends
who were not good guys, according to Fedell." One person who
spoke on Marino's behalf was Tony Dungy, then serving as
the team's defensive back coach. The now Hall of Famer was
impressed with the quarterback's arm as during a tryout as
"the wind was more like a gale, and Marino was firing missiles
into its teeth."[19]

Another method the Steelers used to check up on Marino
was more clandestine in nature. In late March or early April
1983, Art Sr. called his son (who was in charge of scouting)
into his office and two plainclothes police officers briefed the
Rooneys. "'These men,' he [Sr.] went on, 'have something to tell
you about Danny Marino.' It was this: 'We've been looking into

rumors about him, and we find no evidence that he is using, selling or transporting hard drugs like cocaine. There aren't any maybes about this. He may have puffed on some marijuana. Most college kids nowadays do.'" Nothing in the materials available to me indicated that the Steelers were aware of the real reason behind Gabe's suspension prior to the 1982 season.

Although the Rooneys kept this information in-house, the rumors reached Marino's ears, and when the team went to scout him at an all-star game, he was demonstrably upset—storming off the practice field in front of scouts from various clubs. Fedell approached his former teammate and reminded him of the gravity of the situation. "Hey Danny, you can't behave like this. No matter how you feel. This is your showcase. The scouts and coaches from the pro teams are down here to learn who you are." Later that evening, Rooney Jr. recalls, "I saw him [Marino] that night in the hotel lobby with Don Shula . . . and he was noticeably more cheerful and relaxed."[20]

A final reason for why the Steelers passed on Marino was based on the experiences and judgment of Coach Noll. Back in 1969, when he took over the club and went 1–13, the team's first draft choice was Joe Greene. Now, in 1983, with the team at another crossroads, the field general wanted to begin the rebuilding process in the same way: through defensive strength—particularly on the line. Thus, the decision came down to picking between the native son and Gabe Rivera from Texas Tech. Rooney Jr. recalled the conversation with Coach Noll in this way:

> "Both of you know how I feel about Marino," Noll continued. "He's a marvelous talent. But look—we're overloaded with quarterbacks. We have Bradshaw. We have Malone. We have Stoudt." Cliff Stoudt had been with us since 1977, but all he needed, Noll thought, was a chance. . . . "It could be OK," Noll allowed. "Anyhow," he said, having finished his review of the quarterback situation, "let's go the way we started." The way we started back in 1969, was by drafting

a defensive lineman. . . . "Let's take Rivera." I didn't argue. I didn't ask questions. . . . Chuck Noll had given his reasons for making Gabe Rivera our number one pick, and I thought they were sound reasons. . . . And the whispered allegations that Marino was using drugs had nothing to do with it.[21]

Before moving beyond this discussion on how and why the Steelers came to select Gabe, it is also worthwhile to provide one last bit of information—from the MacCambridge biography on Chuck Noll. Just as he was loyal to Joe Greene and wanted to follow the pattern that proved so successful in the 1970s, Noll also was very devoted to another key piece of the Pittsburgh dynasty: Terry Bradshaw, the first selection of the NFL draft in 1970 by the then one-win Steelers. MacCambridge quotes a conversation he had with Tony Dungy, which sheds critical insight on what may have been the ultimate reason why, even after 14 years with the team, the head coach still had confidence in the abilities of Terry Bradshaw. "'It was a weird time,' added Dungy. 'And Chuck was very loyal to those guys. Drafting Marino, as much as Bradshaw says he didn't care about his feelings and stuff, that would have killed Bradshaw, and he still thought he could play a couple more years. There was a lot to that. It changed the course of the franchise, for sure.'" Six picks after the Steelers took Rivera, the Miami Dolphins selected Dan Marino. The Steelers' coaching staff, confident in Noll's judgment, cheered when Commissioner Pete Rozelle announced their pick.[22]

The local papers in the Steel City were supportive of the choice, though some felt that it would have been better to have selected a wide receiver (given that Lynn Swann retired after 1982 and John Stallworth had been injured and missed almost half of the contests that year). John Clayton, for example, then with the *Pittsburgh Press*, prognosticated that the team's selection would have been Gary Anderson, a receiver from the University of Arkansas (though he went to the San Diego Chargers with the 20th selection of the round).[23] Another reporter for the same publication, Jim O'Brien, however, highlighted some of Gabe's abilities in his article—in particular noting his amazing play to tackle Razorback quarterback Tom Jones in the 1982 contest against Arkansas. Additionally, O'Brien stated that the Steelers' choice, in workouts for the Philadelphia Eagles, had improved upon his speed from his college days and reportedly "ran 40-yard dashes of 4.66, 4.64, and 4.69. He can bench press between 450 and 480 pounds and has the ability to dominate a game." This article even went as far as to quote assistant defensive coach Dennis Fitzgerald using some very provocative language. "Didn't I say we would take Joe Greene with our first pick?" Defensive coordinator Woody Widenhofer was just as effusive, stating, "He can tear up an offensive line all by himself; he's a force. He can mess up a team's offense. He's that kind of player. Offensively, you'd have to take Stanford's John Elway, but defensively, Señor Sack is my man."[24]

Even more positive press followed on the day after the draft's conclusion. Again, O'Brien led the charge and even noted that this was the first Mexican American to ever play for the Steelers. He then went on to mention Gabe's father's role as a player and coach in "the Texas flatlands." Most significantly in this article, Gabe, well aware of the rivalry between his future employer and the most famous and successful NFL franchise in his home state, made a statement that was certainly music to many an ear in western Pennsylvania. "I was always for the Steelers when they played against the Cowboys."[25] This certainly sounds like something that Doc Daniels, an agent wise and experienced in the ways of the NFL, would have advised his client to pass along to the Pittsburgh media.

The team's specific plans on how to use their new behemoth appeared in a *Post-Gazette* article on April 27. The defensive schema for 1983 was going to change to a 3–4 alignment. Among the reasons for the selection of Rivera was that management believed "he can play all three positions on the line, although he seems best suited for nose tackle. The Steeler incumbent at that position is Gary Dunn, who remains an unsigned free agent." Interestingly, this article also featured the first mention of Gabe's suspension. Reporter Tom McMillan asked him about the "mysterious 'rules violations'" that had occurred. Rivera deftly brushed it off as a minor matter that was now in the past, although he also incorporated some of Norbert's wisdom in his answer. "They were some team rules. It's something I really don't want to talk about. But it made me finally realize what I wanted."[26]

A final article from a local paper dating to before contract negotiations is from the *Tribune-Review*, written by Dave Ailes and, again, quite encouraging—and not just about Gabe. In addition to all of the statistics about his play at Tech, and how the Steelers perceived him as the second coming of Joe Greene, Ailes noted two other positives. First, he indicated that the Denver Gold (which selected Rivera in the USFL draft) had approached Rivera about jumping to the upstart league. Wisely, Gabe said exactly the right thing. "Better yet, Rivera said he has no intention of playing in the United States Football League. 'Pittsburgh has always been on my mind. I grew up watching the Steelers on TV. I'm not much of a Cowboy fan.... I'll be glad to get out of Texas.'" Second, in another article on the same day, Ailes commented on the positive relationship that existed between the team and Doc Daniels, who "has always had a good working relationship with Steeler brass. Daniels is also the agent for former No. 1 draft choice Robin Cole."[27] With both sides seeming quite happy and ready to proceed, now the work of hammering out a contract commenced. Although Gabe and Doc claimed no interest in the USFL, that league was a wild card that 1983 draftees could use to extract better deals from their respective NFL teams. Gabe certainly understood how this strengthened his hand. Norbert recalled that at about this time his younger brother turned to his future wife and stated gleefully, "How does it feel to be getting married to a millionaire?"

Gabe was not off base with his comments to Kim regarding the possibility of his chance of achieving a major payday. In July 1983, as many of the first-round draft choices had inked deals, an article by Will McDonough of the *Boston Herald* appeared in one of the Riveras' hometown papers, the *San Antonio Light*. Here, McDonough provided readers with a sense of the importance of the USFL's existence to players such as Gabe, John Elway, Curt Warner, and Billy Ray Smith. In total, the need to keep top talent away from the upstart association helped boost the pay of the current year's top draftees by six figures. "A survey of salaries paid to first-round draft choices this year—compared with those of 1982—shows the members of the Class of '83 are the biggest winners ever, averaging $135,148 more per year than their peers of a year ago." A key point in this article noted that nose tackle Lester Williams—selected late in the first round by the Patriots in 1982, who filled the same assignment that the Steelers envisioned for Señor Sack—signed a contract with New England that averaged $214,000 per season. Given the fortuitous timing of the USFL's birth, Gabe hoped to sign for much more than what was now seemingly a paltry figure.[28]

Having an experienced and savvy negotiator such as Doc Daniels in his corner boded well for Gabe. From the start of discussions, as would any good representative, Daniels played up his client's talents to John Clayton. Of course, Daniels was quick to recall the exploits of the Tech–Washington contest of 1982 as well as to compare Rivera to some of the legends of the game (some of whom Doc had "supposedly" played with during his time in the NFL). "Gabe has the intensity of Merlin Olsen, who never gave up. . . . He has the quickness of Deacon Jones." On the one hand, the Steeler management had compared Gabe to "Mean" Joe Greene, and then his agent likened him to two members of the legendary Fearsome Foursome. Now that's how to pump up your client's abilities! Additionally, as noted above, the Denver Gold was always in the background. When it came time to discuss numbers, Daniels hoped that Pittsburgh would be reasonable, but "I'm not saying that it [negotiations] won't be a problem. If there weren't problems, there would be no need to negotiate."[29]

At least one member of Pittsburgh's population of sport scribes felt that Gabe, and Daniels in particular, were overplaying their hand. Pat Livingston, the sports editor for the *Press*, touched base with Clayton and tried to confirm some of what Daniels had told the young reporter about his athletic background. Livingston checked with the Rams, who indicated that Daniels had never played for them. The reporter also contacted the Chargers, another club that Daniel reportedly played for. This time, the team stated only that Daniels had been there for a "cup of coffee." The story was likewise with the Broncos, yet another team for which Doc supposedly suited up. Thus, Livingston warned the Steelers and their loyal fans that the agent might not be all he claimed. During our interview, Kim also indicated that she was concerned, but given her youth, and Gabe's, they allowed themselves to be guided by Doc's counsel.[30] Could the same thing be said about Rivera? "Chuck Noll might want to look more closely at his game film. . . . Prudence is urged for bull marketers thinking of investing in chili or hamburger franchises. Don't start any runs on black-and-gold serapes just yet." What were the Steelers actually in the process of "buying" here? "There are whispers that Daniels acts more like a flesh-peddler selling a stiff to a ring promoter . . . than a representative negotiating a contract for a client."

Thus, for the Rooneys, Livingston was suggesting more research before signing on the dotted line. John Clayton seemed to agree with his editor, as he graded the 1983 overall draft for the Steelers as a C. The main reason for the mediocre mark was his questions about Gabe. He summarized his feelings this way: "Gabe Rivera has been inconsistent in college but could be a dominant defender." Hardly a ringing endorsement.[31]

Still, the overwhelming majority of the local press was excited about the possibility of Señor Sack lining up in black and gold, no matter who represented him. The day following Livingston's harangue, articles by Dave Ailes and Mark Dudurich in the *Tribune-Review* countered the negative portrayal. First, Ailes brought up Rivera's dislike of the Cowboys. If anything would make a newcomer to the area welcome in Western Pennsylvania, that statement certainly would. Additionally, this article reiterated the story of Tom Jones in Arkansas, focusing exclusively on the damage Gabe did to the Razorback quarterback after his legendary pursuit and tackle. Finally, Ailes provided another quote by Rivera designed to melt the heart of the Steeler faithful, so used to rugged defense over the 1970s. "The noise of cracking helmets, I like a lot," he is reported to have said. Additionally, Dudurich reminded fans that it was imperative, given the new defensive scheme, to put pressure on opposing quarterbacks, activity the 1982 version of Pittsburgh's defense had sorely lacked. "All you have to do is think to last year's sub-par pressure on the quarterback . . . to see there was a genuine need there also. . . . Rivera is certainly a unique athlete, one Noll and his scouts felt they could not pass up." Given the obvious talent, Noll's appraisal thereof, and the clear needs on the defensive line, was putting up with an agent who was a bit over the top worth it? Most folks in Pittsburgh seemed to agree that it was.[32]

In early May, Gabe sat down with yet another reporter, Jim O'Brien of the *Press*, for a question-and-answer session. He struck all the right chords. First, O'Brien reminded him not only that Joe Greene was from the Lone Star State, but so were fellow Steeler defensive legends Dwight White and Ernie Holmes. Gabe indicated that he hoped to follow in their gigantic footsteps: "I'm hoping to keep up the tradition." When he was asked about his inconsistency, he acknowledged that this was an appropriate assessment of his play at Texas Tech. "I'd have to admit that. It's something I've been aware of. . . . It's something I need to work on, to get myself mentally ready to play, and keep my mind on it." O'Brien then went on to question Gabe about his seeming popularity with the local press, with the possible exception of Pat Livingston. "I've always had quite a following . . . wherever I've played, people always wanted to see me. . . . So I've always had people keeping an eye on me." O'Brien, in an earlier article, even alluded to the possibility that Pittsburgh fans, famous for "keeping an eye" on specific players through their "Franco's Army" and "Gerela's Gorillas" banners, might come up with something original to celebrate Gabe's heritage.[33] Finally, in this interview, the questions turned to Gabe's uniqueness as a Mexican American in the NFL. Rivera noted that both Max Montoya and Anthony Muñoz were of the same background, and "there are some Mexican kickers, like Rafael Septien, Efren Herrera, and Frank Corral, and maybe some others. But that's about it." Although Gabe failed to mention a few other notables—such as Jim Plunkett and Tom Flores, for example—here was a chance for yet another Mexican American to make his mark at the highest levels of professional football. Gabe would, he stated, hold up his end of the bargain once he signed with Pittsburgh. "I'm going back home and start working out again. Now I know where I'm going, and I've got some motivation. I wasn't too interested for a while, but motivation will be better now."[34] As proof of his conversion to Steeler Nation, when Norbert picked up Gabe at the San Antonio airport after his initial trip to Pennsylvania, he recalled that Gabe walked off the plane covered head to toe in black and gold. It seems that Gabe was fully committed to his new team and was more than willing to show off his allegiance to his fellow Texans.

Toward the end of May, the Pittsburgh papers reported that contract negotiations were proceeding apace and could soon culminate. While no specific figures were mentioned at that moment, Gabe stated that, as of the 24th of the month, "I'd sign today if I could. We're close to an agreement." As a final incentive to the Steelers, he indicated to local media that he had been working hard in Texas to get into the best shape of his life. "My goal is to go to camp in good shape and learn the techniques and Steeler terminology. The mental preparedness is a lot harder than college." Gabe certainly made an impression on Terry Bradshaw the first time the legendary quarterback saw him at Steeler minicamp. "I never saw him play, but . . . down in the Southwest Conference . . . they talk about him like he's a god. . . . Really, I was sittin' next to him. . . . But I was saying all good things about him. Good thing. He was pickin' his teeth with a knife."[35] Shortly after this, on the 28th, Gabe and the Rooneys came to an agreement and signed on the dotted line. He became the 15th member of the first round to ink a deal.

The final figures for his contract included some lofty numbers: a $400,000 bonus and a total of $1.090 million over four years, which worked out to $272,500 per annum. Clearly, none of Gabe's ancestors, when they arrived from Mexico, could have envisioned such a windfall. But here he was, Señor Sack from Texas Tech University, among the elites of the NFL, ready to begin his professional career. The Steelers' preparations for the 1983 NFL campaign were scheduled to begin on July 8, and Gabe was ready to start earning his money.[36]

Once in the fold, some Steeler fans reached out to Gabe to welcome him into the black-and-gold family. The Riveras saved two of these correspondences, and they provide a sense of the hopefulness and fondness that aficionados had for their No. 1 pick. One note, from a San Antonian transplant to western Pennsylvania, offered good wishes and sought to provide Gabe with a sense of home. "My daughter and I came out to St. Vincent's . . . just to see you and caught your attention for a fleeting second when I called out your name and said 'NIOSA.' Thank you for your recognition." As if having a bit of home present in Latrobe, another letter-writer seemed to be on par with his fellow Steeler fans who belonged to Franco's Army or Gerela's Gorillas. Bill Kauffman actually penned a poem in honor of Gabe titled "Señor Sack Attack." While probably not a masterpiece, the ode praised Rivera's prowess while at Tech, and was hopeful that this would continue at Three Rivers Stadium. A small sample of the verse went like this: "With a massive body and a whole lot of speed, it's only your progress we're sure he'll impede." It certainly was part of a heartfelt welcome to Gabe from a loyal fan in his new city.[37]

As if his salary were not sufficient incentive, just a couple of weeks before the start of training camp, Gabe got some extra encouragement for the start of his career: a hearty endorsement from Joe Greene. The man to whom he was being compared provided compliments concerning the newly signed Rivera. "I saw him play against Washington and SMU, and he had great games. . . . He was aggressive, and he was all over the field. He has the kind of nasty attitude you have to have to be a great defensive lineman." No pressure. Now all Gabe had to do was live up to standards established by a future Hall of Famer. Additionally, Greene went to training camp to serve in a coaching capacity and worked directly with the prized rookie. When he retired after the 1981 season, "Greene expressed disappointment that no young lineman had emerged as his heir apparent." Now he would be helping to mold a player whom both team management and "Mean Joe" indicated might be his successor on the Steelers' defensive line.[38]

Finally the big day arrived, and Gabe pulled up to St. Vincent College in Latrobe and checked in to begin his time at what one reporter referred to as "Chuck Noll's Summer Camp for Boys." At weigh-in, he registered at 293 pounds but insisted that he had been working out religiously in San Antonio since leaving mini-camp. "I wish it would be under 290. . . . It will go down from there, hopefully." Although reporters continued to express concern about his eating habits (and many actually lined up at the camp's cafeteria that first day), Gabe got off to a decent start, reportedly consuming only one cheeseburger

Gabe getting pointers from Texas and Steelers legend "Mean" Joe Greene
(Southwest Collection, TTU University Archives)

at the facility that day. Still, reports expressing concern about
Rivera's weight persisted.[39]

Parts of the first three weeks of camp did not go well, however, as Gabe suffered strained ligaments in his chest that
severely limited his participation in drills. The fans visiting
at camp were a bit annoyed at the lack of involvement by the
highly paid No. 1 draft pick. "I've heard them, but I can't let that
bother me. Not being able to practice has been frustrating. I
usually try to stand there and pick up something from looking
at the coaches. . . . But it makes for a long day. . . . I hurt the

chest pulling out on one drill then I reinjured it the following Thursday. I guess I came back too soon." About one week later, however, he managed to take the field as the Steelers played the New Orleans Saints at the annual Hall of Fame Game in Canton on July 30. Pittsburgh won the meaningless contest, 27–14.[40]

Early the following week, *Post-Gazette* scribe Gary Tuma provided an in-depth essay on Gabe's first outing at this level. Overall, it was a fairly positive assessment. Tuma quoted Rivera saying that he was less nervous taking the field against fellow professionals than he was playing at Jones Stadium. Steelers' defensive coordinator Woody Widenhofer's appraisal was fairly positive. "He played about the way you'd want him to play at this stage. He put pressure on the quarterback, and he played the run well. I don't think he was spectacular, but we expect a hell of a lot out of him." One of the key aspects of the story concerned the techniques Gabe and his fellow young linemen were learning, and how they differed from the collegiate level. "The Steelers are teaching . . . to use arm extensions against opposing blockers . . . and using the leverage generated from their legs for force, similar to pressing in weightlifting." Considering how much Gabe could lift, this method, once perfected, would likely be of great benefit. Of course, as a rookie, he made mistakes. "A few times against the Saints, Rivera caught himself reverting to old habits, using the forearm and head butt that he used at Texas Tech instead of locking out his arms."

Gabe indicated that the time he had missed due to his injury actually might have been beneficial to learn the new procedure. "Even though Rivera says he would have preferred to practice, he thinks watching instead of participating . . . aided him in absorbing many of the things he had to learn." A final aspect of this story concerned the picture that accompanied the article. In the photo, Gabe's belly protruded under his t-shirt, and his pants seemed to be straining to contain his girth. Just to put

Steeler fans at ease, given the amount of coverage concerning his weight, Widenhofer reminded aficionados that "Joe Greene had a gut, too. Gabe has a soft body, but he runs well, and he's got good strength."[41]

In order to counter some of the misperceptions (deserved or undeserved) surrounding Gabe, *Pittsburgh Steelers Weekly* printed a short article on his activities at camp in its August 15 issue. Here, along with substantial photographic evidence, was Gabe running and participating in activities. Further, author Vic Ketchman provided extensive details about a "typical day" in the life of this rookie:

> But this Gabe Rivera . . . has quartered himself reclusively in his room, where he has prepared for each practice with a religious fervor for his playbook. This Gabe Rivera would seem to be a Chuck Noll disciple, though it would be expected of a rookie in his first fling with the big time to not be nearly as subdued as Rivera has proven to be at camp. Their schedules are full. Up at seven, to bed at 11 . . . Rivera has breakfast by 7:30 a.m. It's followed by a trip to the training room, relaxing with the playbook and dressing for morning practice. Team meeting is scheduled for 9:30 a.m., with Rivera's defensive line meeting immediately following Noll's team address. Morning practice follows meetings, with lunch at noon. The early afternoon is for the training room, and relaxing in bed, with the playbook, of course. The meetings begin at three p.m., with practice following at about 3:30. Dinner is at six and evening meetings occupy the time between 7:30 and 9:45, with curfew set for 11 p.m.

In summary, Steeler fans were led to believe, Gabe had settled into the pattern of behavior expected out of a newbie by Chuck Noll and his staff. He would continue to work, improve, and justify his draft status and salary.[42]

As the Steelers approached their final tune-up contest for 1983, against their cross-state rivals, the Philadelphia Eagles, it appeared that the defense was shaping up to be well improved over the 1982 edition. In an article by John Clayton, Jack Lambert (yet another future Hall of Famer), now at the tail end of his illustrious career, was asked to comment on whether the "new" version of the defense could approach the legendary Steel Curtain. Not surprisingly, Lambert objected to the question. "I don't think there will ever be a defense like the Steel Curtain again." Still, Coach Noll was happy with the progress after the squad generated 19 sacks and 14 interceptions over the five-game preseason. This tilt against the Eagles was no contest. Indeed, Clayton referred to it as a "massacre," as demonstrated by the eight sacks of Ron Jaworski and Joe Pisarcik. "The Steelers spent so much time in the Eagle backfield, they were running into each other. In the fourth quarter, [Keith] Willis... ran into... Gabe Rivera. 'I thought I had the quarterback, then I hit into Gabe. . . . When you run into Gabe's ribs, you are not going to run around and remember it. . . . I can't remember some of the things that happened.'" Although not naming Gabe specifically, defensive coordinator Widenhofer praised the amount of pressure that the line, regardless of the configuration, got on the Philadelphia signal callers. "We are better than most people think we are. . . . We got real good pressure whether we used a three-man, a four-man, or a five-man rush. But we still have some things to work on." After completing a 4–1 preseason and with the defense playing at a high level (some players began dubbing the squad "Steel Heat"), it appeared all was ready to go for the season opener on September 4 against the Broncos.[43]

As the Steelers broke camp and prepared to play meaningful contests, Clayton produced a lengthy article focusing on Gabe and fellow lineman Keith Gary—another first-round selection by Pittsburgh, but who spent his first two years as a professional playing in the CFL with the Montreal Alouettes. Once again, Gabe's bulk was a principal topic of conversation. Some of the Lubbock-based stories concerning his prodigious appetite were reiterated for the local aficionados, though

Rivera discounted exaggerations such as that he consumed 23 cans of tuna and the same number of enchiladas in a single sitting. "I never really ate that much. I think people think about my size and start talking. They make believe a lot of things." By this stage of the game, it appeared that he was getting a bit ruffled by the constant questions on this topic. "I go up and down between 280 and 284. But I haven't gotten much more weight than that." The story also noted how Gabe had resisted temptation concerning overeating. "At lunch and dinner, cooks constantly ask Rivera, 'Don't you want any more?' Rivera shakes his head." Gabe even abstained, according to teammates, from consuming pizza during a group visit to a Latrobe Pizza Hut.

The story then shifted to a discussion of the two injuries he sustained during training: the first on his chest, which limited him for two weeks, and the second, a sprained knee, which kept Gabe off the field for a similar length of time. Still, the team was pleased with the performance of its No. 1 selection. "Despite Rivera's limited exposure, Steeler coaches still discuss him with Joe Greene reverence. Rivera has handled his frustrations with discipline. His waistline hasn't expanded. His enthusiasm hasn't wilted. He hasn't become a recluse." In addition to performing well when on the field, Gabe continued to work on, and improve, his technique. "There's a lot to learn. It's not too hard even though I didn't practice much. The only thing I need to do is stay a little lower." Finally, Clayton then questioned Rivera concerning his overall assessment of his rookie camp. In his response Gabe indicated that he would continue to work hard to earn his place on the Steelers.

> The only pressure I have is my personal pressure. It really hasn't affected me. I realize it's there, but I'm not going to worry about it. No, I'm not satisfied with myself on the field so far. I'm just going out there to perform. My main goal is to help as much as I can. I didn't think I was going to come in and get the starting job. In the meantime, I can learn the techniques.[44]

Things did not get off to a good start for Gabe or the Steelers for the regular season. Pittsburgh lost its first game of the year, 14–10, against Denver at Three Rivers. Gabe did not register a sack, but he did suffer a concussion that kept him out of the following week's game against the Green Bay Packers.[45] Rivera returned to action for the third game of the year, against the Houston Oilers, in Texas. In this tilt, a 40–28 Pittsburgh victory on September 18, Gabe recorded the first sack of his career, tackling Archie Manning. Unfortunately, the limited activity, plus the move away from the regimented setting of training camp, inevitably led to overeating and gaining weight. Just before the next contest on the schedule, a home clash versus the New England Patriots, John Clayton brought up the issue of how much weight Gabe had gained since the start of the campaign. By the middle of the first month of the season, Rivera once again topped the 300-pound mark.

It was not just the lack of supervision by staff but also the temptations available in the big city. One major factor was that Gabe discovered a restaurant that offered some of the tastes of home: "I found a place in the North Hills that serves burritos." The team quickly stepped in and exerted control over their investment. "Walt Evans, a fitness and conditioning coach . . . devised a diet that includes plenty of chicken, salads, fruits, and juices. 'We want him down to 280 or 285. He's really working hard on it. He is exercising and getting in good shape. . . . We got him going well right now.' The first 15 pounds lost, mostly water weight, came off two weeks ago. Now, Rivera is trying to lose a couple of pounds a week."[46]

The efforts began to pay off, and by the sixth week of the season, in a game against the Bengals in Cincinnati, Gabe collected his second, and what turned out to be his final, sack of an NFL quarterback. After that game, Widenhofer once again reiterated, "He has a chance to be one of the great ones." Overall, the coordinator argued that this was Rivera's best game as a professional. "His run play was average, but his pass rush was great. He was one step away from a sack two or three times. . . . A lot of times, those pressures can be just as important as the sacks. When you get good pressure inside, it forces the quarterback deeper. It makes it easier for your outside pass rush." Gabe agreed with his coach's assessment. He also credited the loss of weight, and the fact that the Steelers settled on leaving him at end when they lined up in the 3–4 and at tackle when they utilized the standard 4–3 alignment. "It's hard to concentrate when you're moving all around. It's a lot easier when you have to worry about one thing."[47]

After a series of stops and starts, Gabe appeared to be finding his place on the defensive line. He was happy with his weight loss, as well as with his more definitive assignments in the Steelers' defensive scheme. In what turned out to be his final game, Pittsburgh defeated the Cleveland Browns, 44–17, on October 16. In the lead-up to this game, John Clayton spelled out how Widenhofer was utilizing Gabe and some of his line mates in order to confuse opponents. "The Steelers' defense can be infuriating to an offensive lineman. On first downs, John Goodman . . . gives right tackles problems. Keith Willis . . . [then] might come on to rush the passer on the next down. The next play the confused tackle might be lined up against the 285-pound Gabe Rivera." In this game, he did not record a sack.[48]

This would be the last mention of Gabe Rivera as an on-field competitor for the Pittsburgh Steelers. Over the next few days, the local papers noted that the team, after its victory against the Browns, was now in first place in the American Football Conference (AFC) Central Division. As usual, the players had Monday off and would return to their scheduled meetings and practices starting on Tuesday, October 18. Gabe participated in these routine events as Pittsburgh prepared to travel cross-country in order to play the Seahawks at the Kingdome in Seattle the following Sunday.

After practice on Thursday, October 20, Gabe got into his new Datsun 280ZX and went out to get dinner as well as a

Gabe's Datsun after his accident (Southwest Collection, TTU University Archives)

few drinks at Julian's on Foreland Street. He left the restaurant/lounge at around 7:30 or 7:45 p.m. He was then headed on Three-Degree Road toward Babcock Boulevard in Ross Township. There, he had a head-on collision with another vehicle. The police arrived at the scene at approximately 8:55. At that moment, Gabe's potential as the next Joe Greene took a backseat to the hope that the Steelers' No. 1 draft choice for 1983 would simply survive the night.

Unfortunately, as local papers noted, the Pittsburgh NFL franchise was well acquainted with tragedy in the late 1970s. Offensive lineman Randy Frisch was killed in an auto accident on August 7, 1977, and then on November 17, 1978, special-teams player Randy Reutershan suffered traumatic injuries in another crash. Now, yet another catastrophic mishap had befallen the black and gold. Shortly thereafter, team president Dan Rooney, Franco Harris, Mel Blount, and defensive line coach Jon Kolb all gathered at Allegheny General to check on the status of their fallen teammate, as well as to console Kim Rivera, who was due to give birth around early November.[49]

CHAPTER 7

THE DAY EVERYTHING CHANGED

THE ACCIDENT AND ITS AFTERMATH, 1983–1999

AS HE HAD DONE THROUGHOUT the draft, training camp, pre-season, and the regular campaign, John Clayton was one of the writers who covered Gabe's accident. While many of the stories in the morning papers of October 21 gave particulars of the collision, Clayton's article for the *Pittsburgh Press* took a different tack: he brought his readers into the Steelers' locker room a few hours before the crash. Gabe was fitting in nicely with his teammates and settling into the routine of a player in the NFL. "Five hours before he nearly met death, Gabe Rivera was full of life. As always, he was the brunt of harmless jokes among his Steeler teammates. . . . 'Going to lift weights, Gabe?' asked one Steeler. A weightlifter he is not; a weight-carrier he is."

During this week, leading up to the Steelers' contest versus the Seahawks in the Pacific Northwest, Rivera had been participating in all of the normal activities (both preparatory and childish) that characterize life in a professional team's facility. On the business side of the equation, he worked with offensive lineman Tunch Ilkin, who wanted a bit more work in order to be ready for the Seattle defensive line. "He's a load. He comes right at you. You can't help but get better going against someone like him." On the juvenile/playful side of locker-room life, other teammates joked about the size of Gabe's contract, indicating that the "mistake jar" money for the defensive line of the Steelers certainly would contain more funds than that of their offensive cohorts at the end of the season, given the size of Rivera's (whom another player called "Señor Burrito") and Keith Gary's paychecks. Another Steeler legend quoted in the article was Jack Lambert, who indicated that Gabe was becoming an important part of the defense, after a difficult start at Latrobe. "He had a rough go of it in training camp, several injuries, but he's lost weight and played well and got a lot of people excited."

At the time of his accident, Gabe had recorded a total of five tackles, including two sacks. Coach Widenhofer summarized the rookie's progress in the following way: "The only reason he isn't getting more sacks is because Gary and Willis are getting to the quarterback faster. But he is just pushing people back." Clayton, toward the end of the piece, gave readers a sense of what might have been had Gabe continued to play. "Rivera's accident came at a time the Steelers' defense was becoming an intimidating unit. Rivera's talents were becoming more and more noticeable."[1] Alas, the statistics generated over those six games with the Steelers would be the sum total of Gabe's professional output.

The structure of this chapter is different from that of previous sections of this work. Certainly, it provides chronological information concerning the crash and its aftermath, including the end of Gabe's marriage to Kim and beyond. But in order to properly contextualize life between his accident and 1999 (the reason for ending the chapter here will become evident shortly), it is necessary to bring in stories and academic materials that shed light on the ordeal of athletes who are confronted by a traumatic spinal cord injury. In order to do this, I include

the words of another NFL alumnus who suffered similar injuries, though on the field, and then wrote a book about his experiences: the late Darryl Stingley of the New England Patriots.
His tome, ironically, appeared the same year that Gabe had his
accident.[2]

Additionally, it is necessary to provide a more scholarly
angle to the discussion. I look at a few sources from the profes-
sional/academic literature on psychology and physical therapy,
most directly a master's thesis titled "Athletes' Experiences
of Leaving Sport Due to Spinal Cord Injury: A Multiple Case
Study Examination," by Derek Michael Zike, an athlete who
suffered a traumatic spinal cord injury.[3] Thus, the chapter first
proceeds by covering the accident and the time period shortly
afterward. Then it transitions to a discussion of Gabe coming
to grips with his situation. The chapter next visits the Zike,
Stingley, and other materials to provide a brief overview of
how persons who were athletes (and their families), and who
suddenly find themselves as paraplegics or quadriplegics, deal
with the emotional and physical upheaval now present in their
lives. The chapter continues by chronicling Gabe's life through
the raising of his son, Tim; the passing of Juan and Maria
Antonia; a second, albeit brief, marriage; and some legal and
personal troubles that brought Gabe to a nadir. Finally, the discussion moves on to a decision in 1999 that gave purpose and
meaning to the last two decades of Rivera's life: his starting
to work with children at a charity organization located in an
inner-city San Antonio neighborhood.

In an ironic and poignant lead-up to the catastrophe,
Norbert Rivera recalled his sibling, while in San Antonio on
his way back to Pittsburgh from California, taking him on a
cruise in the 280zx. Gabe, Norbert indicated, was "simply too
big for that car, I mean, we were shoulder to shoulder during
our drive. I kidded Gabe because his Datsun felt even more
cramped than the small pickup I drove as a company vehicle." Additionally, Norbert, recognizing that driving in winter

weather was not something a life in South Texas had prepared his brother for, warned Gabe concerning road conditions in Western Pennsylvania. "I advised him to get a four-wheel-drive truck in order to deal with the inclement weather." Gabe agreed with his brother's assessment and indicated he would look into purchasing a vehicle more capable of dealing with the region's snow and ice. Unfortunately, he never got the chance.[4]

Another aspect of this trip came into focus during the interview with Kim. She recalled going out to California to pick up the vehicle and then driving back east. The couple stopped in Albuquerque, which is where Kim's parents, Jim and Karan Covington, were living at the time. During this visit, Jim noticed something concerning about the couple's finances. He stated that Gabe and Kim had previously borrowed a few hundred dollars from him. When Gabe wanted to pay his father-in-law back, he had difficulty writing out the check. It seemed that he was not well versed in this basic aspect of financial life. How would the young pair deal with the complicated finances of an NFL first-round pick?[5]

Not surprisingly, there was much confusion, and even outright misinformation, in the hours shortly after Gabe's accident. As the local papers scrambled to place this story on their front pages, some of the facts presented were quite muddled. Probably the most egregious report indicated, sadly, that Rivera was actually "walking after the collision."[6] Of course, that was not the case. A thorough, early overview of the circumstances appeared in an article by William Mausteller in the *Pittsburgh Press* on October 21. Gabe's 280ZX was headed northbound on Babcock Boulevard in Ross Township. His vehicle crossed the median strip and crashed head-on with a much larger car, a 1979 Ford LTD, driven by a gentleman named Allen Watts who suffered only minor injuries as a result of the collision. "I saw this car coming in the opposite direction, at a high rate of speed, and it crossed into my lane. I didn't know what happened. I didn't know where the car went (after the collision) or where the driver went." Given this information, investigating officers requested that Gabe be given a blood-alcohol test as soon as he arrived at Allegheny General. Their reason for this demand was because of "physical evidence they found" at the scene.[7]

Further details provided in Mausteller's article shed light on the severity of the impact between the two vehicles. "J. R. Henry, director of the Ross-West View Emergency Services . . . said Rivera was about 25 to 30 feet away from where the car came to rest. . . . Henry said that it appeared that Rivera had been thrown from the car, although he was lying on the ground on what would be the passenger's side of the vehicle." The first individual to come upon Gabe after the crash was a carwash attendant who was nearby. John Wolfe stated, "I heard screeching and a bam and boom and more screeching. . . . [upon finding Gabe] He was having trouble breathing, he looked like he was tossed from the car. His eyes were swollen, and his side was all scraped."[8]

Once the initial shock of the accident, and its possible severity, sunk in with the Steelers and their fans, subsequent stories focused on what had precipitated the crash. In an October 22 story in the *Post-Gazette*, Jim Gallagher and Andrew Sheehan's headline placed the responsibility for the mishap squarely upon Gabe's broad shoulders. "Steeler Gabriel Rivera yesterday was charged with drunken and reckless driving and speeding in the crash that may have left him partially paralyzed." Gabe was seen at a restaurant/bar named Julian's, alongside teammate Lou Rash (who was on injured reserve) and others, two hours after the team's practice ended at 4 p.m. The tavern's owner indicated that Gabe and Lou were both drinking beers and interacting with customers. "He (Rivera) was a perfect gentleman. He was . . . just generally being a pleasant guy. . . . I'm not going to serve someone who can hurt themselves. I'm the first one to shut them off."[9] A second story in the *Pittsburgh Press* was even more specific, stating that Rivera "sat in a North Side restaurant trading ethnic jokes with drinking companions and consuming four or five draft beers." One of Gabe's drinking colleagues indicated to reporters that "if I were put on the spot, I would say he wasn't drunk when he left." Owner Jim Julian, likely fearing possible legal reprisals, again reiterated that his policy was to deny further beverages if a customer appeared to be tipsy. "My bartenders shut people off. I make it a practice to call the police and get them to back me up whenever I'm going to tell somebody that they've had enough for the night. Neither of those things happened, because there wasn't the need for it."[10]

The story, of course, also made headlines in San Antonio and Lubbock. The *Avalanche-Journal* simply inserted a wire story that indicated only that Gabe was in critical condition after undergoing several hours of surgery. A story in the *Light* on October 22 stated that the accident was still "under investigation," but also mentioned "DWI" in its headline. This article also provided the first information concerning the family's response to the tragic event. Adrian, who had been in touch with Kimberly, stated that Juan and Maria Antonia were both already on their way to Pittsburgh, and that "my dad will be up there until either (tomorrow) or Monday. My mom says that she will stay there until he gets better."[11]

Within 72 hours of the accident (by October 24), however, it was clear that Gabe's career was over. Then medical personnel first articulated the high probability he would never walk again. Joe Gordon, the Steelers' spokesperson, was upset that the term "paralysis" was being bandied about, but an unnamed doctor in Pittsburgh (who claimed to be "very acquainted" with the situation) stated, "I don't think the question about him ever playing again is even legitimate . . . at this point. It's more a question of whether or not he'll ever walk again." Then, the unnamed neurosurgeon went on to provide analysis of the prognosis in extensive detail:

> If he doesn't show any improvement, even the slightest improvement in the first day or so, he's not likely to make any. . . . He had what we call a physiologically transected

(spinal cord). That means his spinal cord is not working. There has been an interruption of the electric impulses. The impulses aren't going through the damaged part of the spinal cord. It's like a short-circuited cable. You can't patch that. You can't change that. The spinal cord will heal and be sturdy, but whether the function returns is a matter of nature. In most cases, the chances are not very promising. . . . He'll have total loss of function below the injury. We're talking about the lower limbs. He has had movement in the upper body.[12]

The very next day, Gabe went from being the Steelers' first-round draft pick to a dire warning to the parents of youths in Western Pennsylvania. Indeed, an opinion piece in the *Post-Gazette* can rightfully be perceived as the first step toward the process of designating Rivera as the "Steeler Who Never Was." "Tragedy is no respecter of persons. . . . No doubt a few Pittsburgh parents used this grim and startling accident to make a point to their children. . . . It is a huge pity that something like this should prove a veritable superman so frighteningly mortal. It can be fondly hoped that this . . . young athlete recovers his health. . . . In the meantime, perhaps others may learn something from it all."[13]

On the same day as the op-ed, local papers carried yet another item that surely damaged Gabe's reputation among at least some of the black and gold's diehard faithful. In an Associated Press piece, Steeler Nation was informed about a variety of mishaps Rivera had had behind the wheel in his home state. According to research by a reporter from the *Light*, between March 1979 and January 1983 Gabe had five incidents and "was charged and pled guilty in at least four of them." He was cited for speeding in San Antonio on March 1, 1979, when he was 17. Police records did not indicate that he had been charged. There were two other such run-ins, which took place in western Texas, one on October 10, 1980, in Tom Green County, and another in Lubbock on December 9. Two other violations occurred while he was at Tech, the last being when he ran a stop sign back in the Alamo City shortly before the draft. "Rivera . . . pleaded guilty and paid fines on all three speeding charges and the stop sign violation."[14]

On October 26 Dr. Daniel Diamond, head of general surgery and trauma at Allegheny General, indicated that Gabe's paralysis extended from his chest down, and that it was permanent. "We feel that Mr. Rivera will live. His prognosis for walking again is not good and becomes worse each day in which we see no return of function below the chest level." The physician also noted that it would be necessary to perform a second surgery in order to perform bone grafts on three damaged vertebrae so that metal rods could be inserted and to stabilize the spine. The key concerns at this point were Gabe's risk of pneumonia and lung infection due to immobility. "We don't expect the operation would result in improvement of his paralysis. . . . Nothing would change from a functional standpoint." Stabilizing the spine would allow doctors to stand Gabe and better treat his lungs. On this day, for the first time, a quote appeared that articulated just one aspect of the difficult road that lay ahead for Gabe, Kimberly, and the rest of the clan. "Many basic functions will have to be learned all over again once his right arm becomes functional again. He will have to learn to feed himself, for example."[15]

While there was criticism concerning Gabe's responsibility for the accident, there were also heartfelt expressions of sympathy for his predicament. One of these came from a former NFLer, Steve Little from the University of Arkansas, a kicker who was the first pick of the then St. Louis Cardinals in 1978, and whose auto accident in 1980 (after being released by the franchise) left him a quadriplegic. He summarized what Gabe would face by saying, "It's tough. Very tough. When you can move one day and the next day you can't, that takes a lot of spirit out of you. It sure did me." This quote, which comes from a *Post-Gazette* article, also mentioned other issues Little endured that foreshadowed what was to come for Gabe. The kicker's marriage, for example, did not survive, and he also suffered from depression. The former Razorback star knew how Rivera would feel after leaving a rehabilitation facility. "I know he is hurting real bad inside. He's upset. He's probably angry with himself. Going through it really messes up your mind. But if I could tell him one thing, I would tell him to be patient. . . . In time you realize that it's not the end of the world." It would take many years for Gabe to come to grips with the final portion of Steve's advice.[16]

Another former football player reached out to the stricken rookie all the way from South Florida (in a letter originally published in the *Miami Herald*). George Cunningham,[17] who suffered a broken neck while playing defense for Miami Pace Senior High School, offered even more direct, and medically relevant, advice that is worth quoting at length.

> You have to take care of the things that sound trivial, such as your skin and lungs, so cooperate with your [medical] team when they want to turn you over and suction the fluid out of your lungs. I know how much it hurts, I know what a pain it is, but you've got to help. By doing this, you can overcome the losses you had no control over, defeat them by making many small gains at a time. Remember how . . . you had to build up your stamina by doing many wind sprints? Eventually, you noticed that . . . [they] became easier because you got yourself in condition. Well, the same thing is going to happen when they wean you off the respirator. At first, you might only be able to take a few seconds. But in a short time, you will be able to stay off it for longer periods, leading up to the point where you become victorious by beating the respirator. . . . I wish I could give you the game plan you will need to get you through this, but the best plan that I could come up with is to take one obstacle at a time and conquer it.[18]

Probably one of the most touching and heartfelt articles concerning Gabe's situation came from the wife of his former

Tech coach, Wallene Dockery, who would, in just a few weeks, endure an even greater tragedy. In an opinion piece in the *Memphis Press-Scimitar*, the former first lady of Red Raider football reminisced about Rivera's arrival on the Lubbock campus, the constant battle he had with his weight, and his determination to succeed on the field. One time during pre-fall drills, she recalled, Gabe ran three miles, instead of the required two, so as to show off how much weight he had lost over the summer, despite living at home and being tempted by Maria Antonia's wonderful tortillas and other Mexican delicacies. Then Gabe went one better and when "the tight ends needed encouragement . . . Gabriel jumped in and ran with them. The whole team applauded. He never said much. He was real quiet, but he was a great leader." Mrs. Dockery then touched upon a topic that would be very significant to the last decades of Gabriel's life, his connection with kids. "When children came to practice, they'd head straight for Gabriel. In a flash, he'd have one youngster slung over his shoulder, another draped from his hip. He didn't seem to need words to communicate with them. He just grinned . . . and they adored him." Finally, Wallene recalled how Gabe played Santa at a team function that included the Dockery children. "Dee crawled up on his lap. He looked at Santa and laughed with delight. 'Momma,' he said as he turned to me. 'This Santa looks just like Gabriel!'" Despite the medical odds, the Dockery clan continued to believe that somehow the "gentle giant" would pull through. "Despite the odds, I'd bet the farm on Rivera. He's a fighter. Rex and I know. We've seen his iron will and determination first-hand."[19]

Still others from San Antonio and Pittsburgh offered prayers on Gabe's behalf. A former classmate from Jefferson High, Stacy Perez, was sufficiently moved to write a letter to the stricken lineman offering her support. "If you just keep faith in Jesus, no matter how hopeless it may look, I know you will come through this. . . . Your life is precious and valuable and people won't stop caring for you even if you can't play football again. Don't look back. Look ahead to a bright future." Steeler fans Joan Caruso and the Morrone family even sent perpetual enrollment cards to Gabe at Allegheny General. These documents were from the Passionists, a missionary order of Catholic priests with a monastery in Pittsburgh, which enrolled the recipient "perpetually in the benefit of daily Mass."[20]

The well wishes and prayers, though no doubt of benefit, did not change the reality of what happened on the evening of October 20. Gabe was paralyzed; his career over; and he, Kimberly, and the rest of the Rivera clan would have to adjust to the new realities of the life of a paraplegic. Additionally, it was time to start thinking about the financial repercussions of this calamitous event. Two articles from the *Pittsburgh Steelers' Weekly* of November 7, 1983, shed light on these considerations. Vic Ketchman discussed, with great specificity, the injuries Gabe suffered as a result of the collision. "In the accident, Rivera suffered: Nerve damage to the right arm, resulting in weakness of the arm; a bruised heart; fractured ribs on both sides; a puncture wound of the right lung; serious contusions to both lungs; fractured and dislocated vertebrae in the upper back, resulting in paralysis from the mid-chest region down." The doctor who performed the surgery to stabilize Gabe's spine, Daniel Diamond, described the effects that acted upon Rivera's body as he was ejected from the Datsun that fateful night: "The forces to do this are tremendous, especially for a man of Mr. Rivera's size. And those forces are transmitted to the spinal cord. It's kind of like stripping the bark from a tree."[21]

Now it was time to turn to the cost, both in expenses and lost wages, of the accident. First, Gabe's agent Ray Galindo indicated during an interview that the Steelers consented to pay their first-round draft choice the total salary for his rookie season—approximately $250,000—on top of the roughly $400,000 signing bonus (which netted out to around $323,000—a copy of this check is included in the Rivera Collection at Texas

Tech). That would be the end of the Steelers' financial responsibilities. Given that Kim gave birth to the couple's son, Tim, on
November 11, these monies would be of critical importance.[22]

Next, as indicated in the *Pittsburgh Steelers' Weekly*, monies
would be coming from the NFL Players Association (NFLPA),
as well as medical coverage. The article quoted Miki Yaras, the
director of benefits for the NFLPA since the early 1980s (she
is known as "the queen of benefits" for the union and is still
employed by them), and laid out how major medical insurance
would work in Gabe's case. "The policy . . . has a $25 deduct-
ible . . . with 80% of the first $3,000 covered and 100% of every-
thing after that initial $3,000 [up to $1,000,000] . . . 'The bottom
line is that someone like Rivera would be responsible for something like $625 for the $1 million coverage.' Beyond those benefits, Gabe, if permanently disabled, would also be eligible for
$725 a month under the terms of the retirement board." The
key issue with this situation, however, was that Gabe's injury
(as was the case with Steve Little) was non-football-related.
According to Yaras, a player who became disabled through
an on-field injury was due $4,000 per month as of 1983. She
indicated that Little, though paralyzed in an auto accident, was
receiving that amount. The NFLPA, Yaras indicated, would
strive to get the same for Rivera. "We'll follow the same strategy we followed in the Little case if we have to. If we have to
go to the media, we will, but I don't know if that will happen."
While not afraid to use the union's leverage if necessary, Yaras
"praised the Rooney family and the Steeler organization for
their care and aid in the situation."[23]

One of the most interesting aspects of this misfortune was a
unique relationship that developed between an unlikely pair:
Steelers' owner and founder, Art Rooney, and Maria Antonia.
As Norbert indicated during our interviews, Rooney spoke
no Spanish, and his mother hardly spoke English, yet the two
bonded over their Catholic faith, as well as the tragic circumstances of a son and first-round draft pick.[24] Maria Antonia

recorded in a diary her thoughts concerning her stay in Pittsburgh right after the accident, and then during a one-week period, from November 18 through November 25. Additionally, Gabe's family kept a series of letters from Art. These items provide great insight into the behind-the-scenes (both positive and negative) goings-on during Gabe's early period of recovery and convalescence.[25]

Before hearing from Art and Maria Antonia directly, it is necessary to bring in the words of Kim Rivera.[26] On the night of the accident Kim recalled that she was in bed, but awake, concerned that her husband had not yet called at around nine o'clock. "The thought always crosses my mind that something could be wrong. Then the police came for me. They said that he had been in a bad accident, but I didn't know how bad until I got to the hospital." Kim recalled that the couple planned to stay in that evening and watch a show on television. She waited for Gabe to arrive, but after a while, she went to bed to await his return. Kim noted during our interview that she had a nightmare that evening wherein she was awakened by police at the couple's front door who informed her that her husband had been in an automobile accident and had been killed. Her recollection of that horrible night was that she was roused from this frightening trance by the actual knocks on her door by authorities there to inform her of the accident. Indeed, she awoke from one nightmare only to enter into a real-life calamity. When Kim arrived at the hospital, Gabe was lucid enough to tell her that he loved her, but it was clear to her that he was deathly afraid of the situation. "He looked at me and I saw a tear roll down his face."[27]

According to Norbert, Kim called the Riveras in Texas and passed along word of the accident. Norbert found out via that phone call, as well as early news reports by local radio stations. Maria Antonia, as expected, was in tears. The fact that Kim did not speak Spanish limited her ability to interact with the distraught mother in the critical early hours; this, no doubt, helped widen a rift that existed previously between the two women (more details are discussed shortly), at least from the mother-in-law's perspective. Norbert also indicated during our interview that when Gabe came out of his coma, the first person he called for was his mother, not Kim, which added to the already tense situation.[28] After the first days, Kim drew some comfort from the fact that after coming out of the coma Gabe was able to converse, if only via a few words. "I'm just happy now that we can communicate. I began to get more rest once Gabe seemed better. Or at least he seemed better to me."

Some of the improvements included regaining limited movement in both arms, though the left was the stronger limb. There is also mention in Sam Blair's article in the *Post-Gazette* that Maria Antonia and Kim's father, Jim Covington, had gone to visit a rehabilitation facility in nearby Harmarville. While there was some optimism that Gabe's condition could improve to an extent, this article also reiterated the financial impact on the young family. "Wherever he goes, of course, there will be tremendous expenses. These will be covered by insurance provided in the 1982 agreement between the NFL Players Association and management. But what about future income? 'If he's permanently disabled,' said . . . Dan Rooney . . . 'he will receive monthly income for life. We want to be sure it's enough.'" Meanwhile, Rivera's teammates and coaches continued to check in and pray on behalf of their stricken comrade. One particularly poignant sentiment came from running back Walter Abercrombie, who played against the Red Raiders while in the backfield for the Baylor Bears: "We're praying for him and his wife. We all liked him. He not only was a great person, but he was really beginning to contribute to the team."[29]

Blair also provided some insight from Gabe's spouse as well as a brief glimpse into the developing relationship between the Steelers' patriarch, Art Rooney, and a housewife from South Texas, Maria Antonia. They both drew much comfort and fortitude from their shared Catholic faith. Each morning during her time in Pittsburgh, the two would see each other at Mass in St. Peter's, the owner's home parish. Then they would often share coffee or breakfast in the rectory alongside the priest or Monsignor who said Mass. Mr. Rooney was heartened by the devotion Maria Antonia displayed; she even brought a statue of Our Lady of Guadalupe (the patroness of Mexico and the Americas) into Gabe's room at Allegheny General. "She has tremendous faith, but I believe she understands what's going on. It's so pathetic. We thought he was going to be a great player. And on top of that, he's a fine person. Everyone liked him."[30] While the diary and letters show the positive, even tender, interactions between Art and the Riveras, the same cannot be said about Maria Antonia's feelings about Kim and her family. Maria Antonia's diary begins on October 21, shortly after the family received the news about the accident. From the very start of her narrative, three themes become evident: her strong Catholic faith, her apprehensions about Kim, and her interactions with Mr. Rooney.

Soon after the Riveras' arrival in Pittsburgh, the family visited Gabe in the hospital. Maria Antonia brought not only a Lady of Guadalupe, but also statues of the Infant of Prague as well as one of Mary, Help of Christians. Seeing her powerful and athletic son in such a state was certainly a shock, and Maria Antonia noted that "he looked very bad and I prayed with great faith that they would do a miracle to save his life, he was hooked up to the necessary equipment (respirator)." Then she, Juan, Norbert, and Adrian went to St. Peter's and found it closed at the conclusion of the midday Mass. Ray Galindo, who had flown in from California, reached out to the Monsignor to open the church, and shortly thereafter the Riveras visited with Mr. Rooney (she indicates that they had previously interacted with Dan at the hospital). After visiting in the rectory, the Steelers' owner put up the family of his stricken player at the Hilton. Previously, the Riveras had been at the young couple's house, and this was not a pleasant experience as far as Maria Antonia was concerned. Her principal recollection of the time spent there was that "her [Kim's] father and mother only spoke about business, as they were certain that Gabe was going to die. I do not know of what they discussed with Galindo, but as Galindo...[does not know] how things will turn out financially, they wanted to visit with the lawyer who works with Galindo." Next began a daily pattern: early Mass, time with priests and visits with Gabriel, then often either breakfast or lunch with Art. There were also visits to social workers and psychiatrists assigned to the case.

Maria Antonia noted that Norbert and Adrian got along well with the Steelers' representatives, particularly with the patriarch. The brothers, Juan, and Maria Antonia were even invited to visit Three Rivers Stadium and hosted to a Steeler home game. By the start of the week after the accident, the medical team informed the family that Gabe needed to have surgery to stabilize his spine; his mom described the operation in her journal as being "a great success." Meanwhile, there were also comments concerning the problematic relationship with Kim. First of all, there were tensions about who would make decisions concerning Gabe's treatment, which, of course, Maria Antonia felt entitled to do. However, this assumption was incorrect. "I believe that Kim and her family believe that she, as the spouse, has the right to decide what to do in this case and I decided not to return to their house." Maria Antonia was also concerned, since Kim did not have family in the Pittsburgh area, that she would likely take Gabe back to Texas, not to San Antonio, but rather near her family's domicile in Fort Worth. She then went on to describe how she felt she was treated by the Covingtons in the couple's house. "Here in the hospital they have treated me like someone special, if I had stayed at her house, I would not have had the blessings I have had." There were also concerns expressed about financial matters.[31]

The diary then picks up again on November 18, and Maria Antonia proceeds to provide a daily accounting of her movements in Pittsburgh, her visits to the hospital, and also clearly articulates the growing strain in the relationship with her daughter-in-law. That day, Maria Antonia visited Gabe, joined by Mr. Rooney. Kim was already in the room when the two arrived. Maria Antonia noted that "she did not seem to like that we arrived and did not want for me to stay.... She [indicated that] she wanted me to return to San Antonio immediately.... [She believed] that I made Gabe think differently and that [this] was going to ruin her marriage." She then goes on to accuse Kim of trying to force the Riveras to return to Texas in order to convince Gabe that he did not matter to the rest of the family. A further issue concerned the upcoming Thanksgiving holiday, which, Maria Antonia asserted, Kim wanted to spend alone with her husband.

Another point of contention during what must have been a heated exchange, from Maria Antonia's perspective, was the fact that Kim indicated to her devout mother-in-law that she did not wish to have Tim baptized in the Catholic Church. This was yet another major disappointment, as Maria Antonia was still upset about how Gabe and Kim had married. "I believe that Gabriel said that he wanted the baby baptized because I told Gabriel that I accepted the marriage in a civil ceremony but when I saw there was a minister who was marrying them I was very displeased and want the baby baptized. Kim had previously told me that she wanted to convert.... I hope that this does not affect Gaby because he is progressing well. The social worker told me that I have the right to stay by [his] side as long as I wish.... I hope that tomorrow will be a better day."[32]

On November 19, Maria Antonia turned her attention and annoyance toward Jim Covington, indicating that when he arrived in Gabe's room he was discussing, "like always, with the business" (meaning the issue of how to sustain the family now that Gabe could no longer play). This seemed to be a harsh assessment of Kim's father's concerns; after all, with a

one-week-old baby and a disabled husband, it was only logical that the grandfather thought about how his daughter
and grandson would be provided for. Another issue that Jim
seemed to be focusing on was whether there was some possibility of suing Datsun due to what Maria Antonia referred to
as "a defect in the car." The issue of money and Kim's family's concerns along those lines come up in the diary on several
occasions.

On a more positive note, a couple of Gabe's teammates visited this day, one of them being Franco Harris, who signed a
football for both Norbert and his mother. Maria Antonia then
left the room at around 8:45 but indicated that she was constantly asking the nurses about the spouses' interactions. She
found reason to be concerned here as well, implying that Kim
was not as attentive as necessary. "The nurses realize what is
happening. In the morning that I arrived they told me that
[Kim] was going to speak with them at 10:00 and she did not
until 11:30."[33] On this day, Maria Antonia also summarized
her feelings about Mr. Rooney, noting that, "since I met him
he has treated me very well, to me he is a saint and the Msg.
[Monsignor] as well." The diary's notes about November 20 are
quite short, with Maria Antonia noting only that Jim brought
the baby and she had the chance to hold him for a while.[34]

The entry from November 21 provides quite a bit of information concerning some important topics: Maria Antonia's
interaction with a psychiatrist assigned to Gabe's case and,
yet again, a discussion about Kim. The writings clearly show
Maria Antonia's stress with all that had occurred and what
would follow. Once more she defended herself against the
notion of being an intrusive parent who was interfering in her
son's marriage and the decisions that needed to be made, given
the new realities. "I responded that I had not ruined her marriage and that before they married they already had difficulties. . . . Since that day [of the accident] I am not important to
her and she did not care what would happen in this city where

I don't know anyone. . . . She once again says that she wants to spend Thanksgiving only with him. I told her . . . I am not leaving until Gaby goes to the other hospital."

On this same day, Maria Antonia had a run-in with Gabe's psychiatrist, who, she felt, was selling short her son's ability to overcome the psychological issues associated with his paraplegia. Earlier in her diary, she had made her impression of this individual quite clear: "I do not like him, and he does not like me." Apparently, the physician tried to explain to Maria Antonia some of the problems that Gabe would likely encounter as he moved to the Harmarville Rehabilitation Center. "He tells me that we need to prepare him because when he goes to the other hospital . . . it will be very difficult and he will have to do what they tell him to do there, in case he is not prepared for that. . . . I told him that Gaby does not need help. That is because Gaby has the determination to recuperate, I have told him that he will be able to walk but that he will have to put forth his effort, he will walk soon, even if it takes months or years."

The discussion then turned to what Gabe would do now that football was no longer an employment option. Maria Antonia, it seems, took this to mean that the medical professional intimated that Gabe did not have the intellectual capability to do anything else. Her response was harsh. "The Dr. let me know that Gaby is smart only for football and not other things. . . . I believe that he is incorrect and that [Gabe] will surprise us and do other things besides football."[35] While it did take many years, Gabe finally found a niche in working with children, though it would come after several starts down other paths.

On November 22, Maria Antonia and Juan arrived at the hospital at 9 a.m. and were informed that Gabe would be transferred to Harmarville on the following day. The hospital personnel indicated that both Maria Antonia and Kim would be able to ride in the ambulance that would take Gabe to the rehabilitation facility. The following day started much the same as had the others: Maria Antonia went to Mass and was able to visit with Mr. Rooney. The preparations for the transport were under way. "They told me that Kim would come with me in the ambulance, but she did not appear, so I went by myself." When they reached their intended destination, Maria Antonia was pleasantly surprised to find some personnel who spoke Spanish, including a doctor from Costa Rica and a nurse from Ecuador. Kim arrived at around 2:30 and stayed with her husband for two hours.[36]

Covering the last two days in Pittsburgh, the diary entries provide a glimpse of how this tragedy had impacted Juan. Here was a man who had dedicated his life to sport, particularly to football, and had helped guide his sons in the ways of the game since their earliest days. While Juan and most of his offspring had had an opportunity to play at the collegiate level, the one member of the family who had achieved the ultimate prize, making it to the NFL, now lay in a rehabilitation center far away from Texas, his professional career ended barely after it had begun. On November 24, after spending time with a priest from St. Peter's and visiting with the cleric's family, Maria Antonia asked him to bring her back to the Hilton. The reason she wanted to return was that "I was very concerned about Juan." Later, the two returned to the facility and visited with Gabe. Kim and her father were there with the baby. Again, Maria Antonia expressed concern that Jim wanted to discuss financial matters, this time with Juan. In a tangent to her narrative, she implied (in a disdainful tone) that Mr. Covington was quite proud of how well he was handling all of the financial issues. "Kim's father gave Juan quite a bit of information and told him of all the good that he had done." While he may have been acting in his daughter's and grandchild's best interests, Maria Antonia could not move beyond her negative feelings about Kim and her parents. "I know that I am the only person whom they want to be far away."

Juan and Maria Antonia visited Gabe one final time on November 25, but only after Mass and spending time at the motherhouse of one of the sisters whom they met at St. Peter's. The Riveras then had lunch with the mother superior and all of the members of the convent (Maria Antonia estimated that there were around 250 nuns), and Maria Antonia was comforted by the fact that they "were sad about what had happened to Gaby, but all of them were praying for his recovery." At the rehabilitation center, she was further gladdened by the fact that Gabe was sitting, seemed to be doing "well . . . was dressed and seated," and was on his way to be X-rayed. She did notice that Gabe had lost a great deal of his girth. From his playing weight of around 285, he was now down to below 244 pounds. This was the last positive aspect noted in this entry. After returning to the hotel at around 5 p.m., "Juan left and had not yet returned [by a quarter to eight]." After dinner, "he wanted me to go with him to the bar and he said that I never liked to [go to] the bar. Later when he arrived, he became very upset."[37] These were the final entries to Maria Antonia's diary. They are significant as they foreshadow various critical points that take place in Gabe's life after his accident. Ultimately, the marriage with Kim ended, there were bumps along the way in regard to his relationship with Tim, there was one more desperate attempt at a "cure," and finally several problems arose once Gabriel returned to Texas.

Before moving on to that part of the story, it is important to hear Art Rooney's voice and his feelings for the Riveras. The family saved a total of six letters from the Pittsburgh patriarch, and the ties that developed between him and his player's clan are very evident. The documents, dating from December 1983 through Christmas 1984, show Art's concern and strong bond, particularly with Maria Antonia. The first such correspondence, dated December 8, 1983, leads off, "I have missed you, especially when I am at St. Peter's at Mass. I keep you and most of all, Gabriel, in my prayers." Rooney indicates in this document how much all of the persons the Riveras interacted with in

Pennsylvania miss and admired them. "You are wonderful and kind people—everyone I know who met you throughout your terrible ordeal were happy to get to know you." He then goes on to talk a bit about how the team is doing: "Since you left and before, our team has not played well but we have [a] big game in New York on Saturday." He then promises to update them after visiting with Gabriel the following week and passes along a "hello" from the Monsignor. With the coming of Christmas, Art sent another letter on December 16 and reminded Juan and Maria Antonia to remain hopeful. "This year and this time of year especially, I know it could be happier for you—pray and hope and all will be well. There is always hope." Along with this letter, Art included a story on the "great work" that was being done with spinal cord injuries at Harmarville. Lastly, he indicated that his son Dan had visited with Gabe recently and that "They were all pleased with Gabe's progress. He was in good spirits."[38]

Letters during 1984 provided further updates on Gabe's progress. The first item from this year, dated January 4, stated that "Father Mikonis drove me out to visit with Gabe and I thought he was well. He seemed spirited and cheerful; I was pleased he does so good. His wife and baby were there as well and they both looked fine." With this correspondence, Art included a program from the Steelers' playoff game (which they lost to the Los Angeles Raiders, 38–10). A follow-up arrived before the end of the month, on January 27. This communication once again reiterated that both Art and clergy from St. Peter's (this time, he was accompanied by the Monsignor) had visited. The owner sought to encourage the family in Texas concerning Gabe's progress. "It was wonderful to see him looking so trim and in such good humor—he is a wonderful influence on others there too—he visits and cheers up his fellow friends there." Additionally, Rooney sought to remind the Riveras that Gabe's teammates had not forgotten him. "A player, Keith Willis, was there when we arrived and they were still there when we left.

Many of the players visit regularly, and I know they enjoy seeing and talking to Gabe."

Finally, there was a handwritten mention that indicated
that Father Mikonis had also visited and continued to keep
Gabe and his family in his prayers. One item on letterhead
is dated February 24 and mentions that Gabe was interviewed on local television and that Art thought "he looked
and spoke so well; I was proud of him. . . . It took a lot of
courage for Gabe and if you would have seen him—well he
was just wonderful." Mr. Rooney also included a copy of an
article on Gabe from one of the local papers. A concluding
piece of correspondence arrived for the Christmas season,
just before Pittsburgh played against the Denver Broncos in
a playoff game on December 30. One particularly important point Art mentioned here was that Gabe was attending
some games at Three Rivers Stadium. "I see Gabe at almost
all of the games and he is a wonder. I believe he is doing well,
and Tim is fine—he was in the office with him and Kim and
it was good that all is as good as it is—Gabe is a strong person who has a wonderful disposition." Rooney then passed
along well wishes to the Riveras from the Monsignor and
Father Mikonis.[39]

While Maria Antonia and Art Rooney continued to boost
each other's morale about Gabe's condition and circumstances,
an article from December 15, 1983, provided an on-the-ground
assessment of how he was doing at Harmarville and what the
future portended. Henry W. Pierce's article in the *Post-Gazette*,
"Gabe Rivera May Go Home after 'Battle,'" indicated that at
least a few more months of rehabilitation still lay ahead. Here
we get a specific mention about the psychological impact of the
accident and how Gabe was coping. Pierce quotes Dr. Gilbert
Brenes, the director of the spinal cord program at Harmarville
(who mirrored some of Steve Little's views): "He's depressed,
but that's to be expected. He's a quiet person, I don't notice
any difference in his behavior. Neither does his family." The

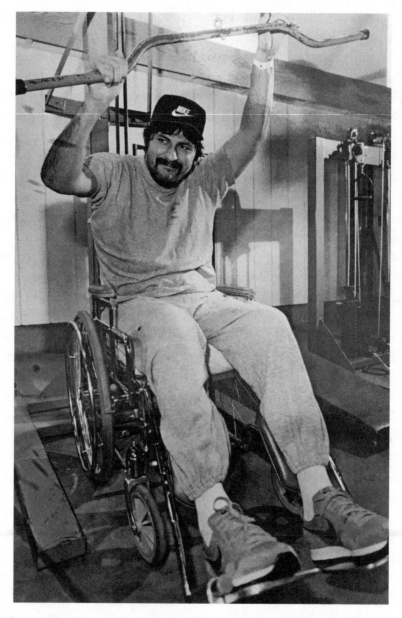

Gabe working out to rebuild strength in his arms after his accident (Southwest Collection, TTU University Archives)

therapy involved weightlifting in order to regain strength in his arms. Other therapy included exercising in a pool so as to keep Gabe's joints and muscles as limber as possible. Ultimately, the goal of these varied endeavors would be so that he could be responsible for tasks such as "grooming, bathing, and home-making." Dr. Brenes noted that the injured lineman would also be able to drive once again, "but in a special car he can control entirely with his hands." The physician expected that Gabe would be able to leave the facility in about three months. The attending doctor sounded an optimistic note at the end of the article, stating, "He had the potential for being an inspiration to others for the rest of his life." This would be true, but there would certainly be bumps along the way.[40]

Having heard Maria Antonia's perspective on the hellish days right after Gabe's accident, we also need to understand the perspective of both Kim and her parents and their recol-lections of these days. Jim and Karan were in Albuquerque and, like the Riveras, took the first flight possible to Pittsburgh. When they arrived to see their son-in-law and to comfort their pregnant daughter, Gabe was stable but still critical. Once in Pennsylvania, one of the things that Kim's family did was to purchase and bring furniture to the Rivera household. Kim and Karan spent some of the time in late October putting together Tim's nursery. When I mentioned to the Covingtons that Maria Antonia had complained about their daughter not converting to Catholicism, they stated that they had never heard about this possibility. Kim asserted that she never made her mother-in-law such a promise.

One thing that did create tension, according to the Covingtons, was that Juan and Maria Antonia had Tim bap-tized in the Catholic Church without Kim's permission. The family also argued that the Thanksgiving issue Maria Antonia mentioned in her diary did not occur. They did invite the Riveras over to the young couple's domicile for dinner that evening. Another, and major, bone of contention was that all of the social workers and counselors indicated to Kim and her family that, when Gabe came out of his postsurgery stu-por, he would likely bond with whomever was in the room.

These professionals recommended that, logically, that person should be Kim, not Maria Antonia. Finally, contrary to the diary entries, the Covingtons indicated during our discussions that Jim never mentioned finances directly in front of Maria Antonia. Instead, he talked with Gabe as he recovered, and his son-in-law was amenable to Jim stepping in to help with managing the couple's finances.[41]

The local media visited with Gabe once again approximately three months later, when he had his first interview with reporters. Here, he spoke about his short-term goals, which included being able to hold Tim and change his diaper (which, Gabe noted proudly, he was able to do the week prior), not to be a burden to Kim, and to help in raising his son. "One of my goals is to do the things a father should do to help out." In addition, by the time of his visit with the press, he had learned to dress himself, transfer to and from a wheelchair, and swim. As far as being able to move about in public, Gabe had visited some local malls, attended a movie theater and restaurant, and even gone to (and received a standing ovation from the fans at) a Pittsburgh Penguins game.[42]

Further on, he stated he wanted to complete a college degree in recreational management, not what he had majored in at Texas Tech. Of course, while his insurance and pension from the NFL would help (as the article noted, "he has enough money for now"), Rivera also discussed the necessity of getting a job at some point. Dr. Brenes praised Gabe's progress and determination. "It was a new teaching experience for us. We're not used to working with someone so organized in terms of goals. The majority try hard but go in circles for a while. Gabe knew from day one which direction he was going to go." Gabe spoke positively about his current state of mind, though he continued to hold out the possibility of someday walking again, while simultaneously recognizing he had to learn to live with the results of the accident. "I know there's hope . . . for a cure. . . . But realistically, this is the way I'm going to be from now on, until I die. I can accept that. It was hard trying to accept that. But then all of a sudden you say, 'What am I going to do, lie around and do nothing?'"[43]

There were also stories about this press conference in the San Antonio papers. Kevin O'Keefe, writing for the *Express*, attended the Harmarville presser and presented an upbeat assessment of the former Texas Tech and Jefferson High star. "There wasn't a trace of bitterness in his tone. He expressed himself well before the reporters, despite the fact that the press conference was not really his idea." O'Keefe also mentioned that one of the great joys for Gabe during his convalescence was receiving letters from the kindergarten students in Mrs. Flanagan's class back in Pittsburgh. "I look forward to those. They're an inspiration." Later on in his life, Gabe would likewise draw encouragement from working with children back in San Antonio.[44]

Another article in the same paper a few days later, this one by Gene Wojciechowski, recounted the tragic events of the autumn night but also featured a unique perspective: briefly giving voice to Juan, a person who, Norbert indicated more than once during our interviews, was just as quiet, if not more so, than his famous son. Wojciechowski's essay took Juan back to when the family arrived in Pittsburgh and first saw his son, thinking death was imminent. "Me, his father. Even I didn't think he was going to pull through." When his son lived, Juan believed an even worse fate awaited. "He didn't remember nothing. The psychologist told us that if he came back, he was going to come back like a baby. . . . Yes, sir, I still asking myself, why him? Why us? I've still got a question mark." Fortunately, this was also not the case, though having to deal with a paraplegic son would present its own challenges. Even in his darkest hours, however, Juan drew upon common wisdom from his ethnic background in order to retain a shred of expectation. While Maria Antonia gained solace from Mass, the Eucharist, Our Lady of Guadalupe, the Infant of Prague, Mary, Help of

Christians, and visits with Mr. Rooney, Juan drew strength from his culture. "Sir, I was born and raised in Texas. My parents are from Mexico. In Spanish, we have a lot of sayings, like proverbs. We have a saying that goes something like this if I can translate: 'If something bad will come, something good will come later.' I keep repeating that to myself." Gabe, it seemed, was on the path toward some positive outcome from the horrific accident. In just a few years, he would wind up living with Juan and Maria Antonia, who would deal with both the good and bad of their son's circumstances for the remainder of their lives.[45]

By the middle of March 1984, Gabe and Kim attended his first court appearance to face charges of drunk driving. The assistant district attorney, John Zottola, recommended that the former Steeler be placed in Accelerated Rehabilitative Disposition (ARD), which meant Rivera would admit guilt for the accident and driving while impaired. The county would then offer entry into a probationary program for first offenders. Stanley Stein, Gabe's attorney, indicated the couple would "think it over. We have time before we decide anything." At this session, Gabe waived his right to a preliminary hearing. His arraignment was then set for April 19. This article also indicated that Gabe was still at Harmarville, though he "expected to be released shortly."[46] During this time, Gabe still received correspondence from Art Rooney. One postcard that the family saved arrived toward the end of March. Art complained about some issues with his knees but indicated that he would be by to visit Gabe in the near future.[47]

By the time of Gabe's scheduled arraignment on the drunk-driving charges, district attorney Bob Colville decided it was in the best interest of justice to drop the case against the injured former player. To some, this smacked of favoritism due to the Steelers' connection, but Colville countered, and rightfully so, that "If this were a regular Joe, we would have dropped the case a long time ago." How much more, he argued, should Rivera be punished? He was now paralyzed from the waist down, his career gone, and his family faced an uncertain financial future. Was that not sufficient chastisement? The leadership of the *Pittsburgh Press*, in an editorial dated April 18, agreed with the county's chief prosecutor's assessment of the situation. "But if the punishment is meant to fit the offense, then Mr. Rivera has more than paid for whatever wrongs he committed. . . . In this accident, at least, the most pain and suffering came to the person causing it. That's not always the case. But when it happens, as it did so appallingly to Mr. Rivera, it's the most fitting justice of all."[48]

By the middle of June 1984, Gabe had been released from Harmarville and was back at the Riveras' domicile in the Franklin Park area of the city. At this time a writer for the *Light*, Jim Lefko, came by to visit with the former Jefferson High star. The article noted that Gabe was adjusting and planned to attend some Pirates games over the summer, and that the family had just returned from a one-week vacation in California with Kim's parents. Gabe did share some of the frustrations that came along with being confined to a wheelchair. It was a hassle getting in and out, and Kim had difficulties when the ground was not level. It seems that the couple spent as much time as they could at places that made pushing the chair as easy as possible. Gabe noted, "Malls are fun, though." The article also noted other key complications that were now part of everyday life. For example, their house was certainly not an ideal setup for a paraplegic, as all four bedrooms were upstairs. Since returning from rehabilitation, Gabe and Kim had moved into the ground floor game room. Tim slept in the nursery, which was in one of the bedrooms.[49]

One of the more interesting aspects of this story comes from Lefko's description of the relationship between the spouses. Contrary to some of what Maria Antonia noted in her diary, the journalist painted a picture of a young couple facing the difficulties of their new circumstances with love, grit, and determination. For example, since Kim and Gabe did not yet own a hand-controlled van, she drove her husband to and from rehab on a daily basis. Lefko summarized the relationship by stating, "While the house may be half-full, the Riveras' marriage is complete." Gabe chimed in that, since the accident, "You know, it's not only me that's injured. It's Kim having to cope too. . . . It's hard to figure out what she's thinking sometimes, but it helps having somebody that cares for you. We're getting a lot closer in our relationship. We're seeing more of each other now during the day than the average person does."

Although Kim is not quoted directly in the article, Lefko summarizes Kim's dealing with her husband's situation by noting that "for a woman who won't turn 20 for another month, she has been a blessing for Rivera. Kim is the motivation for Gabe's daily workouts, his inspiration when fatigue and despair begin to overwhelm everything else." The author presented Gabe as hopeful and looking forward to a positive future (including the possibility of walking again) and not fixating on "what ifs."

> Now, there's a lot of things I want to do, maybe something in football like scouting or something with computers.

> I accept it [the accident] now. . . . What if I had decided not to go out that night? There's always going to be the "ifs." But I don't dwell on it.

> It takes two years after the accident to do a lot of things on your own.

> I'm capable of anything. It's a dream, but it can be a reality. Right now, I ain't going to get up and walk. And if it comes back, I'll be in braces awhile. I'll have to get my legs strong. But the dream is always on your mind, no matter what.[50]

Our chronology of events has now arrived at the moment in time when Gabe faced the critical issue of going home and beginning his new reality as a paraplegic. Here we temporarily set the story aside and bring in some academic and anecdotal materials concerning the effect of this radical change of life. For this perspective, we turn briefly to the work of Darryl Stingley and various academicians whose research focuses on the psychological, familial, and rehabilitative aspects of life after a spinal cord injury (SCI).

Stingley's injury occurred during a contest as he attempted to make a reception over the middle of the field in an exhibition game between the New England Patriots and the Oakland Raiders on August 12, 1978. He was 26 years old at the time of the incident. When Stingley died in 2007, an Associated Press story recounted the hit as follows: "With one jolt, his life was forever changed. His neck was broken; he was left a quadriplegic. In time, he regained limited movement in his right arm and was able to operate his electric wheelchair on his own." The hit by Jack Tatum did not draw a flag. After realizing the circumstances he found himself in, Stingley's thoughts mirrored those of Steve Little, and most certainly, Gabe's. "What's going to happen to me? If I live, what am I going to be like?"[51] Five years after the incident, Stingley published an autobiography; not surprisingly, his words when recalling the realization of his predicament were gut-wrenching. It is not difficult to assume similar thoughts were present in Gabe's mind in late October 1983.

> All this time everything in my life was changing radically. I had to find a way to cope, to continue living. I had to develop an ability to adjust to the obstacles that presented themselves. I was in a totally adverse environment, and the only way to approach it was to try to make as many adjustments as necessary to survive, to function, to communicate. I had no choice. It was up to me.

> After four or five days in the hospital, I realized I was paralyzed and that I probably wouldn't be walking out of the hospital any day soon—if ever. No one told me that. They didn't have to. I still couldn't move a muscle. My whole body was virtually useless. I wasn't stupid. I had a pretty good

idea of what was happening to me, and what had happened to me.[52]

Next came the torturous period of rehabilitation. One of the moments that Darryl recounts in his book is instructive, not only for his achievement, but how it helped lead him, after a period of denial and internal struggle, to reconcile to the reality of his condition. Not surprisingly, at first, Stingley's demeanor was not the best. His attending physician at the rehab institute made it abundantly clear that the injured player would have to change his attitude and interactions with the facility's personnel. "So, my advice to you, Darryl, is to get smart. Don't fight the therapists. Work hand in hand with them. You and everyone else will be a lot better off in the end." Some stern words from his wife reinforced the doctor's advice. Stingley took this to heart and eventually began to make progress. He began to work with his therapist, whom he had previously regarded as little more than "one tactless bitch." One particular day, Stingley recounted, the patient took the initiative and asked his tormentor to do a particular exercise—one in which he would sustain himself using his right arm. The attendant rolled Stingley on a mat and asked him to hold himself up for five seconds. "She let go. I felt as though I was holding up the John Hancock Building—all 103 stories." They had hoped he would sustain himself for five seconds—Stingley managed four. While he did not meet the target, something changed in Darryl's mindset: he would beat his quadriplegia. "Only my definition of 'beat,' in this case, was 'accept.' . . . I knew I wasn't a quitter. . . . I learned later that six of ten quadriplegics attempt suicide. . . . I never once thought of taking away the life that God had twice given me."

Resolving to make the best of his situation, Stingley then considered what he would do with his life. He eventually worked as a scouting consultant with New England, a job he held until 1990. He finished his college degree in 1991 and also received a pension from the NFLPA, which at the time was around $48,000 per season (the updated benefit was around $225,000 per season at the time of his death). Finally, Darryl also thought about what he could do to help his fellow man. "As for what that new career would be, I didn't know the answer yet.... I'd be active in the community. I'd try to be a humanitarian.... It would be silly not to take the lead in various ways."[53]

While the tragic consequences of Darryl's accident helped to reshape rules and policies in the NFL, they did not dissuade his offspring from following in his footsteps. His youngest son, Derek Sr., played Minor League Baseball and also in the Arena Football League (AFL), starting with the Albany Firebirds. He also coached in the AFL for more than one decade. Derek eventually wound up prowling the sidelines of Dunham High School in Louisiana, where he helped coach his son, Derek Jr.[54] If the name sounds familiar, the grandson of Darryl Stingley was, in 2019, a consensus All-American as a cornerback with the Louisiana State University Tigers. He was part of a team that finished the season undefeated and won the college football national championship.[55] This last aspect of Stingley's story would be of significance to the rest of Gabe's life. Rivera did not ever work again (except briefly for the Steelers), nor did he finish a degree. For a while, he was without much direction—that is, until he found his place in working with children in inner-city San Antonio (discussed at length in chapter 8).

Wendy Armour's work, *Remaking the Body: Rehabilitation and Change*, provides important insights into various aspects of the reality that Gabe lived after his accident. At the start of the work, she quotes Professor Bryan S. Turner, a scholar who has written extensively on the sociology of the body. In the foreword to Armour's study, he effectively summarizes some of what Gabe must have been thinking as he headed home from Harmarville in 1984. "Who I am depends upon a unique and particular form of embodiment, *my* body in this place and time." How dramatically had the former defensive lineman's sense of his own body (and its capabilities, or lack thereof) changed from the night of October 20, 1983! One moment he was a player in the NFL with a great career to look forward to; the next, he was in a wheelchair dependent on his wife, family, and the league for his care and future financial wherewithal. Seymour's own assessment of such patients ties in directly with what Gabe was experiencing, particularly since he had been defined by his presence on fields of athletic competition from a young age. "To be an adult male is distinctly to occupy space, to have a physical presence in the world. Sport is a critical vehicle of conventional masculine body appearance.... It is the body that constitutes the most striking symbol as well as the material core of sporting activities."[56] Considering that Gabe was playing football at its highest level, the end of this aspect of his life had to have been greatly distressing.

Beginning to move forward and rebuild a life after an SCI is, to put it mildly, exceedingly arduous—for an athlete of Rivera's caliber, even more so. What could have been, had he remained with Pittsburgh instead of becoming known as "the Steeler who never was"? This question, in addition, was compounded by feelings of dependency and preoccupation with functions that able-bodied individuals take for granted. Seymour deals with these issues at various points of her work. First, how does one rebuild a self-image, given that one can no longer perform the sport in which one previously participated and earned a living?

> Rebuilding the embodied self after such disruptions is an extremely difficult task. A person's self-image has been developed over a lifetime in relation to particular social ideas in terms of a body with certain skills, abilities and appearances. To confront, and to gradually let go of, those aspects of self-identity that now can never be consummated is the most difficult task of rehabilitation.[57]

From being an individual who had excelled in various sports, Gabe now was greatly dependent on Kim and others for a variety of chores. Although he eventually had the use of his arms, he would be limited in how he could interact with his spouse, his child, and others. He would be able to drive, but that would require the purchase of a van with specialized features, yet another financial burden. Seymour's research acknowledges the psychological impact that this would have had on Gabe and those with whom he interacted:

> Dependency is the antithesis of personhood. To be dependent on professional workers may be costly enough; to have to rely on friends, relatives, children and partners may dramatically alter the delicate structure upon which relationships are based. . . . Independence is highly valued, dependence is a costly state.[58]

> But it is the necessity for life-long preoccupation with bodily eliminations that many people in this study claim is the worst problem of all. Even those . . . whose bladder and bowel function are unimpaired must still deal with the difficulties with the lack of movement, sensation, or access . . . Whether such people are paid professional workers, friends, family or loved ones, the obligations engendered in this kind of intimate work may be enormous.[59]

While Seymour's work deals with issues of dependency and rehabilitation, an interesting dissertation by Maria Doelger Anderson provides insight into how the end of an athletic career (whether by retirement, release, or injury) can impact the psyche. Given that Gabe, and Juan as well, had worked a lifetime to hone athletic skills—and indeed, had achieved the pinnacle of anyone who plays football—how did the sudden end of Gabe's career, just as it was beginning, impact him? Doelger Anderson's work studies the end of such dreams and how former athletes come to grips with having to move on to the next part of their lives. Her purpose is "to identify and examine the characteristics and experiences that affect the creation of a new, acceptable self-concept by failed professional athletes."[60]

For some, the transition is smooth and leads quickly to another successful profession (think, for example, of Tony Romo and, as noted above, Darryl Stingley). For others, the abruptness of the "end" creates a downward spiral that often culminates in tragedy (think, for example, of the 2019 death of former Michigan State University and Detroit Lions player Charles Rogers).[61] Doelger Anderson's research stipulates that for former athletes, "most land somewhere in the middle" of this spectrum. That seems to have been the case with Gabe, although part of this scholar's work also noted that players such as Rivera, with a sudden career-ending injury, would "have the most difficulty moving on."[62]

Two points brought up in this project are worth noting as we cover the final three decades–plus of Gabe's life. First, Doelger Anderson discusses how the level of education of former players influences the outcomes of their postplaying days. She hypothesized that the impact of the level of educational attainment before the end of the career would be important. Indeed, all of her respondents noted that "regardless of the sport played, the level of educational attainment . . . there is overwhelming support among the interviewees that getting a solid education benefits life after sports."[63] As is apparent over the remainder of this chapter, Gabe mentioned on several occasions, and Norbert encouraged him, that finishing a degree was critical. The fact that he never did may be a reason why it took so long for Gabe to finally find a niche in his life away from football. When he did find his place in the community, it was highly beneficial and clearly made the last two decades of his life more fulfilling and productive.

A second important issue brought up in Doelger Anderson's work, and which ties in directly with the point noted above, is an examination of how a sudden end to a career impedes progress toward moving on to the next chapters of life. Gabe went from being a professional football player to a paraplegic in one brief moment as his Datsun crashed into the larger

LTD. Postaccident, he had no degree or clear occupational path. While the Steelers were gracious in allowing him to keep the salary for the rest of his rookie season, the team did not bring Gabe on as a scout permanently, as the Patriots did with Stingley (although Gabe did do scout work via game films for some time). There are three possible reasons for this: first, Stingley was already established with his team at the time of his injury (which happened as he was going into his fifth year in the NFL). Second, he was injured on the field, while plying his trade for the Patriots; this was certainly not the case with Gabe. Finally, it may have been that Gabe did not want to work for the Steelers, as he focused on possible treatments that, he hoped, might make it possible for him to walk again.

This crucial circumstance only increased concerns about his and the family's financial future, making the transition away from football all the more complicated and lengthier. As Doelger Anderson argues, "Those athletes whose careers ended with little warning, and thus had little time to prepare for life after sports, had difficulty in abandoning their sports identity and creating a new one." This makes it challenging for the individual to move on from spending time thinking about their "nostalgic self." As one of the subjects in her project stated, "It took me a while to be satisfied with my new identity as it took me a while to get comfortable with my life." Being able to move on to something else would have great benefit in the long run as these athletes could "work for success and recognition in a new field, and then are able to look back happily on their athletic careers with pride." Of course, there is no set time frame for such a metamorphosis. A good way to summarize Doelger Anderson's research, and how it applies to Gabe, can be found at the end of her dissertation, when she states, "Those who were able to move on to activities—careers, volunteer or charity work, or family life—that afforded them the opportunity to feel that they mattered seemed to be among those who made the transition to a new identity most effectively."[64]

A final instrument of professional research with which to contextualize Gabe's postaccident life comes from Derek Michael Zike's thesis, "Athletes' Experiences of Leaving Sport Due to Spinal Cord Injury: A Multiple Case Study Examination," which he completed at Miami University in 2016. Additionally, Mr. Zike was gracious enough to complete an interview with me on his research and experiences as a former athlete who suffered an SCI. One of the most important topics we discussed was the matter of coming to terms with the result of the injury and hope (no matter how fleeting) that somehow there is a possibility to walk again, something that Gabe experienced during a trip to China (discussed below). "At first, you hold on to hope that you will recover, but after a certain time you know you have to deal with daily functioning."[65] Much of Derek's experiences and research supports the points brought up in previous portions of this chapter. Coming to deal with the lack of independence in many aspects of life is difficult, but it is imperative that one learn to rely on others for what needs to be done. Zike took it upon himself to work diligently to be able to graduate with his high school class (his accident took place when he was 16) and achieved that goal. He then pursued and earned undergraduate and graduate degrees. He is currently working on his doctorate at the University of Wisconsin–Milwaukee.[66] Therefore, this ties in with the "reconceptualization" process to which both Seymour and Doelger Anderson allude.

Zike's work cites a 1994 study by Taylor and Ogilvie that presents a framework these authors called the Conceptual Model of Adaptation to Retirement among Athletes. This instrument concerned competitors whose careers had come to an end. It mentions five phases or characteristics of this process: (1) reasons for termination; (2) adaptation to career transition (self-identity and perceptions of control); (3) available resources, such as coping strategies, social support, and preretirement planning; (4) the quality of the transition; and (5) intervention strategies to help the athlete with the transition.[67]

The success, or lack thereof, with these numerous variables would have a significant impact upon how well the athlete (in the case of Zike's subjects, one who had suffered an SCI) would handle posttrauma life.

As we have seen, there were crucial issues for Gabe with many of these stages. First, the reason for termination was sudden and traumatic. Second, his self-identity was completely wrapped up in being a football player. While he also saw himself as a husband and soon-to-be father, how would he support his family, as his notoriety and social status all were tied to being a member of the Pittsburgh Steelers? As Zike argues in his thesis, "A single-minded pursuit of excellence that is rooted in an athlete's earliest experiences may lead to personal investment that restricts development in other areas of life." As noted in the discussion of Maria Antonia's diary, this may have been part of what the psychologist was referring to when he brought up the question of what Gabe would do beyond football.[68]

Third, there was no time for preretirement planning. A good portion of the signing bonus was gone in the purchase of the Riveras' domicile in Pennsylvania as well as the Datsun 280ZX involved in the accident (and a car that Gabe bought for Juan). Further, Kim indicated that, given the limited financial understanding on both of their parts, the couple might have overpaid for their house in Pittsburgh, as well as signed off on investments that they did not fully understand.[69] Fourth, the quality of the transition was, as can be seen from Maria Antonia's diary, anything but lacking in stress. How would Gabe provide for his newborn child? What would happen to his relationships with Kim and Tim? The tension between his mother and wife must have also been evident to him. Finally, what type of postretirement mediation would there be? This final stage of the process would end up being highly problematic, as it featured not one, but two divorces, the death of Juan and Maria Antonia, as well as an inability to be as involved in Tim's life as Gabe would have wanted.

Zike concluded his work with ten findings drawn from his subject interviews, all of which applied to Gabe's transition and later life. The first two dealt with the passage of time and the need to regain some measure of independence. It took many years for Gabe to find himself and be productive off the football field; the fact that he ultimately succeeded in this endeavor was a sign of his personal strength and motivation, which he certainly learned on the field of athletic competition. In regard to independence, the Steelers purchased a van for him to be able to move about and get to his physical therapy appointments. They continued to do this throughout the rest of his life.[70] He also had to confront the need for independence once Maria Antonia passed away in 1997 (Juan had died in 1990, shortly after his retirement from the SAISD).

Findings three and four—the shared experience and guidance of those in the adaptive community and using what was learned in competitive sport as an aspect of rehabilitation— were also present in Gabe's life. As noted earlier, he was already working with and encouraging other patients at Harmarville; he would continue this pattern and would do the same type of work with inner-city children. Gabe would also be forced to turn to some of what he disliked as a player—weightlifting, in order to maintain strength in his arms. While this may not have been a favorite pastime while he played for the Red Raiders or Steelers, the habit of having to complete certain tasks in order to improve performance was certainly part of his football playing (and now rehabilitation process), no matter how unpleasant he may have considered the task.

Findings five through seven proved more problematic, as the rest of this chapter shows. Number five was the availability of counseling services, which Gabe apparently did not pursue. Instead, as Norbert mentioned in our interviews, his brother sought help by interacting with some questionable friends and continuing to smoke pot, both of which led to negative consequences. Kim confirmed this matter. She added that Gabe also drank a great deal in addition to his use of marijuana.[71] Finding six concerned the satisfaction of achieving career milestones as part of the transition process. Again, there were major stumbling blocks here. As mentioned above, Gabe did not work again, nor did he finish his degree. There were several educational starts over the years, but they did not lead to accomplishing the ultimate task. Finding seven dealt with focusing on limited goals as part of the transition. One of Zike's interviewees decided not to take time off from school, using the need to study and keep his grades up as motivation and for focus, for example. This did not happen with Gabe. In some of his interviews with newspaper reporters, we hear that he changed career and academic goals over the years but did not follow through.

Findings eight through 10 were the value of involvement in adaptive sport; relationships with friends (former teammates and persons connected to football at the high school, collegiate, and professional levels); and the importance of the concerns expressed, and assistance provided, by others. Gabe used his wheelchair as a training vehicle. He participated in activities to keep himself in shape and often brought Tim along with him for rides. Thus, he was able to maintain a modicum of fitness and also interact with his son. With the passage of time, Gabe's accomplishments on the football field came to be recognized by the school district in his hometown, his university, and eventually the College Football Hall of Fame. These honors, as well as his induction into the College Football Hall of Fame, are discussed in chapter 8.[72]

As the one-year anniversary of his accident approached, Gabe was once again in the news as Dan Donovan visited and described his current circumstances. It was a mixed bag. His spine was stable, and while he was fairly strong due to an irregular schedule of working out and pushing his wheelchair, just as during his years at Texas Tech, the issue of his weight came up. Dr. Brenes from Harmarville indicated that Gabe was at around 200 pounds but should have been down to around 180. "I tell my patients that they don't have to eat every day, just every other day. He still needs to think in terms of activity. He sees daily activity in terms of pushing his wheelchair and thinks that's enough. He has to organize his life during the day—15, 20, 30 minutes he has to spend exercising. He could become a lot stronger." Still, Dr. Brenes noted that he felt Gabe was doing well psychologically. "If you look at his eyes now, they are different. You can see that behind them there is something different, that he has more meaning than before. His eyes are happier, looking more to the future." Rivera did do some scouting for the Steelers, via analyzing game films, which helped keep him connected to the game he loved. Brenes argued,

> He's beginning to see his value and discover he is valuable to other people. He's seeing that he can share his ability with others and there are challenges he can take on. He recognizes he is important to other people and that he's doing an important job (for the Steelers). He's beginning to look at himself as a man, as a person who has a function, an active role in society.[73]

Gabe noted how difficult the transition had been, and how he was still unsure of what to do moving forward. "It's kind of hard right now to know what to do. When you are a teen-ager, you figure out what you are going to do with your life. You make some choices. Now I have to redo it again, there's a lot of things going through my mind." He spoke about finishing his degree and possibly following his father into coaching—though he recognized that profession would be difficult, particularly given how much he missed being on the field. Among the other things occupying his time was looking forward to seeing Tim walk, as well as dealing with a house full of pets, including three dogs, two cats, and house-sitting a friend's black Lab. He did also begin to see himself as, like Stingley, a wheelchair-bound individual who could help others by sharing his experiences with others in similar circumstances. "Because of his high profile, he said he thinks he can be a good example for people who suffer tragedy. 'I think other people can come back and see what I went through. I guess I can be a role model or something.'"[74] Shortly after this interview, Gabe and Kim returned to Lubbock and were treated to press-box seating to watch Tech take on Texas. Unfortunately, though inspired by it being Gabe Rivera Day at Jones Stadium, the homestanding Red Raiders fought hard but fell to the Longhorns, 13–10.[75]

Two months later, Phil Musick visited with Gabe and covered many of the same topics, but the subject of his article sounded quite upbeat during this particular interview. Indeed, the title of the article mentioned that Rivera was "seeing the sun again," and the conversation took place in the Steelers' offices. "I'm getting better daily. I'm getting to where there aren't those mornings when I'd think, 'God, another day!'" Again, Gabe discusses what he will do with his life, particularly his determination to finish a degree. "Just to see if I can do it." He talks about being able to drive a car, becoming more adroit at moving from his chair to the floor and other surfaces. Jokingly, given his penchant for visiting malls, Gabe did acknowledge that he has become a bit of a nuisance to clerks by knocking down clothes racks. "I've knocked down a few." His main concern, however, is to be able to get a job. "What do I want to do? There are a lot of possibilities. I don't know yet. I do know I've got a wife and a son and that I need a paycheck." Still, now 14 months beyond October 20, 1983, he continued to ponder what might have been. "I think about how good of a player I might've been. Who knows? I could've been a flop. But we will never know, will we?"[76]

By the time the 1985 NFL draft came around, as the Steelers began the process of rebuilding their defensive line again, Gabe's name and accident took center stage. The Rooneys, as usual, were gracious, but acknowledged that the team had to draft to replace the giant hole left by his departure. "I know

Gabe had a bit of a weight problem . . . but he would have been a top player for at least five years." Part of what the team did in order to work around the issue was to switch from the traditional 4–3 defense to a 3–4, emphasizing the play of linebackers to generate the pass rush. This worked to an extent, as the number of sacks recorded by the second level of the Steelers' defense increased from 11 in 1983 to 23.5 in 1984. The linemen's contributions in this area decreased substantially, however, down to 19.5 from 36. Chuck Noll, as usual, noted that he did the best he could with the players on hand. "I don't care where the pass rush comes from, just so we get one." Part of the lack of heat on opposing quarterbacks was evident in the American Football Conference (AFC) championship game that year, as a ghost from Pittsburgh's past, Dan Marino, sat comfortably in the Dolphins' pocket and shredded the Steelers for 421 yards in a 45–28 victory that sent Miami on to the Super Bowl. Thus, Art Rooney Jr. was open to the notion that it was necessary to seek a direct replacement for Gabe. "But if a Gabe is still available when we pick, I think you'll see us take him. Those big, strong, fast guys are hard to find."[77]

While the Steelers moved on, as any franchise would have to when a player dies, retires, or is let go, Gabe continued to hold on to the hope that he would walk again. Shortly after the NFL draft, Gabe and Kim made two fateful decisions: the first was to leave Pennsylvania and return to Texas, particularly to the Fort Worth area in order to be closer to the Covingtons. Second, by the fall of 1985 Gabe, having spoken with a friend who put him in touch with an acupuncturist from Santa Monica, California, decided to seek treatment for his paralysis at a hospital in Kuangchou, China. He traveled to the facility in November 1985.

Jim and Karan Covington spoke extensively about the context concerning Gabe's trip to China. When Gabe asked his father-in-law to assist with finances, Jim began working with some brokers in California, presumably at Doc Daniels's recommendation. Jim declared during our conversation that these advisers invested Gabe and Kim's money in some risky instruments, including options and complicated tax shelters. In short order, the account was, in his words, "drained." Additionally, one of these brokers mentioned that it might be advisable to consult with an acupuncturist in Santa Monica who provided some treatments that could help Gabe recover at least some mobility. Jim was not initially sold on this course of action, but after consulting a few other medical professionals, he brought the proposal to Gabe. Jim went so far as to work with Rivera's insurance provider to get the company to pay for his travel to China as well as his medical treatments and interpreter there. The insurer, however, did not pay for Kim and Tim to visit with Gabe overseas; Kim footed that particular bill. Lastly, there was a need for Gabe to have a specially built bicycle as part of his treatment. Given his size and condition, this item was custom made using the frame of a Schwinn Airdyne Exercycle. A friend of Jim's worked on the frame, but the Covingtons absorbed the cost of sending the machine to China. After Gabe's return to the United States, that item was left behind in China.[78]

The regimen at this facility was grueling physically and emotionally, and very taxing financially. In a May 1986 article in the *Express-News* Gabe described what his days were like while in China:

> "I have 12 days of acupuncture and then three days rest," he said. "Don't ask me what Chinese herbal medicine is because I don't know. All the treatments keep me pretty busy." When Rivera isn't undergoing treatment, he usually stays in his room on the third floor of the hospital and reads or watches television. "I have had a lot of time to think. China isn't too accessible for wheelchairs. . . . The people here are very friendly. They make you feel at home. I have an interpreter and there are other people who speak English." Rivera said he wonders what might have been if there never had been an

accident. "What would life be like," he said. "Where would I have gone? What would I have accomplished?"[79]

By the start of 1986, reports in the *Light* indicated some progress, but it was limited. Kim was quoted as saying, "The doctors are very excited about the way his nerves have reacted to treatments, and Gabe is excited, too. . . . He wants this very badly, he's never lost confidence. But he understands that it might not lead to him walking. The treatments are more successful on people with lower back injuries. We're praying that it's his turn to get better." Unfortunately, given the scar tissue that had developed over the damaged part of the spine, Gabe was only able to get to a point where he could lift himself up to a vertical position. Certainly progress, but not what he and Kim had hoped for.[80]

Gabe returned to Fort Worth, after not seeing his son and wife for months, in August 1986—still unable to walk but, as far as he was concerned, better off. "It helped. My body seems . . . different. It functions better than it did before. Really, I just went over there to try to see what chance and stuff I had." Whatever benefits Gabe gained from this extended treatment needed to be counterbalanced by the costs, the separation from his wife and child, and the apparently minimal results. As Kim noted, "It's been hard on the pocketbook, especially the phone bills." Fortunately, Gabe's insurance company ultimately agreed to pay for the medical expenses overseas above and beyond the policy limits. Still, as a result of the sojourn, Gabe and Kim were stretched very thin financially. One option was to trade in the van purchased in Pittsburgh for a smaller car. Given all of the stress concerning these matters, Kim recalled that Gabe continued to drink and smoke pot.

The young pair now also had a mortgage on their house and the only extra income was from Kim's part-time job with her father's firm. In an article in the *Post-Gazette* shortly after Gabe's return to Texas, Ed Bouchette detailed the family's current financial situation and Gabe's desire for a job. More importantly, this article addresses some of the psychological issues that Gabe was enduring. The Steelers, Bouchette noted, "offered Rivera some kind of a scouting position," but Gabe did not accept it. Why he did not isn't clear, but it may have been due to his suffering from depression. The article discusses that Gabe was experiencing a period of "low motivation," an issue that had come up earlier in life. "I don't know, maybe I've had motivation problems most of my life. Maybe if I could fight the motivation problem, it could be easier." Part of the unhappiness could also be tied to the fact that Gabe had not been able to spend extended time with Tim. "He's almost three years old. . . . First, there was the rehabilitation at Harmarville. Then the past nine months. I've only been with him 15 months."[81]

Before turning to my interview with Tim Rivera, we need to briefly examine the end of Gabe's marriage—and his return to San Antonio to live with Juan and Maria Antonia. The trip to China not only failed to fundamentally transform Rivera's physical circumstances, it—plus the costs and the long separation from Kim and Tim—was the final impetus that brought about the couple's divorce. In a *Houston Chronicle* article in December 1987, reporter Erin Powers interviewed Gabe and detailed his circumstances four years after his accident. The piece, titled "What Could Have Been . . . ," presented readers with detailed information concerning Gabe's personal struggles, specifically an overview of his depressive state. One of the key statements in this article regards Gabe questioning whether surviving his accident was actually a positive outcome. "Whether Rivera was lucky to be alive was debatable. He has wondered in his mind on the base days. 'A lot of days I've had the hardest time finding something good in all of this,' he says."

By this time, Tim was four years old and living with Kim in Fort Worth as the couple had divorced shortly after Gabe's return to the United States from his sojourn to Kuangchou. "The trauma of the accident, raising Timothy in what Gabe called the 'diaper years,' and the frustration of her husband's paralysis—physical and otherwise—apparently proved too much for her." Gabe's response to Powers's question in this regard is very revealing, as he acknowledges his failings in the marriage and the postaccident relationship. "She figured she could do better than being around me. In a way, I understand. When things go so bad, she put a lot in—you know, mental kind of things—and didn't get anything back. She was like everyone else. It was easy to get sick of it. Everything anyone suggested went in one ear and out the other. . . . I couldn't pick myself up much at all. Nothing looked too good. It was bad."

In the interview with Kim, she noted that the continued use of pot, the drinking, and yes, the depression all contributed to the end of their relationship. One final element to the separation mentioned by both Kim and her parents was the result of some of the investments made while Gabe was with the Steelers. The Covingtons indicated that, having filed joint returns during their marriage, Kim wound up being billed for a substantial amount of money by the IRS a few years after the divorce. A final, and important, point that Kim made to this author concerned Maria Antonia. Although they did have their run-ins, she never felt animus toward her mother-in-law. Kim resented some of her actions, such as baptizing Tim and moving a bed into Gabe's hospital room. Still, she understood that Maria Antonia was acting as many mothers would, given such traumatic circumstances. As proof of her feelings, Kim indicated that she attended the funerals of Juan in 1990 and Maria Antonia in 1997.[82]

Gabe eventually asked Norbert and Adrian to bring him back to San Antonio after daily life with Kim reached its nadir. In addition to the financial and personal stress between the couple, Norbert believed, was the fact that Gabe was constantly asked about "what might have been." The reminder of his lost career caused him to brood constantly and to become detached from his wife. Eventually, Gabe returned to Juan and Maria Antonia's house. A retrofitting of their domicile ultimately made it possible for Gabe to manage his personal needs and training regimen (with the couple's garage becoming his weight room). This arrangement, though positive to a certain extent, led to three major problems. First, Maria Antonia wanted to "do everything for him," but Gabe sought to be as independent as possible—certainly understandable actions and beliefs by both parties. Second, according to Norbert, Juan never did accept his son's situation, which led him to drink even more than usual, as well as made him more detached from the reality of the situation before him. Last, in hopes of forgetting and dealing with his circumstances, Gabe continued to smoke pot and drink—and Adrian participated in this practice as well. This behavior eventually led to encounters with the police. Norbert also indicated that while he did visit his brother often, he limited how often he brought his own children over, given the odor of marijuana present in the Rivera house.[83]

As the five-year anniversary of the car accident approached, Jim Lefko from the *Light* once again visited with Gabe. Both the reporter and the interviewee sounded a bit more upbeat than they had back in 1984. Lefko, perhaps not wanting to scratch too much under the surface, argued that Gabe had, indeed, turned the corner. "During an interview in June of 1984 . . . Rivera was withdrawn, subdued, introverted. He answered questions politely, but with little enthusiasm." Now, the reported indicated, "he is a new person. The gleam is back in his eye. And his spirit in strong again." Part of the reason for this change was that Gabe was working out consistently, as well as working on his relationship with Tim. In regard to his physical training, the former Red Raider was spending time outside of Alamo Stadium "using the sloping parking lot . . . as his personal training ground." While he had previously done only eight trips up the pavement, Gabe indicated that he was now doing twenty per day. "The reason I'm doing this, is I'm thinking about marathons and maybe a 10K. . . . It's been a while since I've had the win/loss thing."

Once again, Gabe indicated that he was taking classes and wanted to return to work. "Rivera is working on his mind too. He is taking nine hours of classes at San Antonio College and hopes eventually to earn his degree at one of the four-year institutions in the city." Gabe even looked back on his trip to China more positively than he previously had. "I did a lot of soul searching over there. And now, I think I am different than I was before. I'm not as depressed any more. Now I feel fresh." Even Juan chimed in with some positive statements, noting that his son "is making it on his own. He's doing all right. He's getting along fine." Of course, as noted previously, this was still a period where Gabe was struggling. Norbert's assessment of the situation was that Gabe was "lost" before he began his work with children with the Inner City Development organization in 1999 and was never truly interested in completing his degree.[84]

As the 1980s drew to a close, Gabe was granted some significant recognition for his athletic accomplishments. First, in December 1989 he was named to the All-Decade Team for the Southwest Conference. This was noteworthy, as the defensive squad featured some legendary performers; among them were Billy Ray Smith and Steve Atwater of Arkansas, Mike Singletary of Baylor, Ray Childress of Texas A&M, and Kenneth Sims of Texas.[85] In early 1990 Gabe was honored by the Latin American Sports Hall of Fame (LASHF) in Laredo. Here he noted the importance of being recognized by fellow Latinos. "The award is special coming from fellow Mexican American people." Two stories on this honor appeared in the *Express-News*, and one key detail evident again was Rivera's noting his desire to finish school and go back to work. "One of my main goals is to attend school and be able to get a job. I'd like to be able to do a lot more things. I feel confident that through my rehabilitation I will be able to."[86] In 1993 he was inducted into the Hall of Honor at Texas Tech.[87] A final accolade during the 1990s came with his induction into the Hispanic Sports Hall of Fame in 1999.

The goal of that organization was to serve as an inspiration to Spanish-surnamed youths so that they could identify with Latinos who were successful on and off the field. In 2006 this organization was renamed the Hispanic Sports Foundation for Education and it continues to operate as of 2020.[88]

Unfortunately, in the same year that he garnered two of these important awards, Gabe endured a pair of difficult situations: he was arrested on charges of possessing marijuana, and Juan died unexpectedly shortly after he retired from Edison High School. The arrest occurred soon after Gabe's induction into the LASHF. He was a passenger in a van that police pulled over as a result of alleged traffic violations. When officers peered into the vehicle, they detected the odor of the illegal substance, and Rivera was arrested along with three other men. Norbert's recollection of this event is that Gabe became quite hostile with police and was eventually taken to the city jail. He was charged with misdemeanor possession. As she usually did, Maria Antonia called upon Norbert to assist his brother. When he arrived at the station, Norbert chastised Gabe for getting into trouble and threatened him with not bailing him out of jail, which, of course, he ultimately did. The second traumatic event, Juan's death, Gabe handled in what was his typical manner: he kept all of his emotions bottled up, though Norbert indicated that, deep down, he was heartbroken about his father's passing.[89]

Although Gabe struggled to find his way during these years, he worked diligently to develop a relationship with his son. Given that, as he noted in the article after his return from China in 1986, he had been away for a substantial part of his first three years of life, Gabe wanted desperately to be there for his offspring. His medical realities limited what he could do in this regard, of course. After the divorce, Kim was, according to all sources, cooperative in making it possible for father and son to get together on a regular basis. After the split, Tim went to live with his mom and maternal grandparents. Kim eventually remarried, and the younger Rivera has a half-sister from that union. The interview with Tim revealed mixed recollections about his relationship with "Gabe" (which is how he always referred to his father).[90] Gabe would often travel to Fort Worth in his van to visit, and eventually he and Kim decided to meet in Salado so that father and son could then drive back to San Antonio together. As a child, Tim would play with some of Gabe's Steelers paraphernalia, and the two would also attend games of the Spurs and Missions (a Minor League Baseball team). Still, Tim stated that "he was not able to be there for me" and "could not do the 'dad thing' with me." One point that Tim did specify in his interview was that Gabe's van "always smelled of pot." One of the most gut-wrenching issues for Gabe in his relationship with Tim was trying to teach him about football. As Juan did with his sons, the veteran of the gridiron showed his offspring the "how to" of playing the sport. For Gabe, his injury made it so that all he could do was describe for Tim the techniques of how to tackle and so forth.

Tim indicated that he was not very close to Juan ("I can count on one hand how many times I saw him"), but he had positive recollections of his ties to Maria Antonia. The language barrier that existed between grandmother and grandson created some problems, however. "She cared for me and was trying to learn some English near the time of her passing [in 1997]." Overall, Tim summarized his time with her, as well as with Norbert's children, as providing him with "good memories."

By the early 1990s Gabe had married again, to a lady named Carmela. She had previously served as a member of his physical therapy team in San Antonio. I reached out to her to get input on her life during this marriage, but she decided not to participate in the project. Tim, however, did provide some background about this relationship. Carmela had two children, and he recalled that their relationship was "good." When this second spouse moved with her offspring into Maria Antonia's house, they, Tim recalled, often "butted heads." She eventually

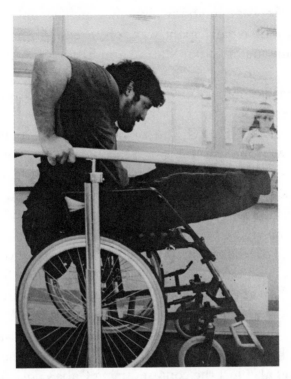

Gabe exercising at a San Antonio facility for individuals with spinal cord injuries in 1990 (Southwest Collection, TTU University Archives)

moved out, and the couple divorced at approximately the time when Maria Antonia passed away.[91]

By the time the 10-year anniversary of his accident arrived, Gabe had settled into a routine of working out at the Rehabilitation Institute of San Antonio. In the spring of 1990 this facility published an article on electrical stimulation for patients with SCIs that described some of the treatments Gabe received. By 1993 he was still attending and was part of a workout group known as the "Four O'Clock Club," made up of members with different types of disabilities. An article in the *Express-News* made the club's sessions sound similar to the banter Gabe would have heard in the Steelers' locker room a decade earlier. It seemed that he had found some valuable camaraderie with the other patients. "'Guys in a chair normally speak a lot of trash to each other,' said Chris Huizar. . . . 'Gabe is no different than anybody else when he's around us. He's a talker.'" Another participant went on to explain the value of having someone of Gabe's stature and history as part of their assembly. "He inspires a lot of us in our daily lives. Knowing what he has come back from pushes some of the other guys around here."

The article by Tim Griffin then shifted to provide some sense of how Gabe was doing. It indicated that, by helping others, he was now in a better place psychologically. "You sometimes think about what would have happened if you did things differently, but I try not to dwell on them. Life goes on." He then noted that he would be traveling to Lubbock for his induction into the Hall of Honor during a Red Raiders' contest versus the North Carolina State University Wolfpack. "That will be exciting. More than anything else, it will be great to hear the roar of the crowd once again. That always was a big rush." That season, under the leadership of Spike Dykes, Tech finished 6–6, losing to Oklahoma in the Sun Bowl, 41–10. Unfortunately, the Red Raiders also lost the contest during Gabe's enshrinement, 36–34.

Two final topics of note in this article centered, not surprisingly, on finances and education. Griffin indicated that the majority of Rivera's funds from his rookie salary and bonus were long gone and that he "lives on an insurance payment and a small stipend from the NFL Players Association." Lastly, the story indicated that Gabe was taking classes, now at UT–San Antonio, and that he was "about 30 hours from receiving his degree." His ultimate goal was "to become a nutrition specialist or a strength coach."[92]

The interlude between his accident and the start of Gabe's work at Inner City Development in May 1999 was certainly very difficult. The adjustments required to accept his paraplegia, endure two divorces and the deaths of his parents, and deal with his failure to complete a degree and find work all impacted Rivera's self-esteem. As his brother Norbert indicated in one of our interviews, "he was lost" throughout many of these 16 years. During these trying times, however, Gabe continued to do the best that he could to develop and sustain his relationship with Tim. Also, he eventually came to be more accepting of his fate. He had made so much progress that he reached the point where he could even joke about and enjoy watching his Steelers play the hated Cowboys in Super Bowl XXX in 1996. If he had continued to play, this would have been his 13th year in the NFL. "The Steelers will win it by four. . . . We'll probably have a little get-together. But if the Cowboys start winning big, I'm going to run everybody off and tell them all the food's gone." Unfortunately, that contest did not turn out as Gabe had hoped, with Dallas emerging victorious by a score of 27–17. When asked if he still continued to think about what might have been, he was contemplative. "I have good days and still have bad days. The only difference is I don't have bad days as often as I used to. . . . I'm beyond that now. At first, I blamed God, but not anymore."[93]

It seemed Gabe was finally ready to try something new, and in May 1999 the opportunity presented itself. His love for and ease in working with children had been evident since his college career at Texas Tech. One day he saw an ad in the paper about volunteer opportunities with Inner City Development to work with children in their summer recreational program. Encouraged by his fiancée, Nancy Morris, he answered the ad, and it helped to make the last two decades of Gabe's life more meaningful than he could have ever imagined.

CHAPTER 8

"AND WHAT DID IT COST YOU?"

GABE RIVERA'S FINAL YEARS, 1999–2018

AFTER HAVING LIVED AS A paraplegic for around 15 years, Gabe Rivera had settled into a life that featured both positive and negative facets.[1] On the constructive side of the ledger, he continued with a fairly rigorous schedule of exercise, a regimen that made it possible for him to regain at least some use of his right arm (his left arm had suffered no permanent damage in the accident). Additionally, with Kim's cooperation, he spent as much time as possible with Tim. Unfortunately, there were deleterious aspects to his routine as well. In addition to never finishing his degree, as noted previously, Gabe's second divorce took place at approximately the same time that Maria Antonia passed away in 1997. Gabe also continued to smoke pot on a regular basis. He was joined in this preference by his younger brother, Adrian, whose drug use eventually led to his serving a brief period of jail time for possession in 2004. Adrian passed away in 2016 from the last in a series of strokes.[2]

In 1999, however, Gabe found love again, and the initial meeting took place at a most unusual locale: the San Antonio

Zoo. Here, during an outing, Gabe met his third wife after he "accidentally" ran "over my foot with his wheelchair," Nancy Morris recalled. At the time they met, she was the mother of two daughters, Rae (age 15) and Myste (13). The two had an instant connection, and Gabe would eventually adopt Rae and embrace her as his own child; Myste decided not to pursue that option, hoping instead to reconnect with her biological father. By later that year, the couple was engaged, and in May Gabe spotted the newspaper advertisement from Inner City Development that would transform and add great meaning to the final years of his life.

In part, Nancy was responsible for getting Gabe interested in pursuing such work. During our interview in January 2020 she noted that, as the couple got to know each other, she expressed surprise that Gabe did not work or volunteer. "Why do you not look into ways to give back to your community?" Gabe told her that his days were full of a workout regimen designed to stay in the best shape possible, given his circumstances, but Nancy found it odd that he did not challenge himself in other ways. Hence, they made the decision to look into something along the lines of working with Inner City Development. The couple married on November 20, 1999.[3]

Inner City Development (previously called Inner City Apostolate) is an all-volunteer, self-help organization headed by Rod and Patti Radle since 1969. It was previously directed by Father Ralph Ruiz and several other priests and was initially affiliated with the Catholic Archdiocese of San Antonio, starting in 1966. The mission was to assist families living in the city's near West Side, an area about two miles from City Hall, which includes the Alazan-Apache Courts, one of the nation's first public housing projects, built between 1939 and 1942.[4] The organization's center is located near what has always been a predominantly Mexican American high school: Sidney Lanier High (home of the Voks).[5] In the late 1960s the originators established an emergency food pantry, a recreation program for youths (Gabe volunteered to help with this effort for the first time over the summer of 1999), and a mechanism to raise funds to help families in the neighborhood with outlays such as rent, medicine, and funeral expenses. Most importantly, from its inception, the goal of the program was "to develop community leadership to discuss the needs of the neighborhood and to discover what needed to be done to assist their community."[6]

Since Rod and Patti's installment as codirectors, the entity has not been directly affiliated with the Catholic Church, and is, as they describe it, a true grassroots organization with a multitude of endeavors helping people in what is still one of the poorest inner cities in the country. As of the late 2010s, the district served contains schools where 93 percent of the student body is on free or reduced-price lunch, the average family's income is less than $11,000 per year, only about one-third of adults have a high school diploma, nearly 80 percent of households are headed by a single parent, and the teen pregnancy rate is three times the national rate. Over the life of the organization, more than 22,000 children have participated in the recreation and sports programs.

One of the most successful parts of the group's athletic component has been a progressive basketball camp: starting with a developmental effort ("To teach the kids how to dribble," as Rod indicated) all the way up to a competitive program that allows many youths to eventually feed into the Voks' teams. The San Antonio Spurs recently worked with Inner City by donating $25,000 to help renovate the facility's courts. The summer docket also includes trips to the zoo and museums, and fun activities such as roller skating. In other words, the goal is to introduce children to opportunities and interests that they, most likely, have no access to in their neighborhood.[7]

When Gabe first approached Inner City, Patti did not recognize his name. She immediately knew that he was in a wheelchair, as Rivera asked about handicap accessibility to the organization's building. While Gabe was down in weight

Cover of a program put together by staff and children at Inner City
(Southwest Collection, TTU University Archives)

substantially from his playing (and 13-Big-Macs-in-one-sitting) days, Patti was still awed by his size during their first meeting at the initiation and training session for volunteers. Rod, on the other hand, recognized the new recruit immediately and informed his wife about the identity and story of the "big man in the wheelchair." Once Gabe's decision to volunteer was made, Nancy also helped out at Inner City, primarily working with the children in the kitchen, teaching them how to make simple meals that they could whip up for their sustenance in case no one else was home right after school. Nancy also became well known, and highly appreciated, by attendees for a treat she called her "cowboy cookies." These goodies were based on a recipe that Laura Bush often used during her time living in the Texas governor's mansion. Gabe, and also often Nancy, Patti recalled, were among the first people at the facility as the doors opened at 10:30 a.m. over the summer of 1999.

Within a short time, the Radles asserted, Gabe's wheelchair became "invisible" to the kids. They did not know about his storied past at Jefferson or Tech, or with the Steelers. He simply became their friend "Gabriel," who initially helped teach them basketball and other athletic skills, and later assisted with homework assignments. Soon, some of the children became interested in hearing the details of the accident that had happened in that strange, faraway place called Pennsylvania so many years before their birth. Patti noted that one particular interrogator wanted Gabe to use toys to demonstrate the details of the incident. The child was also curious as to the extent of the damage done to the other vehicle involved. When Gabe estimated that there must have been at least $1,000 worth of damage, the youngster innocently replied, "And what did it cost you?" Patti recalled that Gabe just looked at her, smiled, and shook his head.[8] Overall, Gabe's recollections of that summer were very pleasant, and he decided to continue working in a co-op home school that began in the fall.

During this time Edmond Ortiz of the *Express-News* caught up with the former Red Raider. "Rivera is a daily volunteer tutor. . . . He is one of nine tutors who spend 90 minutes teaching junior high school–aged children math and grammar skills. 'I've always wanted to help people, especially children, as much as I could. I think this program has helped me give back to the community.'" This program not only gave him a reason to get out of bed every day, it also was an opportunity for him to move beyond his regret and sadness, both for his physical situation and his not being able to do "dad things" with Tim. "I'm sorry I never had the chance to do normal things with my

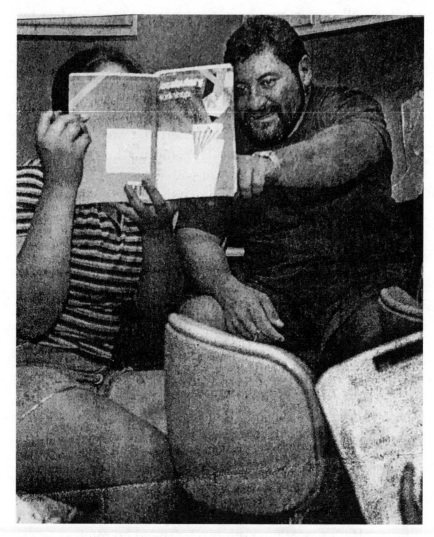

Gabe working with a group of students at Inner City in 1999 (Southwest Collection, TTU University Archives)

kid. He has never known me other than being in a wheelchair." Overall, Gabe benefited greatly from this volunteer endeavor, as "this has helped me deal with my situation to a point where it doesn't bother me as much as before."[9]

This relationship was not a one-way street, however, as the kids grew to love and value Gabe's engaging presence and his assistance with their work. In a wonderful tribute album from

May 2001, Inner City's administrators and children all provided the gentle giant with a keepsake of their appreciation. As Patti noted in an introduction, "Your commitment here has been so wonderful. I really feel God has blessed us greatly by your presence. You have touched the students' lives and hearts deeply. You are an inspiration to everyone around here." There can be little doubt that these wonderful words must have filled Gabe's heart with joy. His love for children, so evident even during his days at Texas Tech, now made it possible for him to assist and encourage youngsters facing difficult circumstances in a desperately poor neighborhood. It is not beyond the realm of possibility that this meant more to him than the cheering crowds at Jones Stadium so many years earlier. Even more wonderful than the kind words of the codirector are the letters some of the young attendees wrote to their wheelchair-bound friend. These heartfelt messages, from children with difficult circumstances at home, had to have made a very positive difference in Gabe's life.

The key theme of the letters was always the same: the kids thanking Rivera for helping them during the school year. Danny Hernandez, who was in junior high school, stated that his mentor had helped "me get through the year to get ready for Lanier. Thank you for helping me with Math and vocabulary." Angela Ybarra appreciated Gabe's attention during her recreation time. "Without you we wouldn't have P.E. and then we wouldn't be able to play soccer and baseball." Angela also welcomed the opportunity to share lunch with her mentor at a local McDonald's. For others, such as a young lady named Melanie, Gabe's presence permitted her to get some family and personal concerns off of her chest. "I want to thank you for everything you have done for me. You are a very important person in my life and I'm glad that I met you. I want to thank you for listening to my problems, bringing treats and letting us play at P.E." This individual also noted the importance of Nancy to Gabe's life. "I hope that you and Nancy stay together for a long time and that you are always happy." Another individual who wrote along these same lines was Joey Estrada, who noted in his letter that he appreciated "the little talks you gave me. . . . I like to tell you about my problems." Additionally, Joey was thankful that Gabe paid to take him to a Spurs game. He summarized his feelings by asking Gabe to "keep helping other people."

Veronica Barrientos very poignantly appreciated Gabe's attendance, recognizing the difficulties he faced in getting ready for the routine aspects of daily life. "I want to thank you for getting up in the morning and coming here every day just to teach us. . . . Thank you for pushing me to do things. I really learned things from you." Gabe even managed to pierce the tough outer shell that some of these kids developed in order to survive in this difficult environment. As Sarah Lucio Duncan noted, "I am sorry for give [sic] you a bad attitude, I just had bad days. So I am very sorry. But thank you very much for what ever [sic] you helped me on." Lastly, Sarah's sister Priscilla acknowledged the difficulties Gabe faced in getting to Inner City as well as appreciated his efforts to help improve her life. "I just want to thank you for all you done for us and thank you for coming all the way over here. I'm sorry for all the rude stuff I've done to you."[10]

While Gabe helped many children at Inner City between 1999 and his passing in 2018, he and Nancy formed a special bond with a particular young man named JR Cisneros. In an interview years later, he expressed his feelings about Gabe and how significant he was to JR's life. This was one of the youths whose letter was part of the "Thanks, Gabriel" document from May 2001:

> You mean a lot to me because you are a very good friend to me. Thanks for taking me to the Spurs game with you. Do you know what I like about you? What I like about you is how you teach me here to play sports. I hope that you will [illegible] your feet and start to walk, that's my hope for you. Thank [sic] for everything Gabe.[11]

I had the opportunity to interview JR in January 2020. Now in his early 30s, he recalled that he began attending Inner City around the age of eight or nine in 1996. His aunt was a volunteer at the facility, and she advised her sister to start sending Cisneros over with the goal of keeping him away from gangs and other negative aspects of life in the Alazan-Apache Courts by engaging him in both the sports and educational programs.

In 2005, JR's father passed away, and Gabe and Nancy became almost substitute parents. In fact, when we began our conversation, one of JR's first mentions about Rivera indicated that "he was my pops." He also referred to Nancy as being his "mom." This youth first attended Lanier, where he played football for the Voks, but eventually transferred over to Sandra Day O'Connor High School in nearby Helotes. While O'Connor was an opportunity to start over, he indicated that there were many difficulties acclimating to the new environment. Cisneros lived with the Riveras for a couple of years, until around 2008 or 2009. Gabe encouraged the young man to do better in school and to improve himself, but he did not finish his high school education. Still, there was much positive reinforcement, and the Riveras helped Cisneros get a job as a janitor at the Institute of Texas Cultures. The young man was also regularly welcomed in family events that took place at Norbert's house. Gabe and Nancy continued to mentor this young man, who eventually managed to find work as a general laborer with AT&T. He subsequently trained to become a tower technician and climber. JR credits all of the talks he had with Gabe over the time they shared a household with helping him focus and improve his life. JR is now a father as well, and he and his girlfriend are looking forward to purchasing a house of their own. In the years after he moved out, JR stayed in touch with his "foster parents" and recalled that the last time he saw Gabe was about one month before he passed. Not surprisingly, the two former football players spent time one Sunday watching sports and talking about life and what the future would hold.[12]

In addition to the joy of having Nancy, his family, her daughters, and eventually grandchildren in his life, the last few years of Gabe's life also saw him receive various awards and recognition of his football prowess—proof that even with the passage of time, his city, state, alma mater, and even the sport itself had not forgotten his superb career at Jefferson and Texas Tech. In late 2000, for example, the bible of the sport in the Lone Star State, *Dave Campbell's Texas Football*, recognized Rivera's play in its 40th anniversary commemorative edition as part of their "Super Team" of the 1970s. This article included some of Gabe's recollections of the difficulties of overcoming his injuries and its physical and psychological impacts. "It took me until 1988 just to get over the fact that it happened. . . . Now, I've learned to live with it and move on. I'm exercising, trying to maintain my health and still hoping to walk again. If the good Lord's willing, I will. But if not, I'll be fine."[13]

In the early 2000s, Gabe continued to visit Lubbock on a semiregular basis to keep up with his beloved Red Raiders. Indeed, I had the opportunity to briefly meet him and shake his hand in October 2000 when he came to Jones Stadium to see Tech play the then-number-one-ranked Nebraska Cornhuskers. There was much excitement on the South Plains leading into that contest, as the home team came in with a 5–1 mark, a potent offense, and (believe it or not) a stingy defense, allowing fewer than 10 points per contest up to that time. The locals smelled a possible upset. Unfortunately, the contest was not even close, as Big Red steamrolled Tech, 56–3.

After the game, I had a chance to speak again briefly with Gabe and inquired as to what Tech might have needed to compete against the juggernaut from Lincoln. He made some polite comments about having to recruit athletes with more speed and strength, and we left it at that, given how shellshocked we all were at the outcome. As I walked away, having just recently begun to write on the topic of the history of Latinos and their participation in American sports, the thought entered my mind that Gabe's story needed to be told. Here was a Mexican American who had brought great glory to his school. What obstacles did he face in getting here? What had his life been like since his accident? All of these were questions of great interest. Although I did not have the opportunity to share these thoughts or questions directly with him, and I turned to various other projects over the years, it is certainly satisfying to be able to finally complete this endeavor in honor of the great number 69's memory and legacy.[14]

In December 2001, Gabe had another opportunity to root for the red and black when he attended the Sylvania Alamo Bowl in San Antonio between Tech and Iowa. As he had done many times before, David Flores of the *Express-News* visited with the local legend and Gabe got to reminisce about his years in Lubbock. Once again, the story's subject sounded upbeat, but it is possible to detect the longing for what might have been. "Yea, I was big, and I could move for someone my size. But I played with passion. You can have mobility and athleticism, but if you don't have the passion, you can't play your best." (If only he had had the opportunity to display that passion and athleticism at Three Rivers for a longer period of time!) Unfortunately, the Red Raiders once again disappointed Gabe and their fans on this day, losing 19–16 to the Hawkeyes.[15]

Other honors followed. In 2004, Gabe was inducted into the San Antonio Sports Hall of Fame. A story on this honor mentioned his work with local kids and how Gabe continued to remind his charges that he paid dearly for making the mistake to drink and drive. "I hope that at least my accident serves as an example to the youths of the high cost of being irresponsible. I always tell them to give their best, to protect themselves, and to enjoy their lives."[16] The ultimate honor for a collegiate football player followed in 2012, as Gabe earned entry into the College Football Hall of Fame. In May of that year, Ron Cook of the *Post-Gazette* brought Steeler fans up to date with the life and times of the former number-one selection. It just so happened that when Cook called to discuss the honor, Señor Sack was in the middle of changing diapers. "Taking care of the young ones. Three grandkids." While Gabe appreciated the congratulations for the honor, he reminded folks in Pittsburgh that he could have been a great Steeler. "I know I had the skills, but only God knows how it would have turned out." Still, he was also realistic about his circumstances. While indicating that he was doing well financially, his health was a concern, primarily due to sores and infections. "'If I don't stay on top of things, I'm going to have big problems.' He said that doctors told him he probably will live 10 fewer years than usual because of his spinal cord injury." Still, Gabe remained as upbeat and philosophical as possible. "If not for the accident, I wouldn't have met the kids that I'm working with. Hopefully, they can learn something from me. I hope I can make a difference in their lives." A final honor along these lines came in 2016 when he was inducted into the San Antonio Independent School District Sports Hall of Fame.[17]

Texas Tech in 2014 granted Gabe the highest honor it can bestow upon a football player: induction into the Ring of Honor at Jones Stadium. The Ring's website describes the requirements for entry into this august company, in the words of Athletic Director Kirby Hocutt, who stated,

> The Ring of Honor will be a tremendous addition to the legacy and heritage of Red Raider Football. The careers of those that we will celebrate in this Ring of Honor brought national recognition to this university and left an incredible mark on our football program. Their names will become a permanent fixture inside Jones AT&T Stadium so that all who enter will be reminded of their outstanding contributions to Texas Tech University.[18]

The school established this distinction in 2012, with the initial class featuring Donny Anderson, E. J. Holub, and Dave Parks. Gabe was the sole member to garner this acclaim in 2014. He was followed by another Tech (and Miami Dolphins) legend, Zach Thomas in 2016.[19]

In the 2000s and 2010s, Gabe found himself in yet another unanticipated role: that of a sage offering advice and support to athletes who had suffered serious spinal cord injuries. In many ways, he mirrored the guidance received from Steve Little and others for dealing with the life-altering trauma. The first situation he was asked to comment on concerned the tragic case of Kansas City Chiefs' All-Pro linebacker Derrick Thomas, who was ejected from a vehicle during an accident on a snowy highway in Missouri on January 23, 2000. He was paralyzed from the chest down and eventually flown to his hometown of Miami for surgery on his spine. Dave Flores asked Gabe what thoughts he would pass along to the injured player. "As an athlete, he should know what it takes to get up and go again. He knows how hard he has to work. . . . It's going to be a struggle for him right now. You sit there and think a lot of 'what ifs' and ask, 'Why me?' Stuff like that comes to mind." In this article Gabe noted that it took him almost a full decade to truly acclimate himself to his new reality. But, he argued, Thomas would have to keep working on finding meaning for his life. "Thomas probably will feel anger for a while like I did. That's natural. . . . Anger always crept in. . . . You have to do something. You can't always sit back and think about it." Unfortunately, Thomas did not live much beyond the moment of his accident, as he suffered a pulmonary embolism when a blood clot that had developed in his legs dislodged and traveled to his lungs. He died on February 8, 2000.[20]

Shortly before his own passing, Gabe once again had the opportunity to offer good wishes to another athlete. This time, it hit closer to home as the situation concerned a fellow Steeler, linebacker Ryan Shazier, who was injured during a game versus the Cincinnati Bengals in 2017. That incident brought back a lot of painful memories for Gabe. In an article in the *Post-Gazette* by Ed Bouchette, Gabe wished Shazier well, but the piece mostly brought the folks in Western Pennsylvania up on the status of Rivera and his family. Bouchette noted that Gabe was doing okay financially, due to the NFL disability payments and Supplemental Security Income (SSI), as well as noting his work with Inner City. Additionally, the article discussed some of the medical issues Gabe was enduring currently, as well as in previous years. "But getting around is hard for Rivera. He was elected a vice president of the center's board but no longer attends night meetings, as he has scars and bruises on his feet from bumping into things with his wheelchair." Additionally, Bouchette quoted Patti Radle concerning the former Steeler's health. "There are some years where he's had physical challenges and couldn't come for a long time because of tears and infections. He had some challenges over the last year and lost a lot of weight but seems to be doing better now."[21]

While many articles hinted at various medical issues Gabe endured over the years, one piece by David Flores in late July 2005 provided a great deal of specificity on such matters. Flores leads off the article by noting that Gabe was ill during the days just prior to and after his induction into the San Antonio Sports Hall of Fame. "Rivera remembers having a fever that Thursday night in February, but he was too pumped up to worry much." Unfortunately, on Valentine's Day 2004, just four days after the ceremony, he was admitted into the Christus Santa Rosa Medical Center with a serious infection. He would remain in the facility until April 1. "The infection in his chium [sic] bones—the bones on which one sits—was so extensive that doctors removed both of them. They filled the void with muscle flaps from Rivera's hamstrings. 'I had four operations before I came home.'" According to Nancy, in addition to the initial surgeries, he had to have one more due to a problem with one of his incisions. Gabe was, again, philosophical about his situation. "I was sad that it happened, that I got sick, but you have to take it in stride. Any kind of infection is bad for someone who is paralyzed. You have to stay on top of this stuff."[22] Unfortunately, by July 2018, Gabe could no longer fight off the infections and other issues racking his body.

Norbert recalled that Gabe had attended a Fourth of July party at his house and seemed to be doing well, both emotionally and physically. Indeed, Norbert indicated during our interview that his little brother had actually been quite contented over the past year and was truly happy with Nancy. However, over the next week or so, his health took a dramatic turn for the worse. As noted above, a paraplegic such as Rivera is highly susceptible to infection, which had occurred on several occasions since 1983. What was actually happening was that Gabe had developed a perforated intestine since the last time he had visited with Norbert. When Gabe entered the hospital for the final time, on July 13, he was nearly septic and would become so relatively quickly. Doctors informed Nancy that nothing could be done to save his life. Initially she wanted the doctors to perform surgery, but the physicians determined that they could not save him. Nancy then went into Gabe's room and shared the news that the end was near. Both cried over the news and then began to make the necessary calls to family and friends. In a story from the *Houston Chronicle*, Nancy noted, "He has a perforated bowel, a perforated colon, and doctors can't perform surgery because he has no stomach muscle."

True to the pattern of his life over the previous two decades, Patti recalled that Gabe had actually attended to his volunteering at Inner City that very day. He even had stopped to get Nancy some roses, as July 13 was her birthday. Nancy contacted Norbert, who then passed word to Tim; he had to fly back to San Antonio from Houston, where he was spending time with his daughter at an Astros game. Thus, Gabe prepared for the end of life. As Patti described it, he "was functional, but knew he would be dead in a couple of days."[23]

Tim arrived in time to visit with Gabe and got to spend two hours with his father, who was in and out of consciousness. A stream of visitors also came from Inner City. Patti and Rod stopped by on Saturday morning and recalled that the visit was "very emotional. [But] he was in good spirits." They made sure to remind Gabe of what he had meant to them, to the program, and most of all, to the children he worked with over the past nearly two decades. Given their faith, the Radles talked with their friend about the hereafter, and inquired as to whether he was frightened by impending death. They recalled that he answered with a hearty "No!"

Upon their return to the facility, there was a general call for prayers and then an inquiry as to how many wanted to visit with their friend. In total, it necessitated two 15-person vans to transport all of the children to the hospital. The kids were informed that this would be their final visit with Gabe, and Rod encouraged them to share their feelings. One final person who was present was JR Cisneros, who stopped by on Sunday. The boy whom Gabe and Nancy mentored had a final opportunity to visit with Pops and told him how much he appreciated and loved him. During my interview with JR, he noted that Gabe's final piece of advice was for him to be strong and continue to move forward. The two then held hands for a final good-bye. Having had time to visit with grandchildren, his son, brothers, and Nancy and her children, Gabe slipped into a coma and died on Monday, July 16, at 9:25 p.m.[24] More than 200 people attended his memorial service at University Methodist Church. Nancy recalled that among the mourners were representatives of Texas Tech University and the Pittsburgh Steelers. Gabe's body was cremated.[25]

CONCLUSION

THE LIFE AND LEGEND OF SEÑOR SACK

AS PART OF THE MEMORIAL services for Gabe Rivera, JR Cisneros composed a poem for his mentor. Just like the "Señor Sack Attack" noted earlier in the text, the words were most certainly heartfelt and would have struck a chord with all of the individuals present. Titled simply "Gabe Didn't Say Goodbye," it appears here in its entirety:

> It's hard not to cry, but Gabe is okay.
> He went to heaven with Jesus, where you'll be another day.
> I know that you're lonely and I know you will cry
> But always remember Gabe didn't say goodbye
> Death is not the ending. It's the beginning of life
> In heaven it's forever. It's a life without strife.
> There is no pain in heaven, and you'll cry no more tears
> One day you'll see Gabe, but for now his memory is here.
> When you're sad, close your eyes
> And think of the times you shared.
> Can you see Gabe smiling?
> Can you feel how much he cared?
> Live your life to the fullest.
> Take time to laugh, it's okay.
> One day you'll be with Gabe and he'll never go away.[1]

Not surprisingly, tributes for this great athlete came from various sources. Texas Tech, of course, paid homage with a statement from the communications wing of the school's Athletic Department. Ron Reeves, Gabe's teammate from so many years before, and now the head of the Double T Varsity Club, stated, "He was obviously a big name in Texas Tech history. . . . I think he did a great job of staying involved at Tech. It was a highlight for us every time Gabe came back for a weekend." In order to honor this legendary player, the Tech football team wore a #69 helmet sticker during the entirety of the 2018 campaign.[2] Similar tributes appeared on ESPN and KSAT, and in the *Pittsburgh Post-Gazette* and the *Express-News*.[3]

Of course, the most heartfelt acknowledgments came from his wife, Nancy; his family; and all those associated with Inner City Development. "He was a good man, who cared very much for his family and the children at Inner City," Nancy noted during our interview. When asked about his father's legacy, Tim Rivera was cautious and argued that, on the football field, it was hard to judge, given the brevity of his professional career. He did state that his father's life was "a testament to the fact that choices have consequences." Norbert's perspective was framed by the history of Mexican Americans in the state of Texas (and elsewhere) when he stated that this was the "story of a man born in 1961 when many places were segregated. There were things that a Mexican American could not do, or dream of doing. . . . He was a hero because he made it possible to believe that 'we can do this [play football at its highest levels] and be part of this.'"

Rod and Patti Radle stated that Gabe's tale was an example to the children in the neighborhood about the value of good habits and making the most of what life deals you. "Yes, I guess you can deal with a major crisis. . . . As time went on, he always got more out of it [the interaction with the kids] than he put into it. . . . It brought him a lot of happiness." Lastly, JR Cisneros noted how both Gabe and Nancy benefited from their relationship. "She made him strong and pushed him. She helped him get his act together." As a result, many people gained from the final years of Gabe Rivera's life.[4]

Another glowing homage came from Ray Galindo, who managed to visit with his former client just a couple of weeks prior to his passing. In a long email, Ray recalled,

> I spent 2 days and maybe 10 hours of conversation with Gabe a few weeks before he passed away. Gabe was a man of few words from the first time I met him until the last time we saw each other. I believe he wanted to hear things that happen[ed] after the accident that he was not aware [of] and perhaps no one had told him. In my conversations with him, he would say that he didn't remember, or it sounded familiar but wasn't sure. . . . That first night it seemed he was at ease and those 30+ years of being estranged never happened.

> When I first flew him out to California, he stayed at my beach house and my kids were just in total awe of his size and how friendly he was to them. I remember and so does my son how he tried to sneak up on him while he was sleeping, Gabe opened one eye while they hovered over him and then caught one and lifted him up with one hand. The son that he lifted came back with me to San Antonio the month before we lost Gabe. He honestly did remember that day and was happy to see him. We talked about our adventures in New York, Hollywood and Disneyland and he did remember some of it.

> In the two days I spent with him he never let on how sick he was but was looking forward to my return to San Antonio. As we were leaving his home he escorted us out to the driveway and sat in his wheelchair just staring at us as we walked to the car, once I started to pull away and he was still staring at us, then suddenly an odd thought crossed my mind that this could be the last time I would see Gabe. The last correspondence I received from Gabe was a text 2 weeks before he passed away. . . . It was actually for my son congratulating

him on his success at the Special Olympics National Games at the University of Washington since he told Gabe he was dedicating his competition to him.

It was that son who told me Gabe passed away when a flash came over ESPN that Gabe had passed away. I then received a call from Nancy. You know it is still hard for me to think he is gone.[5]

A wonderful example of Gabe's legacy appeared less than two weeks after his passing on KENS in an article by David Flores, a writer who had covered so much of Gabe's story. The article discussed Rivera's work with the children of Inner City. It also quoted Patti Radle concerning the last bit of advice that Gabe wanted to leave for his charges at the organization. "That's when, right away, Nancy just offhand, said, 'Yeah, don't drink and drive.' Gabe shook his head, yes, the same message."[6]

Finally, what are we to make of the life, athletic career, tragic accident, struggles, and redemption through volunteer work that constituted the life of Señor Sack? We can make a few points. First, as Norbert has attested, Gabe's success on the football field—being a first-round selection of an NFL franchise—provides an important example to the growing body of Latinos who are playing the sport at all levels at the start of the third decade of the 21st century. As Mario Longoria and I note in *Latinos in American Football: Pathbreakers on the Gridiron, 1927 to the Present*, Spanish-surnamed football players have been making their mark on the field for almost a century. These men, particularly those in the years before the civil rights era, faced many obstacles—as noted in the discussion on Juan's career—simply getting to play. They wanted to play because they loved the sport, and because it provided avenues for some to continue their education (and a few even made it to the NFL or other pro leagues).

Gabe's story was a culmination of the struggles of many. While players such as Tom Fears, Joe Kapp, Jim Plunkett (yes, they are Mexican Americans), Tom Flores, and of course, the legendary Anthony Muñoz are fairly well known, there are many others, such as Joe Aguirre, Daniel Villanueva, "Mean" Gene Brito (all Mexican Americans), George Mira, and Ralph Ortega (both Cuban Americans), who are not as recognizable. What all of these individuals have in common is that they competed at the highest levels and achieved great things on the field. They also all went on to move into other successful careers, in broadcasting, business, and other endeavors.[7] They are all examples of what persons of such backgrounds can achieve if given opportunities in athletics and other fields. Gabe, while not earning a degree, starting a business, or entering politics, eventually turned to the noble path of volunteering in order to serve others and his community.

Second, many items have appeared on the impact and import of athletic heroes to modern culture, in the United States and elsewhere. One work, a dissertation by Keith D. Parry titled "The Bad, the Good, and the Ugly: The Formation of Heroes within the Setting of a New Sports Team," is vitally important to Gabe's story because of this researcher's focus on "how the formation of sports heroes is shaped by established notions of national identity and longstanding mythological archetypes rather than the heroes' personal traits or deeds."[8] In other words, many have argued previously that sports heroes are supposed to look a certain way. What is the impact on a society when a sports hero who, while bringing success and notoriety to a particular team or scholastic institution, does not quite "look" as expected? I've considered this question in research on another Texas Tech hero, Bobby Cavazos.[9] Thus, the mere presence of Gabe Rivera on the field at Jones Stadium argued for the inclusion of Mexican Americans on "our" teams as well as in other facets of Texas Tech's campus life. Given that Tech is now a Hispanic Serving Institution (HSI), it makes sense to present our students and alumni with stories of Red Raider success in as many endeavors as possible.

Third, Gabe was not just a hero on the football field, but a tragic figure due to his accident. Richard Ian Kimball examines the story of great athletes who died young or suddenly, and how they influence our culture in his work, *Legends Never Die: Athletes and Their Afterlives in Modern America*.[10] While Gabe lived another 35 years after his accident, his career certainly did "die" on October 20, 1983. So much was expected for this young man by Steeler fans and also aficionados of the Red Raiders. Here was a Tech player who would play in the NFL and help to carry "our" name to prominence with his success. Who knows, perhaps he might have played on a Super Bowl–winning team or been an All-Pro? He might have even, in our wildest imagination, become a Hall of Famer. All of this success and positivity would have been tied back to the places where he played previously: Jefferson High School and Texas Tech University. To bolster this argument, one need simply think about the reaction of folks in Lubbock and Whitehouse, Texas, to the success of Patrick Mahomes with the Kansas City Chiefs, and particularly his exploits as the MVP of Super Bowl LIV.

In his study, Kimball quotes historian Joseph L. Price about the forceful impression generated by an athlete's death or maiming: "When faced with the death of a physically fit . . . or impressive athlete, we often experience a keener anxiety about our own mortality. For if an athlete can die . . . then how much more are we, who are less physically fit . . . vulnerable not only to the certainty of death but also to its timing, its possible imminence?"[11] Certainly, Gabe's accident had such an influence on football fans in Pittsburgh, Lubbock, and San Antonio. It reminded us that, at any moment—through our own doing or merely by accident—we might cross the center lane on a highway.

The key issue, however, is what does it all mean? Kimball posits that the making of our memories of such athletes is most significant. In a quote that dovetails nicely with Gabe's story, Kimball argues that "the black hole of unfulfilled potential magnifies the energy of the universe of memory."[12] On the Tech campus, and to a lesser degree in Pittsburgh, we continue to see Gabe running down a quarterback after a 60-yard sprint, ripping the helmet off of an offensive player, and finally, crushing a future Hall of Famer with one of his bone-jarring tackles. While his life did not turn out the way that many had expected, one could argue that he did fulfill his potential. True, he did not get a college degree or work after his accident, and he surely did struggle for many years to find his bearings. Still, he eventually, through his own initiative and Nancy's prodding, came to realize that something he loved doing—working with children—was a way to give back and find fulfillment. While the glory that was expected of Gabe Rivera ended suddenly as far as playing the sport he loved, he ultimately made a difference in the lives of many people. What more can be expected from an individual?

Among the stack of the materials Nancy Rivera provided for the Southwest Collection Archive, I came across an undated poem titled "Touchdown" written by an individual named Francisco Machorro. The paper is old and faded, and it is logical to assume that Juan Rivera clipped this verse for his sons at some point. The item is in Spanish, and my translation seems to provide an effective homage for Gabriel Rivera: football player, husband, father, volunteer, and Texas Tech legend.

TOUCHDOWN

FRANCISCO MACHORRO

... Take the football, my son, and I name you quarterback
of your team in the game of life! ... I am your coach and I
give it to you such as it is.
There is only one schedule of games during your entire
life and it is only one contest ... It is a long match, without
time outs, nor substitutions ... You are in the contest for
your entire life.
... You will have a great backfield and you will call
the signals ... Your other teammates behind the line,
also have great value; they are called: faith, hope and
charity ...
You will play behind an extremely powerful line; from
one side of the line to the other, they are called: honesty,
loyalty, devotion to duty, self-respect, study, fastidiousness,
and good conduct ...
... The goal posts are the pearly gates of heaven ...
God is the referee and sole arbiter ... He makes all the
rules and there is no appeal against them. There are ten
basic rules: you know them as "The Ten Commandments"
and you shall follow them strictly ...
There is also another fundamental regulation: "Do unto
others as you would have them do onto you."
... In this game, if you fumble the ball, you lose the
contest ...
... Here is the football: It is your immortal soul, hold it
tightly against you ... !
... Now, son, go out onto the field and we will see what you
can do with your life ... [13]

Gabe Rivera never played quarterback, and though he did fumble the ball a few times along the way, he accomplished great things on the football field, cared for his family and alma mater, and provided much-needed encouragement for children facing difficult circumstances. While this tale is of an imperfect individual, in the end Rivera held on tightly to the ball, and to his soul, and crossed the goal line of life. May the great number 69 of the red and black rest in peace and cheer on his beloved Texas Tech Red Raiders and Pittsburgh Steelers from a better place.

Notes

INTRODUCTION

1. See http://fs.ncaa.org/Docs/stats/football_records/DI/2010/ Awards.pdf. The Texas Tech All-Americans are listed on page 16 of this document.
2. See https://www.cfbhall.com/about/inductees/ and proceed to the specific page of each of the individuals noted.
3. Johnny Campos, "Jeff's Rivera Claims Thom McAn Award," *San Antonio Light*, January 7, 1979. See also "Rivera, Jenkins Top S.A. 'Signees,'" *San Antonio Light*, February 15, 1979.
4. See https://www.ncaa.com/news/football/article/2018-07-31/ college-footballs-9-winningest-teams.
5. For information on Texas Tech's football championships, please see http://cfbdatawarehouse.com/data/div_ia/big12/ texas_tech/championships.php.
6. For information on Texas Tech's participation in bowl games, please see https://www.sports-reference.com/cfb/ schools/texas-tech/index.html.
7. See https://www.sports-reference.com/cfb/schools/ texas-tech/1982-schedule.html.
8. See https://en.wikipedia.org/wiki/1982_Washington_Huskies_football_team.
9. Nick Kosmider, "Saluting Señor Sack," September 12, 2014, https://texastech.com/news/2014/9/12/Saluting_Se_amp_ ntilde_or_Sack.aspx.
10. Norval Pollard, "'Big Foot' Sighted in Pacific Northwest," *Lubbock Avalanche-Journal*, October 26, 1986.
11. Will McDonough, "NFL Draftees Cash in on USFL," *San Antonio Light*, July 13, 1983.

12. David Riles, "Steelers Grab Freight Train," and "Steelers' Draft Aim: Rebuild Defense," *Pittsburgh Tribune-Review*, April 27, 1983.
13. Scott Sinclair, "Señor Sack . . . the Steeler That Never Was," accessed October 26, 2018, https://stillcurtain. com/2013/04/24/senor-sack-the-steeler-that-never-was/.
14. Gabriel Rivera page, accessed October 26, 2018, https:// www.cfbhall.com/about/inductees/.
15. https://www.everythinglubbock.com/news/kamc-news/ former-teammates-reflect-on-legendary-red-raider-foo tball-player-gabe-rivera/1308413533.

CHAPTER 1

1. The amount of work on these topics is quite extensive, and the following list is not meant to be exhaustive, merely representative of the many works available: C. Richard King, *Redskins: Insult and Brand* (Lincoln: University of Nebraska Press, 2016); David K. Wiggins, *More Than a Game: A History of the African American Experience in Sport* (Lanham, MD: Rowan and Littlefield, 2018); Jack Kugelmass, *Jews, Sports, and the Rites of Citizenship* (Champaign: University of Illinois Press, 2007); Gerald Gems, *Sport and the Shaping of Italian American Identity* (Syracuse, NY: Syracuse University Press, 2013); Rob Ruck, *The Tropic of Football: The Long and Perilous Journey of Samoans to the NFL* (New York: New Press, 2018); and Joel S. Frank, *Asians and Pacific Islanders in American Football: Historical and Contemporary Experiences* (Lanham, MD: Lexington Books, 2018).
2. A brief discussion of the debate between *Hispanic* and *Latino* is necessary at this point. This argument has raged for many years. On one side of the equation, critics of the term *Hispanic* argue that it was created by faceless, nameless federal bureaucrats and that it makes better sense to have a term "we" created. Thus, individuals in this camp prefer *Latino* as it is perceived as "more authentic"

because it points toward a specific place: Latin America. Those who embrace "Hispanic," however, note that Latino can be seen as downplaying the Spanish cultural background of such persons, and further that it implies that all Spanish-speakers in the United States have ties to the original natives of this continent. For a fuller discussion of this topic, please see Jorge Iber, Samuel O. Regalado, Jose M. Alamillo, and Arnoldo De Leon, *Latinos in U.S. Sport: A History of Isolation, Cultural Identity, and Acceptance* (Champaign, IL: Human Kinetics, 2011), 6–8. See also https://blogs. usafootball.com/blog/4428/the-8-best-hispanic-players-i n-football-history.

3. Ralph Hickok, *Bibliography of Books about American Football, 1891–2015* (self-published, 2015).

4. Mario Longoria and Jorge Iber, *Latinos in American Football: Pathbreakers on the Gridiron, 1927 to the Present* (Jefferson, NC: McFarland and Company, 2019).

5. Ibid.

6. Quoted in Gerald R. Gems, *For Pride, Profit, and Patriarchy: Football and the Incorporation of American Cultural Values* (Lanham, MD: Scarecrow Press, 2000), 112.

7. Michael Oriard, *King Football: Sport and Spectacle in the Golden Age of Radio and Newsreels, Movies and Magazines, the Weekly and Daily Press* (Chapel Hill: University of North Carolina Press, 2001), 260. For more information, see chapter 8 of Oriard's work, "Ethnicity."

8. David Barron, "The Birth of Texas Schoolboy Football," in Mike Bynum, ed., *King Football: Greatest Moments in Texas High School Football History* (Birmingham, AL: Epic Sports Classics, 2003), 26–39. See also Iber et al., *Latinos in U.S. Sport*, 74.

9. Greg Selber, *Border Ball: The History of High School Football in the Rio Grande Valley* (Deer Park, NY: Linus Publications, 2009).

10. Ibid., 5.

11. Joel Huerta, "Friday Night Rights: South Texas High-School Football and the Struggle for Equality," *International Journal of the History of Sport* 26 (June 2009): 981–1000.

12. Fred Morales, "History of Bowie High School, 1922–1973" (self-published, 2015). See 8, 10, 12, 13, 21, and 23. In author's possession.

13. Ignacio M. Garcia, "William Carson 'Nemo' Herrera: Constructing a Mexican American Powerhouse While Remaining Colorblind," *Journal of the West* 54 (Fall 2015): 40–46.

14. See *El Paso Times,* "Bowie Plays Lanier at 8 Tonight," September 26, 1941, and Grenville Mott, "Bowie Gains Scoreless Tie in El Paso," *El Paso Times*, September 27, 1941.

15. Selber, *Border Ball*, 201–8.

16. Ibid., 77, 87–92.

17. Ibid., 169–71.

18. See the following, all by Jorge Iber: "Mexican Americans of South Texas Football: The Athletic and Coaching Careers of E. C. Lerma and Bobby Cavazos, 1932–1965," *Southwestern Historical Quarterly* 55 (April 2002): 617–33; "Bobby Cavazos: A Vaquero in the Backfield," *College Football Historical Society* 14 (August 2001): 1–5; and "Becoming Raiders Rojos: Using Sport to Claim Hispanic 'Space' at Texas Tech University," *West Texas Historical Association Yearbook* 77 (2001): 139–51.

19. Jorge Iber, "On Field Foes and Racial Misperceptions: The 1961 Donna Redskins and Their Drive to the Texas State Football Championship," in Jorge Iber and Samuel O. Regalado, eds., *Mexican Americans and Sports: A Reader on Athletics and Barrio Life* (College Station: Texas A&M University Press, 2007), 121–44; Selber, *Border Ball*, 164–68.

20. Longoria and Iber, *Latinos in American Football*, 201.

21. Al Pickett, *Mighty, Mighty Matadors: Estacado High School, Integration, and a Championship Season* (College Station: Texas A&M University Press, 2017), 6, 116.

22. Selber, *Border Ball*, 169–71.

23. Ibid., 221–38, 286–87.
24. Kelsey Conway, "Where It All Began for Juan Castillo," July 16, 2015, https://www.baltimoreravens.com/news/where-it-all-began-for-juan-castillo-15492485.

CHAPTER 2

1. Speech by Jose Angel Gutierrez, April 1, 1963, quoted in Marc Simon Rodriguez, *The Tejano Diaspora: Mexican American-icanism and Ethnic Politics in Texas and Wisconsin* (Chapel Hill: University of North Carolina Press, 2011), 46.
2. Jose Angel Gutierrez, *The Making of a Chicano Militant: Lessons from Cristal* (Madison: University of Wisconsin Press, 1998). "Cristal" is the spelling of "crystal" in Spanish. Most individuals of Spanish-speaking background from this area use the Spanish-language pronunciation of the word.
3. Marc Simon Rodriguez, *The Tejano Diaspora: Mexican American-icanism and Ethnic Politics in Texas and Wisconsin* (Chapel Hill: University of North Carolina Press, 2011); Selden C. Menefee, "Mexican Migratory Workers of South Texas" (Washington, DC: US Government Printing Office, 1941).
4. Rodriguez, *Tejano Diaspora*, 17.
5. Rodriguez denotes the Winter Garden District as encompassing the border county of Maverick, as well as Zavala, Dimmit, and parts of LaSalle Counties in Texas. See ibid., 17.
6. Menefee, "Mexican Migratory Workers of South Texas," 1, 3.
7. Ibid., 3.
8. Ibid., 10.
9. Rodriguez, *Tejano Diaspora*, 17.
10. Menefee, "Mexican Migratory Workers of South Texas," 41.
11. Ibid., 42.
12. Ibid., 43, 44.
13. Ibid., 44, 45.
14. Ibid., 37–40; Rodriguez, *Tejano Diaspora*, 25.
15. Rodriguez, *Tejano Diaspora*, 18–20.

16. Ibid., 21–30.
17. See Charles Vale Fitzpatrick, "Latino Empowerment in South Texas: The Crystal City Revolts (1962–1969) as a Case Study," master's thesis, Baylor University, 2004, 19, 20; http://www.cityofcc.org/default.aspx?name=History_Page (accessed April 26, 2019).
18. Rodriguez, *Tejano Diaspora*, 33.
19. Ibid., 22, 23.
20. In addition to the Rodriguez, Gutierrez, and Menefee works noted previously, the following sources are used to support this part of the discussion (with an emphasis on the situation in the local schools): R. C. Tate, "A History of Zavala County, Texas" (master's thesis, Southwest Texas State Teachers' College, 1942); Zavala County Historical Commission, "Now and Then in Zavala County: A History of Zavala County, Texas Written by the People of Zavala County," 1986; Ignacio M. Garcia, *United We Win: The Rise and Fall of La Raza Unida Party* (Tucson: University of Arizona Press, 1989); Armando Trujillo, *Chicano Empowerment and Bilingual Education: Movemiento Politics in Crystal City, Texas* (New York: Routledge, Taylor and Francis Group, 1998); Guadalupe San Miguel Jr., *Chicana/o Struggles for Education: Activism in the Community* (Houston: University of Houston–Center for Mexican American Studies, 2013); F. Arturo Rosales, *Chicano: The History of the Mexican American Civil Rights Struggle* (Houston: Arte Publico Press, 1997); Douglas E. Foley, *Learning Capitalist Culture Deep in the Heart of Texas* (Philadelphia: University of Pennsylvania Press, 1990); John Staples Shockley, *Chicano Revolt in a Texas Town* (Notre Dame, IN: Notre Dame University Press, 1974); Joyce Anne Langenegger, "The School as a Political Tool" (master's thesis, Baylor University, 1993); and Baldemar James Barrera, "'We Want Better Education': The Chicano Student Movement for Educational Reform in South Texas, 1968–1970" (PhD diss., University of New Mexico, 2007).

21. Tate, "History of Zavala County, Texas," 46, 47.

22. James Staples Shockley, *Chicano Revolt in a Texas Town* (Notre Dame, IN: University of Notre Dame Press, 1974), 11, 13.

23. Rodriguez, *Tejano Diaspora*, 40.

24. Ibid., 43.

25. Ibid., 44, 45.

26. Barrera, "'We Want Better Education,'" 193–94.

27. Ibid., 194.

28. Rodriguez, *Tejano Diaspora*, 32, 35.

29. Ibid., 36.

30. Jose Angel Gutierrez, *"We Won't Back Down!": Severita Lara's Rise from Student Leader to Mayor* (Houston: Arte Publico Press, 2005).

31. Ibid., 6, 8, 25, 36, 46–47.

32. Ibid., 49.

33. Ibid., 54–55.

34. See Mario Longoria and Jorge Iber, *Latinos in American Football: Pathbreakers on the Gridiron, 1927 to the Present* (Jefferson, NC: McFarland and Company, 2019) for extensive coverage on this topic.

35. Jose Angel Gutierrez, interview with author, October 18, 2018.

36. Gutierrez, *Making of a Chicano Militant*, 31.

37. Jose Angel Gutierrez, interview with author, October 18, 2018. See also Jose Angel Gutierrez, email to author, May 3, 2019.

38. Jose Angel Gutierrez, email to author, May 3, 2019. See also Marc Simon Rodriguez, email to author, May 1, 2019, and Norbert Rivera, email to author, April 29, 2019.

CHAPTER 3

1. Norbert Rivera, email to author, June 28, 2019. Norbert's contention is that some of the missing birth information mentioned here is due to his inability to find certain

records from that state.

2. Norbert Rivera, interview with author, January 18, 2019.

3. Ibid. See also Maria de Jesus Rivera, interview with author, August 7, 2019.

4. Zavala County Historical Commission, *Now and Then in Zavala County: A History of Zavala County Written by the People of Zavala County* (Crystal City, TX, 1986), 64.

5. Ibid., 225.

6. Jose Angel Gutierrez, email to author, July 15, 2019.

7. For a complete summary of all Texas high school football records through the 2018 season, see https://www.texas-highschoolfootballhistory.com/season_records_-_coolidge. html. The Javelinas have not been a highly successful program over the decades, though the 2014 to 2018 seasons under Coach David Lopez have produced playoff teams (the longest such streak of success in school history). Still, their overall record since 1920 is 310–563–33. Their playoff mark covers only 13 total games, with a record of 5–8.

8. "This Was the News, February 27, 1948," *Zavala County Sentinel*, February 20, 1959.

9. Norbert Rivera, interview with author, January 18, 2019.

10. "This Was the News," *Zavala County Sentinel*, September 26, 1958.

11. Arnoldo De Leon, "Our *Gringo Amigos*: Anglo Americans and the Tejano Experience," *East Texas Historical Association Yearbook* 22, no. 2 (1993): 72–79.

12. Ibid., 72.

13. Ibid., 77.

14. See https://texashistory.unt.edu/ark:/67531/metapth41293/ hits/?q=Rivera; https://texashistory.unt.edu/ark:/67531/ metapth41292/m1/98/?q=Juan%20Rivera.

15. Tom Penn, "Penn Points," *Brownwood Bulletin*, October 28, 1954. See also "Penn Points," November 30, 1954.

16. See Norman Fisher, "Howard Payne Captures 12–7 Victory," *Brownwood Bulletin*, October 30, 1955; "Jackets, McMurry

Expect to Be in Top Shape," *Brownwood Bulletin*, November 2, 1955; "Line Play May Hold Key to Circuit Championship," *Brownwood Bulletin*, November 3, 1955.

17. See Norman Fisher, "Howard Payne Ready for Homecoming Tilt," *Brownwood Bulletin*, November 11, 1955; "Jackets Snuff Out ACC Victory Torch," *Brownwood Bulletin*, November 25, 1955.

18. Norbert Rivera, interview with author, January 18, 2019. See also "Births," *Brownwood Bulletin*, September 5, 1956.

19. Norman Fisher, "Jackets Launch Spring Grid Workouts Tuesday," *Brownwood Bulletin*, April 1, 1956; "Williams 'Well Pleased' with Howard Payne Football Drills," *Brownwood Bulletin*, April 15, 1956; and "HPC Jacket Gridmen, Exes All Set for Annual Tilt Saturday," *Brownwood Bulletin*, April 27, 1956; Jorday Vandagriff, "Elkins, Garms to Lead Howard Payne Gridmen," *Brownwood Bulletin*, May 3, 1956.

20. Norman Fisher, "Brownwood High, Howard Payne Open Grid Drills This Week," *Brownwood Bulletin*, August 26, 1956.

21. Norbert Rivera, interview with author, January 18, 2019.

22. In an email to me on July 15, 2019, Jose Angel Gutierrez noted that 1957–1958 "is when CCISD integrated and moved those of us at the former Japanese concentration camp barracks which was the Mexican Jr. High to Sterling Fly Jr. High. The Japanese camp became the Migrant School thereafter."

23. See the following, all from the *Zavala County Sentinel*: "Grid Practice Starts Monday," August 23, 1957; "Halloween Bazaar to Be Held," October 11, 1957; and Edwina Stocking and Sammy Guyler, "Crystal City Lights," October 18, 1957.

24. See the following, all from the *Zavala County Sentinel*: "Hogs, Cats to Clash," November 15, 1957; "Schools Open Tuesday," August 29, 1958; "Grid Opener Set Friday," September 5, 1958; "Javs Tie, 12–12," September 12, 1958; "Javelins Lose, 18–6," September 19, 1958; "Javs, Cats Due to

Clash," November 14, 1958; "Javelins Defeat Carrizo, 42–28,"
November 21, 1958; and "1958 Graduates, Crystal City High
School," May 23, 1958. Jose Angel Gutierrez, email to author,
July 15, 2019, noted, "They may have been listed and even
photographed but I do not recall many of these names as
'starters' but for three of them who were exceptional: Rey
Villegas, Rey Perez, and Eusebio Salinas."
25. Norbert Rivera, interview with author, January 18, 2019.
See also "Services Thursday for Dr. Sterling Fly," *Hondo
Anvil Herald*, July 26, 1963.
26. For information on Coach Rutledge's record, please
see https://www.texashighschoolfootballhistory.com/
season_records_-_coolidge.html and https://www.texas-
highschoolfootballhistory.com/coaches_-_r_roberts.html.
27. See the info on the Benavides Eagles and Coach Gonzales at https://www.texashighschoolfootballhistory.com/
season_records_-_b.html and https://www.texashigh-
schoolfootballhistory.com/coaches_records__g-.html. For
information on the role and significance of high school
football coaches in Texas during the middle of the 20th
century, see Ty Cashion, *Pigskin Pulpit: A Social History
of Texas High School Football Coaches* (Austin: Texas State
Historical Association, 1998), and Jorge Iber, "The Pigskin
Pulpito: A Brief Overview of the Experiences of Mexican
American High School Football Coaches in Texas," in
Michael E. Lomax, ed., *Sport and the Racial Divide: African
American and Latino Experience in an Era of Change* (Jackson:
University Press of Mississippi, 2008), 178–95. For specific
information on Coach Lerma and his career, see Jorge Iber,
"Mexican Americans of South Texas Football: The Athletic
and Coaching Careers of E. C. Lerma and Bobby Cavazos,
1932–1965," *Southwestern Historical Quarterly* 55, no. 4 (April
2002): 617–34.
28. "Juan Rivera, Jr. Head Coach at Benavides," *Zavala
County Sentinel*, September 11, 1964. See also https://www.

texashighschoolfootballhistory.com/season_records_-_b.
html; "New Eagle Coach Has 17 Returnees," *Alice Daily Echo*,
September 6, 1964.

29. All of these items are from the *Alice Daily Echo*: "Surprise,"
September 12, 1965; "Freer Gets Nod in District 31-AA, Others Might Surprise," September 6, 1966; "Returning Starters to Spark Benavides," August 1, 1967; and "Eagles Can
Soar," September 12, 1968.

30. See Juan Rivera's overall record at https://www.texashigh-
schoolfootballhistory.com/coaches_records_-_neil.html.

31. "Rivera Goes to Edinburg," *Corpus Christi Caller-Times*,
August 1, 1970. See also "20 South Texas Teams under New
Guidance," *Corpus Christi Caller-Times*, September 6, 1970.

32. Norbert Rivera, interview with author, February 22, 2019.

33. "Editorial," *Zavala County Sentinel*, October 2, 1964.

34. See Crystal City's record at https://www.texashighschool-
footballhistory.com/season_records_-_coolidge.html. For
info on Coach Harvey, see https://www.texashighschool-
footballhistory.com/coaches_records__g-.html.

35. "Homecoming Activities Moved," *Zavala County Sentinel*,
November 20, 1969.

36. Ibid. See also "Sweetheart Presentation Due at Game,"
Zavala County Sentinel, November 20, 1969.

37. Jose Angel Gutierrez, *The Making of a Chicano Militant: Les-
sons from Cristal* (Madison: University of Wisconsin Press,
1998), 144. For a full discussion of the 1969 walkout from
Gutierrez's perspective, see 129–39. See also John Staples
Shockley, *A Chicano Revolt in a Texas Town* (Notre Dame, IN:
University of Notre Dame Press, 1974), 127–41.

38. Shockley, *Chicano Revolt in a Texas Town*, 141, 148, 151–54.

39. Jose Angel Gutierrez, interview with author, October 18,
2018.

40. Ibid.

41. "Athletic Director Hired," *Zavala County Sentinel*, February
11, 1971.

42. Gutierrez, *Making of a Chicano Militant*, 204–5.

43. Charlie Robinson, "Unique Brother Combination," *Texas Coach*, April 1973, 34, 35.

44. See https://www.texashighschoolfootballhistory.com/ season_records_-_coolidge.html, and https://www.texas-highschoolfootballhistory.com/coaches_-_r_roberts.html.

45. Gutierrez, interview with author.

46. Norbert Rivera, interviews with author, January 18, 2019, and February 22, 2019. See also "H. S. Coaches Move," *San Antonio Express*, September 1, 1972.

CHAPTER 4

1. Joe Kapp and Jack Olsen, "A Man of Machismo," *Sports Illustrated*, July 19, 1970, 26–31.

2. Ibid., 28.

3. In earlier decades, the term *Chicano* was considered derogatory among Mexican Americans. With the advent of the Mexican American civil rights struggle in the 1960s, the individuals at the forefront of this movement chose to embrace this term as part of their efforts.

4. "Kapp Visit Set," *Zavala County Sentinel*, December 14, 1972.

5. Harry Page, "This Time Lee Rides Mustangs," *San Antonio Express/News*, October 27, 1973.

6. The NAIA is the National Association of Intercollegiate Athletics, and its membership tends to comprise smaller institutions of higher learning. "ENMU Grew from Humble Beginnings," *Eastern New Mexico News*, October 2, 2009, https://www.easternnewmexiconews.com/story/2009/10/02/ publisheducationnews/enmu-grew-from-humble-begin-nings/105533.html?m=false.

7. "Scott Impressed by Scrimmage," *Clovis News-Journal*, March 5, 1975; "And Finally . . . ," *San Antonio Express*, August 11, 1975; "Hounds Seek Sixth Win—Again," *Clovis News-Journal*, October 24, 1975; "Moving Right Along," *San Antonio Express*, November 10, 1975; "Hounds Plan

Silver-Green Game," *Clovis News-Journal*, February 22, 1976; "Greyhounds End Spring Practice," *Clovis News-Journal*, March 16, 1976; "Hounds Open Saturday Night," *Clovis News-Journal*, September 2, 1976; and "Hounds Going After Second Win with WNMU," *Clovis News-Journal*, September 9, 1976. See also https://goeasternathletics.com/alltime.aspx?path=football&record_type=seasons. Norbert Rivera, interview with author, July 22, 2019.

8. See https://www.texashighschoolfootballhistory.com/season_records_round_rock.html.

9. Norbert Rivera, interview with author, February 22, 2019. See also "TCIL 3-AA Team Named," *San Antonio Express*, November 25, 1975; "Jackets, 69–46," *San Antonio Express*, January 21, 1976; John Hines, "St. Anthony's Aiming for the Top," *San Antonio Express*, November 15, 1974; and John Hines, "TCIL Teams in Title Chase," *San Antonio Express*, February 20, 1976.

10. Norbert Rivera, interview with author, July 22, 2019. See also D. L. Grant, "E-N's Most Popular, Hated Employee: 'Wingo Man,'" *San Antonio Express/News—The Inside Scoop*, June 6, 1990.

11. John Hines, "Ponies Off and Running," *San Antonio Express/News*, September 23, 1976.

12. Gallen Wellnicki, "Jefferson Routs Wheatley, 49–14," *San Antonio Light*, October 22, 1976.

13. John Hines, "Jeff Notches Close Victory," *San Antonio Express/News*, October 31, 1976.

14. Harry Page, "Jeff near Title," *San Antonio Express/News*, November 6, 1976.

15. John Hines, "Owls, Ponies to Vie for Title," *San Antonio Express/News*, November 10, 1976; "Owls Advance to Bi-District," *San Antonio Express/News*, November 4, 1976.

16. See "Sports Scoreboard: Track," *San Antonio Express/News*, April 23, 1977; John Hines, "Riders, Jeff Start Bi-District," *San Antonio Express/News*, May 10, 1977; Ray Evans, "Jeff:

Mutts Grew Up Fast," *San Antonio Light*, May 16, 1977.

17. "Schoolboy Football Arrives," *San Antonio Express*, September 1, 1977; John Hines, "Jefferson Improved," *San Antonio Express/News*, September 14, 1977.

18. John Hines, "Jefferson Rolls, 35–7, by Burbank," *San Antonio Express/News*, October 8, 1977; Mike Burton, "Davila, Darr Grab Schoolboy Honors," *San Antonio Express*, October 11, 1977.

19. Betsy Gerhardt, "Edison Upsets Jeff, 23–20," *San Antonio Light*, October 29, 1977. See also Norbert Rivera, interview with author, February 22, 2019.

20. John Hines, "Experience Pays Off for Top 2," *San Antonio Express*, December 15, 1977.

21. Johnny Campos, "Despite His Aching Back: Rivera to Carry Ponies," *San Antonio Light*, August 1978 (clipping in file, date unavailable); Norbert Rivera, interview with author, February 22, 2019. See also https://www.classmates.com/siteui/yearbooks/86872?page=135, and https://www.classmates.com/siteui/yearbooks/86872?page=137. Copy of certificate from KMOL to Gabe Rivera is in author's possession.

22. Johnny Campos, "Jeff's Rivera Claims Thom McAn Award," *San Antonio Light*, January 7, 1979; Norbert Rivera, interview with author, February 22, 2019.

23. Campos, "Jeff's Rivera Claims Thom McAn Award"; Norbert Rivera, interview with author, February 22, 2019.

24. For background information on Coach Laurence, see the Texas Tech Red Raider Game Program for September 15, 1979, 14.

25. Norbert Rivera, interview with author, February 22, 2019; Jerry Briggs, "Texas Tech Should Make Strong S.A. Showing," *San Antonio Light*, February 11, 1979; https://www.sports-reference.com/cfb/players/anthony-hutchison-1.html. See also "Rivera, Jenkins Top S.A. 'Signees,'" *San Antonio Light*, February 15, 1979.

26. Letter from Bob Thomas to Gabriel Rivera, March 1, 1979, Gabe Rivera Collection, Southwest Collection Archive, Texas Tech University.

27. Letter from Ken Murray to Juan and Maria Antonia Rivera, February 27, 1979, Gabe Rivera Collection, Southwest Collection Archive, Texas Tech University.

28. Jerry Briggs, "Did Tech Recruit Rivera or the 'Burger King'?," *San Antonio Light* (clipping in file, date unavailable).

29. See Don Henry, "Weighty Matters," *Lubbock Avalanche-Journal*, July 24, 1979; Norval Pollard, "Freshman Frolic," *Lubbock Avalanche-Journal*, August 12, 1979.

30. Norval Pollard, "Hadnot Optimistic as Tech Season Approaches," *Lubbock Avalanche-Journal*, August 5, 1979.

31. Norval Pollard, "Can't Tell This Book by Its Cover," *Lubbock Avalanche-Journal*, August 30, 1979.

32. Barry Robinson, "USC Holds Off Tech, 21–7," *San Antonio Express News*, September 9, 1979.

33. Barry Robinson, "Big Gabe Sparkles in College Debut," *San Antonio Express News*, September 13, 1979.

34. "Tech Freshmen Turning Heads," *Texas Tech Game Day Program*, October 6, 1979, 34.

35. Roberto Delgado, "Inside Sports," *El Editor*, October 19, 1979. See also Chuck McDonall, "Rivera Earns First Start as a Red Raider," *Lubbock Avalanche-Journal*, October 20, 1979.

36. Norval Pollard, "Dockery to Keep Offensive Strategy," *Lubbock Avalanche-Journal*, October 16, 1979. See also *Texas Tech Game Day Program*, October 20, 1979, 35.

37. Pollard, "Can't Tell This Book by Its Cover."

CHAPTER 5

1. See https://web.archive.org/web/20131012004522/http://www.texastech.com/trads/hoh-eh.html; Norval Pollard, "Raiders Await Draft Call," *Lubbock Avalanche-Journal*, April 25, 1980. Hadnot died in April 2017, just a few months before Gabe Rivera. For an article on Hadnot's passing,

see https://www.lubbockonline.com/news/sports-red-raiders/sports/2017-04-01/former-teammates-mourn-loss-tech-great-james-hadnot.

2. See https://web.archive.org/web/20160304203306/http://www.databasefootball.com/players/playerpage.htm?ilkid=WATTSTED01.

3. See https://www.sports-reference.com/cfb/conferences/swc/1979.html.

4. Barry Robinson, "The Señor Sack Stories Continue," *San Antonio Express*, March 6, 1980.

5. Chuck McDonald, "Rivera Now a Sleek 280," *Lubbock Avalanche-Journal*, August 21, 1980. See also "Junior Raider Program Stated at Texas Tech," *Lubbock Avalanche-Journal*, July 15, 1980; "Junior Raider Club Sets Picture Day in August," *Lubbock Avalanche-Journal*, July 31, 1980.

6. Norval Pollard, "SWC Coaches Face Crucial Season," *Lubbock Avalanche-Journal*, July 27, 1980.

7. Norval Pollard, "Lame Duck in Town," *Lubbock Avalanche-Journal*, July 18, 1980, and "Clause Keeps Tamburo at Tech," *Lubbock Avalanche-Journal*, July 19, 1980.

8. Norval Pollard, "Meyer Not High on Raiders," *Lubbock Avalanche-Journal*, July 20, 1980.

9. Chuck McDonald, "Coogs Equipped for Fourth Straight SWC Title," *Lubbock Avalanche-Journal*, July 24, 1980.

10. Norval Pollard, "SWC Defenders Top All-America List," *Lubbock Avalanche-Journal*, July 30, 1980. See also "Red Raider Grid Squad Begins Fall Workouts," *Lubbock Avalanche-Journal*, August 10, 1980.

11. For information on this rivalry, see http://www.winsipedia.com/texas-tech/vs/utep.

12. Russ Parsons, "Mistakes Cost Tilt for UTEP," *Lubbock Avalanche-Journal*, September 7, 1980.

13. Norval Pollard, "UNC Drops Error-Prone Raiders, 9–3"; Chuck McDonald, "Raider Defense Deserved Better," *Lubbock Avalanche-Journal*, September 14, 1980.

14. Norval Pollard, "Tech Attendance Down," *Lubbock Avalanche-Journal*, September 25, 1980.

15. Norval Pollard, "Raiders' Offense Loses Poise," *Lubbock Avalanche-Journal*, September 29, 1980; "Tech Blockers Must Prove Ability," *Lubbock Avalanche-Journal*, September 30, 1980; Chuck McDonald, "When in Doubt . . . ," *Lubbock Avalanche-Journal*, September 30, 1980.

16. Norval Pollard, "Inconsistent Raiders, Aggies to Battle," *Lubbock Avalanche-Journal*, October 4, 1980.

17. For information on the Owls' 1980 season, see https://www.sports-reference.com/cfb/schools/rice/1980.html.

18. For specifics on this game, see https://stats.texassports.com/custompages/sports/m-footbl/archive/stats/80/ut-tech.htm.

19. See https://www.sports-reference.com/cfb/schools/texas-christian/1980-schedule.html.

20. Norval Pollard, "Tech Loses Poise in TCU Upset," *Lubbock Avalanche-Journal*, November 10, 1980.

21. "Big Play Rivera Shines in Loss," *Lubbock Avalanche-Journal*, November 13, 1980.

22. Norval Pollard, "Tech Aware of SMU Strengths," *Lubbock Avalanche-Journal*, November 12, 1980.

23. Norval Pollard, "Raiders Revert to Upset Tactics," *Lubbock Avalanche-Journal*, November 16, 1980; Chuck McDonald, "Snuff, Snow Steam SMU," *Lubbock Avalanche-Journal*, November 16, 1980. See also "Rivera Wolfs Down Defensive Honors," *Lubbock Avalanche-Journal*, November 20, 1980.

24. Norval Pollard, "No Bowl Bid Disappoints Tech," *Lubbock Avalanche-Journal*, November 17, 1980.

25. Norval Pollard, "Raider Passing Game Sparkles in Defeat," *Lubbock Avalanche-Journal*, November 30, 1980, and "Tech Loss Blamed on Turnovers," *Lubbock Avalanche-Journal*, December 1, 1980. See also Norval Pollard, "Dockery's Job in No Peril This Year," *Lubbock Avalanche-Journal*, December 5, 1980.

26. "Watts, Baker Top Tech All-SWC Honorees," *Lubbock Avalanche-Journal*, November 28, 1980; "Returnees Lead AP All-America Team," *Lubbock Avalanche-Journal*, December 4, 1980.

27. Preston Jordan, Texas Tech Athletic Information Office, email to author, October 3, 2019.

28. Norval Pollard, "In the Note . . . ," *Lubbock Avalanche-Journal*, December 12, 1980. See also "1980 Texas Tech Red Raiders Roster," https://gotigersgo.com/news/2013/10/24/The_Late_Rex_Dockery_to_be_Honored_with_Liberty_Bowl_Field_Rededication.aspx (accessed September 25, 2019).

29. Norval Pollard, "Dockery Takes Memphis Post," *Lubbock Avalanche-Journal*, December 17, 1980.

30. "The Late Rex Dockery to Be Honored with Liberty Bowl Field Rededication," October 24, 2013. See https://gotigersgo.com/news/2013/10/24/The_Late_Rex_Dockery_to_be_Honored_with_Liberty_Bowl_Field_Rededication.aspx (accessed September 25, 2019).

31. Norval Pollard, "Two Raider Coaches to Go with Dockery," *Lubbock Avalanche-Journal*, December 18, 1980.

32. Jim Bates, interview with author, September 27, 2019.

33. Norval Pollard, "NTSU Coach Lands Post at Tech," *Lubbock Avalanche-Journal*, January 5, 1981; Chuck McDonald, "Moore Envisions Changes in Program," *Lubbock Avalanche-Journal*, January 5, 1981. See also https://www.sports-reference.com/cfb/schools/texas-tech/1980-roster.html; https://www.sports-reference.com/cfb/schools/texas-tech/1981-roster.html; https://www.sports-reference.com/cfb/schools/texas-tech/1982-roster.html.

34. All by Norval Pollard: "Raider Offense Coils, Strikes," *Lubbock Avalanche-Journal*, April 5, 1981; "Tech Offense Shapes Up; Injuries Concern Moore," *Lubbock Avalanche-Journal*, April 9, 1981; "Tech Offense Shines Again," *Lubbock Avalanche-Journal*, April 12, 1981; "Raiders Click Right Along," *Lubbock Avalanche-Journal*, April 15, 1981; and

"Reeves Explodes in Scrimmage," *Lubbock Avalanche-Journal*, April 19, 1981.

35. Norval Pollard, "Raiders Click Right Along," *Lubbock Avalanche-Journal*, April 15, 1981.

36. Norval Pollard, "Big Gabe Beckons Blacks to 10–0 Blanking of Reds," *Lubbock Avalanche-Journal*, April 26, 1981. See also Mike Keeney, "Gabe, Black 'Sack' Red," *University Daily*, April 27, 1981.

37. Norval Pollard, "Offensive Lack of Depth Worries Moore," *Lubbock Avalanche-Journal*, September 2, 1981.

38. Norval Pollard, "Tech Awaits New Season," *Lubbock Avalanche-Journal*, September 6, 1981.

39. Randy Riggs, "Moore Has Red Raiders Believin'," *Austin American Statesman*, September 2, 1981.

40. *Texas Tech Red Raiders 1981 Football Media Guide*, 128–29.

41. Nobert Rivera, interview with author, February 22, 2019.

42. See http://cfbdatawarehouse.com/data/div_ia/big12/texas_tech/yearly_totals.php.

43. Norval Pollard, "Gabriel's Key Chances for Tech, UNM," *Lubbock Avalanche-Journal*, September 19, 1981.

44. Ibid.

45. Chuck McDonald, "Tech Bends, But Holds," and Norval Pollard, "Moore Credits Linemen's Play," *Lubbock Avalanche-Journal*, September 20, 1981. See also Ray Glass, "UNM Coach Calls Penalty the Key," *Lubbock Avalanche-Journal*, September 20. 1981.

46. Norval Pollard, "Tech Still a Mystery," *Lubbock Avalanche-Journal*, September 29, 1981.

47. Norval Pollard, "Tech Defense Does Job Well"; and "Tech's Reeves Takes Beating," *Lubbock Avalanche-Journal*, October 25, 1981.

48. Norval Pollard, "Frosh Key to Future," *Lubbock Avalanche-Journal*, November 3, 1981.

49. Norval Pollard, "Tech, TCU Try to Limp out of Cellar," *Lubbock Avalanche-Journal*, November 7, 1981.

50. Norval Pollard, "Frogs Rally to Tie Tech, 39–39," *Lubbock Avalanche-Journal*, November 8, 1981; "Nightmare Finish Frustrates Moore," *Lubbock Avalanche-Journal*, November 9, 1981.

51. Norval Pollard, "Ponies Powder Charitable Tech," *Lubbock Avalanche-Journal*, November 15, 1981; "Cougars Edge Stubborn Tech," *Lubbock Avalanche-Journal*, November 22, 1981.

52. Norval Pollard, "Red Raider Fans Deserve a Big Hand," *Lubbock Avalanche-Journal*, November 17, 1981.

53. See https://www.cfbhall.com/about/inductees/inductee/gabe-rivera-2012/. See also https://s3.amazonaws.com/sidearm.sites/texastech.com/documents/2005/8/29/05 mediaguide-history.pdf, 161.

54. Norval Pollard, "Only One Red Raider . . . UnBaerable," *Lubbock Avalanche-Journal*, December 1, 1981. See also Norval Pollard, "Raider Coaches Expect Banner Crop," *Lubbock Avalanche-Journal*, February 10, 1982.

55. Mike Benton, "Raiders Suspend Rivera," *San Antonio Express-News*, February 13, 1982. See also https://www.upi.com/Archives/1982/02/12/Texas-Tech-University-football-coach-Jerry-Moore-announced-today/6863382338000/.

56. Norval Pollard, "Moore Suspends Gridders," February 13, 1982.

57. Benton, "Raiders Suspend Rivera." See also Norbert Rivera, interview with author, February 22, 2019.

58. Norbert Rivera, interview with author, February 22, 2019.

59. Norval Pollard, "Spring Training Livens Air at Tech," *Lubbock Avalanche-Journal,* March 23, 1982.

60. Norval Pollard, "How's Tech You Ask," *Lubbock Avalanche-Journal*, March 28, 1982; "Tech's Moore Wearing a Smile," *Lubbock Avalanche-Journal*, April 2, 1982; "Reyneveld Eases Tech's DT Woes," *Lubbock Avalanche-Journal*, April 4, 1982.

61. Norval Pollard, "Alumni Face Raiders Saturday," *Lubbock Avalanche-Journal*, April 21, 1982; "Alumni Contest Ticks

Like Clockwork," *Lubbock Avalanche-Journal*, April 25, 1982.

62. Norbert Rivera, interview with author, February 22, 2019. Also, Jim Bates, interview with author, September 27, 2019.

63. Letter from Coach Moore to Juan and Maria Antonia Rivera, June 21, 1982, Gabe Rivera Collection, Southwest Collection Archive, Texas Tech University.

64. Elaine Noll, "Rivera Reinstated," *San Antonio Express*, July 20, 1982. See also "EP's Rothblatt Rejoins Raiders after Suspension," *El Paso Times*, July 21, 1982; "Rivera Reinstated," *New Braunfels Herald Zeitung*, July 21, 1982.

65. Norval Pollard, "Raiders Laud Land, Raider Newcomers," *Lubbock Avalanche-Journal*, August 14, 1982. See also "Raiders Greet Walk-Ons," *Lubbock Avalanche-Journal*, August 31, 1982.

66. Ken Murray, "Rivera Has a Lot to Prove for the Red Raiders This Fall," *Austin American-Statesman,* September 1, 1982.

67. Norval Pollard, "Big Gabe Back in Spotlight," *Lubbock Avalanche-Journal,* September 22, 1982.

68. See "Gabriel Rivera: All America Candidate," publicity sheet. Gabe Rivera Collection, Southwest Collection Archive, Texas Tech University. Most of the individual game tackle totals for this season for Rivera come from this sheet. See also Norval Pollard, "Raiders Attempt to Reverse Fortunes," *Lubbock Avalanche-Journal,* September 18, 1982.

69. Norval Pollard, "Big Gabe Back in Spotlight," *Lubbock Avalanche-Journal,* September 22, 1982.

70. Norval Pollard, "Frosh Cool in Clutch," *Lubbock Avalanche-Journal,* October 3, 1982.

71. Norval Pollard, "Revived Raiders Wrestle Razorbacks," *Lubbock Avalanche-Journal,* October 9, 1982.

72. Norval Pollard, "Gabe Steals Smith's Act," *Lubbock Avalanche-Journal,* October 10, 1982.

73. Norval Pollard, "Offensive Lull Costs Raiders," *Lubbock Avalanche-Journal,* October 11, 1982.

74. Norval Pollard, "Moore Eyes No. 1 Test," *Lubbock*

Avalanche-Journal, October 19, 1982.

75. Norval Pollard, "Raiders Challenge No. 1 Huskies," *Lubbock Avalanche-Journal,* October 23, 1982.

76. Norval Pollard, "Rivera Draws Rave Reviews," *Lubbock Avalanche-Journal,* October 24, 1982. For the comments by the Husky players, see also "Gabriel Rivera: All America Candidate."

77. Steve Rudman, "Señor Sack Gone, But Not Forgotten at UW," *Seattle Post-Intelligencer,* October 24, 1982; John Owen, "Huskies Face Big Gabe, Live to Tell of It," *Seattle Post-Intelligencer,* October 24, 1982; Gil Lyons, "Huskies' Laud Raiders' 'Big Foot' in Wake of Win," *Seattle Times,* October 24, 1982.

78. Norval Pollard, "'Big Foot' Sighted in Pacific Northwest," *Lubbock Avalanche-Journal,* October 26, 1982.

79. Norval Pollard, "Stability Aids in Recruiting," and "Rivera's Play 'Awesome,'" *Lubbock Avalanche-Journal,* October 27, 1982. See also "Señor Sack Succeeds," *Austin American-Statesman,* October 27, 1982; "'Señor Sack' Bags Top SWC Honors," *San Antonio Express,* October 27, 1982.

80. Clifford Broyles, "Rivera Blasts toward All-America Honors," *San Antonio Express,* October 28, 1982.

81. Letter from Coach Frank Howard to Coach Jerry Moore, October 28, 1982, Gabe Rivera Collection, Southwest Collection Archive, Texas Tech University.

82. See "Gabriel Rivera: All America Candidate" and the box score for the game at https://web.archive.org/web/20101125075334/http://mackbrown-texasfootball.com/sports/m-footbl/archive/stats/82/ut-tech.htm.

83. Letter from Jerry Moore to Mr. and Mrs. Juan Rivera, November 6, 1982, Gabe Rivera Collection, Southwest Collection Archive, Texas Tech University.

84. Ray Glass, "Rivera Ends Career in Stellar Fashion," *Lubbock Avalanche-Journal,* November 21, 1982.

85. Norval Pollard, "Gabe Grabs Kodak All America Berth,"

Lubbock Avalanche-Journal, November 23, 1982; Murray Olderman, "Walker, Elway Head NEA Honorees," *Lubbock Avalanche-Journal*, November 23, 1982; "Gabe Rivera Wins Spot on Coaches' All America," *San Antonio Light,* November 23, 1982.

86. Letter from Chuck Knox to Gabriel Rivera, December 14, 1982, Gabe Rivera Collection, Southwest Collection Archive, Texas Tech University.

87. Kim Pappas, interview with author, February 9, 2020.

CHAPTER 6

1. 2019 *Texas Tech Football Media Guide*, 168. The electronic version of this document is available at https://s3.amazonaws.com/sidearm.sites/texastech.com/documents/2019/7/19/Texas_Tech_2019_Media_Guide.pdf.

2. Telegram from Art Rooney Jr. to Gabe Rivera, December 29, 1982, Gabe Rivera Collection, Southwest Collection Archive, Texas Tech University.

3. Letter from Dr. William Elizondo to Principals and Football Coaches of SAISD, December 1982, and Letter from Dr. William Elizondo to Juan and Maria Antonia Rivera, December 17, 1982. Both items are part of the Gabe Rivera Collection, Southwest Collection Archive, Texas Tech University.

4. Copy of press release by the Mexican American Sports Association, Gabe Rivera Collection, Southwest Collection Archive, Texas Tech University.

5. "Gabe Rivera Day" press release, Gabe Rivera Collection, Southwest Collection Archive, Texas Tech University.

6. Letters (all to Gabriel Rivera) from Edward C. Burt Jr., December 21, 1982; Jim Armstrong, December 23, 1982; and Robert J. Komarek, December 27, 1982, Gabe Rivera Collection, Southwest Collection Archive, Texas Tech University.

7. Norbert Rivera, interview with author, March 14, 2019.

8. Duane Plank, "This Professor Deals in Dollars and

Sense," *Los Angeles Times,* January 3, 1992, https://www.
latimes.com/archives/la-xpm-1992-01-03-sp-5617-story.
html (accessed October 29, 2019). See also "Black Sports
Agents Make Inroads in Competitive Field, But Still
Have a Long Way to Go," *Jet,* May 8, 1995, 50. See https://
books.google.com/books?id=ezkDAAAAMBAJ&p-
g=PA50&lpg=PA50&dq=harold+%22doc%22+daniels&-
source=bl&ots=PxEhBt8cLF&sig=ACfU3U3tWVxMt8xvjr
XgClP8DbjnagS-Dg&hl=en&sa=X&ved=2ahUKEwj66JX-
ei8LlAhVHKKwKHUaLCsYQ6AEwAnoECAkQAQ#v=o-
nepage&q=harold%20%22doc%22%20daniels&f=false
(accessed October 29, 2019).

9. Josh Luchs, "Confessions of an Agent," *Sports Illustrated,* October 17, 2010. See https://www.si.com/
vault/2010/10/18/105995454/confessions-of-an-agent
(accessed October 29, 2019).

10. Norbert Rivera, interview with author, March 14, 2019.

11. Ibid.

12. Kim Pappas, interview with author, February 9, 2020.

13. Joe Stein, "Questions Surround Defensive Linemen," *Sporting News,* April 4, 1983.

14. Aaron Tallent, "10 Greatest Draft Classes in NFL History,"
April 23, 2019, accessed October 30, 2019, https://athlon-
sports.com/nfl/10-greatest-draft-classes-nfl-history.

15. Michael MacCambridge, *Chuck Noll: His Life's Work* (Pittsburgh, PA: University of Pittsburgh Press, 2016), and Art
Rooney Jr. with Roy McHugh, *Ruanaidh: The Story of Art
Rooney and His Clan* (Pittsburgh, PA: Geyer Printing Company, 2008).

16. Rooney, *Ruanaidh,* 445.

17. See https://www.sports-reference.com/cfb/players/
dan-marino-1.html.

18. Rooney, *Ruanaidh,* 445.

19. Ibid., 445–46.

20. Ibid., 446.

21. Ibid., 447.

22. MacCambridge, *Chuck Noll*, 293. See also Dave Anderson, "The 'Pittsburgh Guy' Who Got Away from the Steelers," *New York Times*, January 6, 1985, https://www.nytimes.com/1985/01/06/sports/sports-of-the-times-the-pittsburgh-guy-who-got-away-from-steelers.html (accessed October 24, 2019).

23. John Clayton, "NFL Draft Wheeling 'N Dealing," *Pittsburgh Press*, April 25, 1983.

24. Jim O'Brien, "Steelers Choose Texas Tech's Señor Sack," *Pittsburgh Press*, April 26, 1983.

25. Jim O'Brien, "Rivera No. 1 in Size, Speed and Appetite," *Pittsburgh Press*, April 27, 1983.

26. Tom McMillan, "Rivera Seen as Big Factor in Steelers' 3–4 Defense," *Pittsburgh Post-Gazette*, April 27, 1983.

27. Dave Ailes, "Steelers Grab 'Freight Train,'" and "Steelers' Draft Aim: Rebuild Defense," *Pittsburgh Tribune-Review*, April 27, 1983.

28. Will McDonough, "NFL Draftees Cash in on USFL," *San Antonio Light*, July 13, 1983.

29. John Clayton, "Agent Daniels Builds Big Case for Rivera," *Pittsburgh Press*, April 28, 1983.

30. Kim Pappas, interview with author, February 9, 2020.

31. Pat Livingston, "You Can Call Rivera's Agent 'Señor Smoothtalker,'" *Pittsburgh Press*, April 29, 1983. See also John Clayton, "Rating the Winners and Losers in This Year's Draft," *Pittsburgh Press*, May 1, 1983.

32. Dave Ailes, "Steelers' Fans Gonna Love Top Pick Rivera," and Mike Dudurich, "Rivera: Too Good for Pittsburgh to Pass Up," *Pittsburgh Tribune-Review*, April 29, 1983.

33. Jim O'Brien, "Rivera No. 1 in Size, Speed and Appetite," *Pittsburgh Press*, April 27, 1983.

34. Jim O'Brien, "Q & A: Gabe Rivera," *Pittsburgh Press*, May 2, 1983.

35. Dave Ailes, "Steelers, Rivera Near an Agreement,"

Pittsburgh Tribune-Review, May 24, 1983. See also David Ailes, "Steelers: Brad Meets 'El-What's-His-Name,'" *Pittsburgh Tribune-Review*, May 25, 1983.

36. McDonough, "NFL Draftees Cash Ion USFL"; John Clayton, "Draft Picks Signing Contracts Quickly," *Pittsburgh Press*, May 29, 1983.

37. NIOSA is an acronym for "A Night in Old San Antonio," which began in the late 1930s. It is a multiday celebration of the city's historical and cultural legacy. See https://www.niosa.org/p/home/history. Also see letters from Amy Alexander and Bill Kauffman to Gabe Rivera, not dated, Gabe Rivera Collection, Southwest Collection Archive, Texas Tech University.

38. Jim O'Brien, "Will Rivera Make an Impact? Greene Believes He Can," *Pittsburgh Press*, June 28, 1983. See also Gary Tuma, "Mean Joe: He's Back at Training Camp to Sample the Coaching Life," *Pittsburgh Post-Gazette*, July 12, 1983.

39. Bruce Keidan, "Rivera's Arrival Whets Steeler Appetite," *Pittsburgh Post-Gazette*, July 9, 1983; Vic Ketchman, "Top Pick Texas Tech's Gabe Rivera," *Pittsburgh Steelers Weekly*, July 1983 (bonus issue). See also "New 'Jaws' Awes Steelers," *San Antonio Express*, July 14, 1983.

40. John Clayton, "Injuries Changing Picture for Steelers," *Pittsburgh Press*, July 24, 1983. See also https://www.profootballhof.com/hall-of-fame-game-results/.

41. Gary Tuma, "Loose End: Top Draft Pick Rivera Wasn't Uptight for His Steeler Debut," *Pittsburgh Post-Gazette*, August 3, 1983.

42. Vic Ketchman, "Rookie," *Pittsburgh Steelers Weekly*, August 15, 1983.

43. John Clayton, "Steeler Defense Turns on the Heat as Eagles Get Burned," *Pittsburgh Press*, August 26, 1983.

44. John Clayton, "All Eyes Focusing on No. 1 Picks," *Pittsburgh Press*, August 29, 1983.

45. Gary Tuma, "Torn Curtain," *Pittsburgh Post-Gazette*, September 9, 1983. See also "NFL Update," *Sporting News*, September 19, 1983. For the results of the 1983 Denver and Green Bay games with the Steelers, see https://www.footballdb.com/games/boxscore.html?gid=1983090405 and https://www.footballdb.com/games/boxscore.html?gid=1983091106.
46. John Clayton, "Señor Diet," *Pittsburgh Press*, September 25, 1983.
47. John Clayton, "Rivera Weighing Less, Playing More," *Pittsburgh Press*, October 15, 1983.
48. John Clayton, "Warning Shot: After Gary's Tackle, Steelers, Browns Might Play Cautiously," *Pittsburgh Press*, October 16, 1983.
49. "Steelers' Rivera Critically Hurt," *Pittsburgh Post-Gazette*, October 21, 1983.

CHAPTER 7

1. John Clayton, "Full of Life, Rivera Was Always Butt of Steeler Jokes," *Pittsburgh Press*, October 21, 1983.
2. Darryl Stingley with Mark Mulvoy, *Happy to Be Alive* (New York: Beaufort Books, 1983). A similar story can be found in a work by Dennis Byrd (who played with the New York Jets) with Michael D'Orso, *Rise and Walk: The Trial and Triumph of Dennis Byrd* (New York: HarperCollins, 1993).
3. Derek Michael Zike, "Athletes' Experiences of Leaving Sport Due to Spinal Cord Injury: A Multiple Case Study Examination" (master's thesis, Miami University, 2016). Zike is currently working on his doctorate at the Department of Kinesiology at the University of Wisconsin–Milwaukee. Two other works consulted for this discussion were Wendy Seymour, *Remaking the Body: Rehabilitation and Change* (New York: Routledge, 1998), and Maria Doelger Anderson, "The Death of 'the Dream': The Experience of Loss of a Central Identity among Professional Athletes"

(PhD diss., Stony Brook University, 2012).

4. Norbert Rivera, interview with author, March 14, 2019.

5. Jim and Karan Covington, interview with author, February 7, 2020; Kim Pappas, interview with author, February 9, 2020.

6. William Mausteller, "Gabe Rivera Critical after Crash," *Pittsburgh Press*, October 21, 1983.

7. Ibid.

8. Ibid.

9. Jim Gallagher and Andrew Sheehan, "Charged: Drunken Driving Laid to Injured Rivera," *Pittsburgh Post-Gazette*, October 22, 1983.

10. Mary Pat Flaherty, "Rivera Joked, Drank before Crash," *Pittsburgh Press*, October 22, 1983.

11. Stephen Sharpe, "The Gabe Rivera Tragedy: DWI," *San Antonio Light*, October 22, 1983.

12. "Neurosurgeon Doubts If Gabe Can Play Again," *Lubbock Evening Journal*, October 24, 1983.

13. "A Tragic Ride," *Pittsburgh Post-Gazette*, October 25, 1983.

14. "Rivera Cited in Five Texas Traffic Incidents," *Pittsburgh Press*, October 25, 1983.

15. Gary Tuma, "Doctor: Rivera May Be Paralyzed," *Pittsburgh Post-Gazette*, October 26, 1983; Dan Donovan, "Rivera's Chance of Walking Called Bleak," *Pittsburgh Press*, October 26, 1983.

16. David Casstevens, "Injured Former Kicker Offers Encouragement to Rivera," *Pittsburgh Post-Gazette*, November 1, 1983.

17. Information on Cunningham's injury and others like it is noted in John Underwood, "An Unfolding Tragedy," *Sports Illustrated*, August 14, 1978, https://www.si.com/vault/1978/08/14/822885/an-unfolding-tragedy-as-football-injuries-mount-lawsuits-increase-and-insurance-rates-soar-the-game-is-headed-toward-a-crisis-one-that-is-epitomized-by-the-helmet-which-is-both-a-barba-

rous-weapon-and-inadequate-protection.

18. George Cunningham, "You Can Win, Gabe," *Pittsburgh Press*, November 6, 1983.

19. Wallene Dockery, "Steelers' Mountain of a Man Faces a Steep Climb," *Memphis Press-Scimitar*, October 27, 1983.

20. Letter from David and Stacy Perez to Gabe Rivera, October 25, 1983; Perpetual Mass enrollment forms from Joan Caruso and the Morrone family to Gabe Rivera, no dates; Gabriel Rivera Collection, Southwest Collection, Texas Tech University.

21. Vic Ketchman, "Despite Surgery, Rivera Likely Paralyzed," *Pittsburgh Steelers' Weekly*, November 7, 1983.

22. Ray Galindo, interview with author, December 18, 2018.

23. "Rivera Receiving Standard Coverage," *Pittsburgh Steelers' Weekly*, November 7, 1983. See also "60 Heroes: The Queen of Benefits," November 11, 2016, accessed December 11, 2019, https://www.nflpa.com/60-heroes-the-queen-of-benefits; and "Steeler Notes," *Pittsburgh Press*, November 12, 1983.

24. Norbert Rivera, interview with author, March 14, 2019.

25. A copy of this diary was provided to the author by Ray Galindo. The document is in Spanish, and the materials presented here are the author's translation. A copy of this document is in the author's possession. Another copy has been donated to the Gabe Rivera Collection, Southwest Collection, Texas Tech University. From here on, the document is referenced as "Maria Antonia, 1983 Diary."

26. Tim Rivera, interview with author, April 14, 2019.

27. Kim Pappas, interview with author, February 9, 2020.

28. Sam Blair, "Rivera: Every Little Movement Is a Blessing," *Pittsburgh Post-Gazette*, November 23, 1983. See also John Clayton, "Rivera Shows Improvement," *Pittsburgh Press*, November 20, 1983; Norbert Rivera, interview with author, March 14, 2019.

29. Blair, "Rivera: Every Little Movement Is a Blessing."

30. Ibid.

31. These quotes come from the only portion of Maria Antonia's diary that has an October date (the 21st), though it is certain that it is a compilation of her thoughts from the days from October 21 through at least the following Friday, October 28.

32. Maria Antonia, 1983 Diary, November 18, 1983.

33. Ibid., November 19, 1983.

34. Ibid., November 20, 1983.

35. Ibid., November 21, 1983.

36. Ibid., November 22 and 23, 1983.

37. Ibid., November 24 and 25, 1983.

38. Letters from Art Rooney to Juan and Maria Antonia Rivera, December 8 and 16, 1983, Gabe Rivera Collection, Southwest Collection, Texas Tech University.

39. Letters from Art Rooney to Juan and Maria Antonia Rivera, January 4 and 27, February 24 and Christmas card, undated, 1984, Gabe Rivera Collection, Southwest Collection, Texas Tech University.

40. Henry W. Pierce, "Gabe Rivera May Go Home after 'Battle,'" *Pittsburgh Post-Gazette*, December 15, 1983.

41. Jim and Karan Covington, interview with author, February 7, 2020; Kim Pappas, interview with author, February 9, 2020.

42. "Rivera Coping with His Life in Wheelchair," *Lancaster New Era*, February 24, 1984.

43. Dan Donovan, "Hope: Gabe Rivera Optimistic, Sets Goals for Future," *Pittsburgh Press*, February 24, 1984.

44. Kevin O'Keefe, "Gabe Battles Back," *San Antonio Express*, February 24, 1984.

45. Gene Wojciechowski, "Gabe Waits for Something Good to Happen," *San Antonio Express*, February 29, 1984.

46. Al Donaldson, "Rivera Waives Drunk Hearing," *Pittsburgh Press*, March 15, 1984.

47. Postcard from Art Rooney to Gabe Rivera, March 1984, Gabe Rivera Collection, Southwest Collection, Texas Tech

University.

48. "Justice and Gabe Rivera," *Pittsburgh Press,* April 18, 1984.

49. Jim Lefko, "Gabe Clings to Hope of Walking Again," *San Antonio Light*, June 17, 1984.

50. Ibid.

51. Associated Press, "Darryl Stingley, Paralyzed by Tatum Hit, Dies at 55," April 5, 2007, https://www.espn.com/nfl/news/story?id=2826562 (accessed December 27, 2019).

52. Stingley with Mulvoy, *Happy to Be Alive*, 108.

53. Ibid, 145–47. See also "Darryl Stingley," Encyclopedia.com, accessed December 27, 2019, https://www.encyclopedia.com/education/news-wires-white-papers-and-books/stingley-darryl.

54. Jim Kleinpeter, "Darryl Stingley's Story Never Kept His Grandson, LSU Commitment Derek Stingley Jr., away from Football," *The Advocate,* August 11, 2018. See https://lsusports.net/sports/football/roster/derek-stingley-jr-/20303 (accessed December 27, 2019).

55. See https://lsusports.net/sports/football/roster/derek-stingley-jr-/20303 (accessed December 27, 2019).

56. Seymour, *Remaking the Body*, vii, 35. Seymour is citing R. Connell, "Men's Bodies," *Australian Society* 2, no. 9 (October 1987): 33–39.

57. Seymour, *Remaking the Body*, 42.

58. Ibid., 79.

59. Ibid., 158.

60. Doelger Anderson, "The Death of 'the Dream,'" 3, 5.

61. See https://www.nbcnews.com/news/sports/charles-rogers-former-detroit-lions-wide-receiver-dies-38-n1079956 (accessed December 27, 2019).

62. Doelger Anderson, "The Death of 'the Dream,'" 31.

63. Ibid., 87.

64. Ibid., 94, 105, 107, 116, 117.

65. Derek Michael Zike, interview with author, January 28, 2019.

66. Ibid.

67. Zike, "Athletes' Experiences of Leaving Sport Due to Spinal Cord Injury," 12–14.

68. Ibid., 12.

69. Kim Pappas, interview with author, February 9, 2020.

70. This fact was confirmed by Kim and Jim Covington, as well as Nancy Rivera.

71. This fact was confirmed by Kim and Jim Covington, as well as Nancy Rivera.

72. Zike, "Athletes' Experiences of Leaving Sport Due to Spinal Cord Injury," 65–72.

73. Dan Donovan, "One Year Later: Rivera Eyes an Uncertain Future," *Pittsburgh Press*, October 21, 1984.

74. Ibid.

75. "'Pressure' Kick by Ward Keeps Texas Unbeaten, 13–10," *Pittsburgh Press*, November 4, 1984.

76. Phil Musick, "Gabe Rivera Is Finally Seeing the Sun Shine Again," *Pittsburgh Press*, December 12, 1984.

77. Ron Cook, "Steelers Eye Help up Front," *Pittsburgh Press*, April 26, 1985.

78. Jim and Karan Covington, interview with author, February 7, 2020; Kim Pappas, interview with author, February 9, 2020.

79. David Flores, "Faith in Gabe, God Helps Riveras Weather Tragedy," *San Antonio Express-News,* May 4, 1986.

80. John P. Lopez, "Rivera Showing Progress in China," *San Antonio Light*, January 28, 1986. Also: Jim and Karan Covington, interview with author, February 7, 2020; Kim Pappas, interview with author, February 9, 2020.

81. Lopez, "Rivera Showing Progress in China"; also Jim and Karan Covington, interview with author, February 7, 2020; Kim Pappas, interview with author, February 9, 2020. See also Ed Bouchette, "No Miracle Cure," *Pittsburgh Post-Gazette*, August 27, 1986; Tim Griffin, "Rivera's China Odyssey," *San Antonio Express-News*, September 1, 1986.

82. Erin Powers, "What Could Have Been . . ." *Houston Chronicle*, December 17, 1987. Also: Jim and Karan Covington, interview with author, February 7, 2020; Kim Pappas, interview with author, February 9, 2020.

83. Norbert Rivera, interviews with author, March 14 and 21, 2019.

84. Ibid. See also Jim Lefko, "Making It on His Own," *San Antonio Light*, October 24, 1988.

85. "All Southwest Conference Decade," *San Antonio Express-News*, December 17, 1989.

86. Richard Martinez, "Rivera Heads Hall Inductees," *San Antonio Express-News*, January 13, 1990, and "Rivera, Torres Lead Hall Inductees," *San Antonio Express-News*, January 14, 1990. See also Program for Latin American International Hall of Fame induction ceremony, January 13, 1990, Gabe Rivera Collection, Southwest Collection, Texas Tech University.

87. Texas Tech University football program, October 9, 1993.

88. David Flores, "S.A. Group Helping Young Hispanic Athletes," *San Antonio Express-News*, September 23, 1999. See also "Hispanic Sports Hall of Fame" program for September 22, 1999, Gabe Rivera Collection, Southwest Collection, Texas Tech University; and http://www.hsffe.com/about-us/.

89. "Police Nab Rivera on Pot Charge," *San Antonio Express-News*, March 13, 1990. See also Norbert Rivera, interviews with author, March 14 and 21, 2019, and "Veteran Coach Rivera Dies at Age 60," *San Antonio Express-News*, November 6, 1990.

90. Kim indicated during our interview that the reason was that Gabe was in Harmarville and in China for so long that Tim heard her always referring to her husband by his name. Tim picked up on this, and she did not change his habit.

91. Tim Rivera, interview with author, April 14, 2019. The author has copies of the emails to Carmela (to protect her

privacy, I have not used her last name). See also "Spinal Cord Injury and Functional Electrical Stimulation," *Progress Report*, Spring 1990, Gabe Rivera Collection, Southwest Collection, Texas Tech University.

92. Tim Griffin, "S. A.'s Rivera Bouncing Back 10 Years after Tragic Accident," *San Antonio Express-News*, October 6, 1993.

93. David Flores, "A Cruel Twist of Fate: Rivera's Team Is Living His Super Dream," *San Antonio Express-News*, January 26, 1996.

CHAPTER 8

1. One time, as Gabe did his volunteer work at Inner City, he told the students about his 1983 accident. One of the children innocently asked him about how much damage was done to the LTD involved. Gabe provided the young man with an off-the-top estimate of $1,000. The boy's response to this was the quote noted in the chapter title.

2. Norbert Rivera, interview with author, April 14, 2019.

3. Edmond Ortiz, "Rivera Tutoring Youngsters," *San Antonio Express-News*, October 6, 1999; David Flores, "Game Takes Rivera Back," *San Antonio Express-News*, December 30, 2001. Nancy Rivera, interview with author, January 31, 2020.

4. Donald L. Zelman, "ALAZAN-APACHE COURTS," *Handbook of Texas Online*, http://www.tshaonline.org/handbook/online/articles/mpa01 (accessed January 17, 2020).

5. For information on the historical success of the Voks' basketball program, see Ignacio M. Garcia, *When Mexicans Could Play Ball: Basketball, Race, and Identity in San Antonio, 1929–1945* (Austin: University of Texas Press, 2013). Patti and Rod Radle mentioned during our interview that many of the current players on the varsity and junior varsity teams at Lanier honed their skills as youths at Inner City.

6. Patti and Rod Radle, interview with author, January 10, 2019. See also Inner City Development, "50 Years of Service on San Antonio's Westside," 2018, 2 (brochure; copy in

author's possession).

7. Patti and Rod Radle, interview with author, January 10, 2019. See also Inner City Development, "50 Years of Service on San Antonio's Westside," 2.

8. Patti and Rod Radle, interview with author, January 10, 2019.

9. Ortiz, "Rivera Tutoring Youngsters."

10. "Thanks Gabriel." Gabriel Rivera Collection, Southwest Collection Archive, Texas Tech University.

11. Ibid.

12. JR Cisneros, interview with author, January 19, 2020.

13. Rusty Berson, "Gabe Rivera: Working to Walk," *Dave Campbell's Texas Football: 40th Year Commemorative Edition*, Fall 2000.

14. Jaime Aron, "No. 1 Nebraska 56, Texas Tech 3," Associated Press, October 14, 2000. See https://apnews.com/4ee5fc-cocd4eadae4434d3e90697ce04 (accessed January 28, 2020).

15. David Flores, "Game Takes Rivera Back," *San Antonio Express-News*, December 30, 2001.

16. Jorge Oliver, "Una Estrella de Acero Sanantoniano," *Rumbo de San Antonio*, December 24–26, 2004. Author's translation from Spanish.

17. Ron Cook, "Disability Doesn't Stop Rivera," *Pittsburgh Post-Gazette*, May 18, 2012. For information on his induction into the San Antonio Sports Hall of Fame, see https://www.youtube.com/watch?v=M__V16fUoRw. Finally, for Gabe's College Football Hall of Fame page, see https://www.cfbhall.com/about/inductees/inductee/gabe-rivera-2012/.

18. See https://texastech.com/sports/2016/6/8/feature-roh-timeline-html.aspx.

19. Ibid.

20. David Flores, "Rivera Relates to Thomas," *San Antonio Express-News*, January 31, 2000; Mike Freeman, "Pro Football; Chiefs' Thomas Dies Unexpectedly during Hospital Stay," *New York Times,* February 9, 2000, https://www.

nytimes.com/2000/02/09/sports/pro-football-chiefs-thoma s-dies-unexpectedly-during-hospital-stay.html (accessed January 29, 2020).

21. Ed Bouchette, "Gabe Rivera, a Paralyzed Former Steeler, Pulling for Ryan Shazier," *Pittsburgh Post-Gazette*, May 17, 2018.

22. David Flores, "Rivera Remains Upbeat Hombre," *San Antonio Express-News*, July 2005 (clipping in file, date unavailable).

23. Norbert Rivera, interview with author, March 21, 2019; Patti and Rod Radle, interview with author, January 10, 2019. See also Tom Osborn, "Former Texas Tech Star Gabe Rivera Dead at 57," *Houston Chronicle*, July 17, 2018, accessed January 30, 2020, https://www.houstonchronicle.com/ sports/college/article/Former-Texas-Tech-star-Gabe-Rive- ra-Señor-Sack-dead-13082194.php.

24. Norbert Rivera, interview with author, March 21, 2019; Patti and Rod Radle, interview with author, January 10, 2019. See also Osborn, "Former Texas Tech Star Gabe Rivera Dead at 57"; Tim Rivera, interview with author, April 14, 2019; JR Cisneros, interview with author, January 19, 2020.

25. David Flores, "'Don't Drink and Drive' Became Rivera's Mantra after Life-Altering Accident," *San Antonio Express-News*, July 27, 2018; Nancy Rivera, interview with author, January 31, 2020.

CONCLUSION

1. Poem by JR Cisneros. Copy in author's possession.

2. "Texas Tech Mourns the Passing of Gabe Rivera," July 17, 2018, https://texastech.com/news/2018/7/17/double- t-varsity-club-texas-tech-mourns-the-passing-of-gabe-ri- vera.aspx.

3. See the following: "Gabe Rivera, Texas Tech and Steelers Player Left Paralyzed, Dies at 57," https://www.espn.com/

college-football/story/_/id/24122918/gabe-rivera-texas-tec
h-pittsburgh-steelers-player-left-paralyzed-dies-57; Ray
Fittipaldo, "Obituary: Gabe Rivera, Former No. 1 Draft
Pick of the Steelers, Dies at 57," *Pittsburgh Post-Gazette,*
July 17, 2018, https://www.post-gazette.com/sports/steel-
ers/2018/07/17/Gabe-Rivera-Steelers-defensive-lineman-
paralyzed-Art-Rooney-Jr-Woody-Widenhofer/sto-
ries/201807170114; Tom Osborn, "San Antonio Loses Football Legend Gabe Rivera," *San Antonio Express-News*, July 17,
2018, https://www.expressnews.com/sports/colleges/article/
San-Antonio-loses-football-legend-Gabe-Rivera-13083061.
php; Ben Spicer, "Tributes Pour in for San Antonio Football Legend 'Señor Sack' Who Died Monday," *San Antonio Express-News*, July 17, 2018, https://www.expressnews.
com/sports/colleges/article/San-Antonio-loses-footbal
l-legend-Gabe-Rivera-13083061.php.

4. Nancy Rivera, interview with author, January 31, 2020;
Tim Rivera, interview with author, April 14, 2019; Norbert
Rivera, interview with author, March 21, 2019; Rod and
Patti Radle, interview with author, January 10, 2019; JR Cis-
neros, interview with author, January 19, 2020.

5. Ray Galindo, email to author, February 6, 2020.

6. David Flores, "'Don't Drink and Drive' Became Rivera's
Mantra after Life-Altering Accident," July 27, 2018, https://
www.kens5.com/article/sports/dont-drink-and-driv
e-became-riveras-mantra-after-life-altering-acci-
dent/273-577926453.

7. Mario Longoria and Jorge Iber, *Latinos in American Football:
Pathbreakers on the Gridiron* (Jefferson, NC: McFarland and
Company, 2020).

8. Keith D. Parry, "The Bad, the Good, and the Ugly: The
Formation of Heroes within the Setting of a New Sports
Team" (PhD diss., Institute for Culture and Society, West-
ern Sidney University, 2017), iv.

9. Jorge Iber, "Mexican Americans of South Texas Football:

The Athletic and Coaching Careers of E. C. Lerma and Bobby Cavazos, 1932–1965," *Southwestern Historical Quarterly* 105, no. 4 (April 2002): 616–33.

10. Richard Ian Kimball, *Legends Never Die: Athletes and Their Afterlives in Modern America* (Syracuse, NY: Syracuse University Press, 2017).

11. Ibid., 5.

12. Ibid., 4.

13. Francisco Machorro, "Touchdown," undated. Copy in author's possession.

SELECTED BIBLIOGRAPHY

Barrera, Baldemar James. "'We Want Better Education': The Chicano Student Movement for Educational Reform in South Texas, 1968–1970." PhD diss., University of New Mexico, 2007.

Barron, David. "The Birth of Texas Schoolboy Football." In *King Football: Greatest Moments in Texas High School Football History*, edited by Mike Bynum, 26–39. Birmingham, AL: Epic Sports Classics, 2003.

Cashion, Ty. *Pigskin Pulpit: A Social History of Texas High School Football Coaches*. Austin: Texas State Historical Association, 1998.

De Leon, Arnoldo. "Our *Gringo Amigos*: Anglo Americans and the Tejano Experience." *East Texas Historical Association Yearbook* 22, no. 2 (1993): 72–79.

Doelger Anderson, Maria. "The Death of 'The Dream': The Experience of Loss of a Central Identity Among Professional Athletes." PhD diss., Stony Brook University, 2012.

Foley, Douglas E. *Learning Capitalist Culture Deep in the Heart of Texas*. Philadelphia: University of Pennsylvania Press, 1990.

Frank, Joel S. *Asians and Pacific Islanders in American Football: Historical and Contemporary Experiences*. Lanham, MD: Lexington Books, 2018.

Garcia, Ignacio M. *United We Win: The Rise and Fall of La Raza Unida Party*. Tucson, AZ: University of Arizona Press, 1989.

———. *When Mexicans Could Play Ball: Basketball, Race, and Identity in San Antonio, 1929–1945*. Austin: University of

Texas Press, 2013.

Gems, Gerald R. *For Pride, Profit, and Patriarchy: Football and the Incorporation of American Cultural Values*. Lanham, MD: Scarecrow Press, 2000.

———. *Sport and the Shaping of Italian American Identity*. Syracuse, NY: Syracuse University Press, 2013.

Gutierrez, Jose Angel. *The Making of a Chicano Militant: Lessons from Cristal*. Madison: University of Wisconsin Press, 1998.

———. *"We Won't Back Down!": Severita Lara's Rise from Student Leader to Mayor*. Houston, TX: Arte Publico Press, 2005.

Huerta, Joel. "Friday Night Rights: South Texas High-school Football and the Struggle for Equality." *The International Journal of the History of Sport* 26 (June 2009): 981–1000.

Iber, Jorge. "Becoming Raiders Rojos: Using Sport to Claim Hispanic 'Space' at Texas Tech University." *West Texas Historical Association Yearbook* 77 (2001): 139–51.

———. "Bobby Cavazos: A Vaquero in the Backfield." *College Football Historical Society* 14 (August 2001): 1–5.

———. "Mexican Americans of South Texas Football: The Athletic and Coaching Careers of E. C. Lerma and Bobby Cavazos, 1932–1965." *Southwestern Historical Quarterly* 55 (April 2002): 617–33.

———. "On Field Foes and Racial Misperceptions: The 1961 Donna Redskins and Their Drive to the Texas State Football Championship." In *Mexican Americans and Sports: A Reader on Athletics and Barrio Life*, edited by Jorge Iber and Samuel O. Regalado, 121–44. College Station: Texas A&M University Press, 2007.

———. "The Pigskin *Pulpito*: A Brief Overview of the Experiences of Mexican American High School Football Coaches in Texas." In *Sport and the Racial Divide: African American and Latino Experience in an Era of Change*, edited by Michael E. Lomax, 178–95. Jackson: University Press of Mississippi, 2008.

Iber, Jorge, Samuel O. Regalado, Jose M. Alamillo, and

Arnoldo De Leon. *Latinos in U.S. Sport: A History of Isolation, Cultural Identity, and Acceptance.* Champaign, IL: Human Kinetics, 2011.

Kapp, Joe, and Jack Olsen. "A Man of Machismo." *Sports Illustrated*, July 19, 1970, 26–31.

Kugelmass, Jack. *Jews, Sports, and the Rites of Citizenship.* Champaign: University of Illinois Press, 2007.

Langenegger, Joyce Anne. "The School as a Political Tool." Master's thesis, Baylor University, 1993.

Longoria, Mario, and Jorge Iber. *Latinos in American Football: Pathbreakers on the Gridiron, 1927 to the Present.* Jefferson, NC: McFarland & Company, Publishers, 2020.

Luchs, Josh. "Confessions of an Agent." *Sports Illustrated*, October 17, 2010.

MacCambridge, Michael. *Chuck Noll: His Life's Work.* Pittsburgh, PA: University of Pittsburgh Press, 2016.

Plank, Duane. "This Professor Deals in Dollars and Sense." *Los Angeles Times*, January 3, 1992, https://www.latimes.com/archives/la-xpm-1992-01-03-sp-5617-story.html.

Rodriguez, Marc Simon. *The Tejano Diaspora: Mexican Americanism and Ethnic Politics in Texas and Wisconsin.* Chapel Hill: University of North Carolina Press, 2011.

Rooney, Art, Jr., with Roy McHugh. *Ruanaidh: The Story of Art Rooney and His Clan.* Pittsburgh, PA: Geyer Printing Company, Inc., 2008.

Ruck, Rob. *The Tropic of Football: The Long and Perilous Journey of Samoans to the NFL.* New York: The New Press, 2018.

San Miguel, Guadalupe, Jr. *Chicana/o Struggles for Education: Activism in the Community.* Houston: University of Houston-Center for Mexican American Studies, 2013.

Selber, Greg. *Border Ball: The History of High School Football in the Rio Grande Valley.* Deer Park, NY: Linus Publications, 2009.

Seymour, Wendy. *Remaking the Body: Rehabilitation and Change.* New York: Routledge, 1998.

Shockley, John Staples. *Chicano Revolt in a Texas Town*. Notre Dame, IN: Notre Dame University Press, 1974.

Stingley, Darryl, with Mark Mulvoy. *Happy to Be Alive*. New York: Beaufort Books, Inc., 1983.

Trujillo, Armando. *Chicano Empowerment and Bilingual Education: Movimiento Politics in Crystal City, Texas*. New York: Routledge, Taylor and Francis Group, 1998.

Zike, Derek Michael. "Athletes' Experiences of Leaving Sport Due to Spinal Cord Injury: A Multiple Case Study Examination." Master's thesis, Miami University, 2016.

INDEX

Note: Entry numbers in italics refer to images.